RESEARCH IN PARAPSYCHOLOGY 1978

Abstracts and Papers from the

Twenty-first Annual Convention of the

Parapsychological Association, 1978

WILLIAM G. ROLL

Editor

The Scarecrow Press, Inc.
Metuchen, N.J. & London
1979

ISBN 0-8108-1195-2
Manufactured in the United States of America
Library of Congress Catalog Card No. 66-28580
Copyright © 1979 by the Parapsychological Association

CONTENTS

PREFACE

The Parapsychological Association as an international organization is limited by the fact that most of its members reside in North America. Except for every fourth year, when the conventions have been held in Europe, European parapsychologists as a rule cannot attend. Researchers in such areas as Africa, India and Japan are even more restricted. For the convention in St. Louis this separation was largely overcome. As the result of travel grants provided by the James S. McDonnell Foundation, several overseas parapsychologists were able to participate.

James S. McDonnell, chairman of McDonnell-Douglas Corporation and an honorary member of the Parapsychological Association, attended the convention. At the banquet President K. Ramakrishna Rao paid tribute to McDonnell for his support of the Association and parapsychology. In his reply, McDonnell said he wished he could be of more help but expressed the hope that the support of private persons and foundations, such as the McDonnell Foundation, would soon be augmented by government support.

The flesh and bones of a convention are the research reports and papers to be found in a volume such as this. The lifeblood of the gathering, the energy and sense of common purpose which permeated the St. Louis convention, may not have been caught in these pages. By all accounts there was a spirit in St. Louis which animated and connected the world of parapsychology.

The Editor

THE TWENTY-FIRST ANNUAL CONVENTION

The twenty-first Annual Convention of the Parapsychological Association was held at Washington University, St. Louis, Missouri, on August 8-12, 1978. A total of 168 people attended. K. Ramakrishna Rao was chairman of the Program Committee and was assisted by Edward F. Kelly and William G. Roll. The latter also served as head of the Arrangements Committee with Peter Phillips as local coordinator. They were assisted by Linda Hagans, Joan Krieger and Emily Williams as well as by student volunteers.

Theodore X. Barber of the Medfield Foundation, Medfield, Mass., gave the invited dinner address, "Psychosomatic Effects of 'Hypnotic Suggestion': Implications for Parapsychology and Philosophy," and K. Ramakrishna Rao of the Institute for Parapsychology, Foundation for Research on the Nature of Man, gave the Presidential address, "Psi: Its Place in Nature."

In addition to the printed parts of the program, there were four workshops: "Education in Parapsychology," organized by Martin Johnson and Marian Nester; "Free Response Methodology," organized by Robert L. Morris; "Psychokinesis," organized by Mark Schaefer; and "Practical Applications of Psi," organized by William G. Roll.

The present volume consists of five parts. Part 1 contains the symposia and Part 2, the roundtables, which are similar to symposia but shorter and more informal. The research briefs, which describe exploratory or other short studies will be found in Part 3 and condensed versions of the full papers in Part 4. Part 5 is the unabridged Presidential Address.

Part 1: Symposia

CURRENT DIRECTIONS
IN EUROPEAN PARAPSYCHOLOGY*

GREAT BRITAIN (John Beloff, University of Edinburgh)

This paper will be concerned mainly with the organization, status and funding of parapsychological research in Great Britain rather than with its content. For it is these aspects, I believe, which vary most from one country to another whereas the topics and problems which interest researchers today are more or less universal.

Although the United States still clearly leads the world both in the quantity and quality of published work and as a source of the ideas which dominate parapsychological thinking, the situation in Great Britain is of special interest if only because the British were, by common consent, the pioneers in this field. From the start, parapsychology (or "psychical research" as most people in Britain still prefer to call it) has been closely associated in this country with the Society for Psychical Research of London. The Journal of the Society and its volumes of Proceedings remain the only official organs of British parapsychology and virtually all those who are active in the field are members of the Society. As an institution, it has, regrettably, declined in prestige since its great days before the First World War when its leading investigators included a galaxy of illustrious names and when a number of unusually gifted and co-operative mediums were in full flood. Various causes may be adduced for this decline, not least the rise of the Duke Laboratory and the shift of interest towards laboratory experimentation.

During the 1970s, the SPR, like so many learned societies in Britain, has suffered from the effects of the inflation and economic recession which hit this country with special severity. However, by dint of drastic economies and by raising subscriptions, it survived the crisis and the membership has remained steady at just over the one thousand mark. The research fund of the SPR, together with the Perrott-Warrick fund, a legacy bequeathed to Trinity College Cambridge, represent the main sources in Britain for the funding of parapsychological research. Occasional grants are made by wealthy private individuals but English millionaires have not shown the same readiness to subsidize parapsychology as their American counterparts. As for official government agencies, such as our Social Science Research Council, so far as I know none has ever given

---

*Chairperson: Martin Johnson, University of Utrecht.

any money for parapsychological research. Perhaps the most significant change that has taken place in the funding of research in this
country is that most of such money as is currently available is being
devoted to supporting students who have been accepted at a university
to work on a parapsychological project for their Ph. D. or other higher degree. A small vanguard of such students are at present in-
stalled at Edinburgh, at Cambridge, at Surrey, at the City University
of London and perhaps elsewhere and the practice seems to be spread-
ing. The obvious advantages which such students enjoy is that they
have access to all the research facilities which a university department can provide and they are in a position to devote their full time
to research.

There can be no doubt whatever that the demand exists on the
side of the student body. Rarely a week goes by without my receiving inquiries about the possibility of doing postgraduate work in parapsychology in my department. The limitations are in finding the
necessary financial support for such applicants and in finding academ-
ic staff who are willing and qualified to supervise the work of these
students. I think I may say that, thanks to my personal interest in
promoting research at the university, Edinburgh now leads the country in this respect but even we do not have the accommodations or
facilities to accept more than about five such postgraduate students
at any one time. Two so far have gained their Ph. D. 's. Unfortunately, even those who have the will and the ability to gain a Ph. D.
for a parapsychological thesis are faced with the lack of further op-
portunities for research at the postdoctoral level. (Two of my ex-
students, I am glad to say, have found a temporary refuge in Martin
Johnson's hospitable laboratory in Utrecht but more such openings
are desperately needed.)

WEST GERMANY (Hans Bender and Elmar R. Gruber, Institut für
      Grenzgebiete der Psychologie, Freiburg)

The German scene is characterized by an obvious discrepancy
between institutional parapsychology on the one side and the ever-
growing public interest in psi on the other side. Freiburg continues
to be the center of institutionalized parapsychology. The chair for
Psychology and Border Areas of Psychology which was conferred on
Bender in 1953 has been occupied since 1975 by J. Mischo. In
agreement with Mischo, Bender continues to lecture at the University.
Through Mischo's initiative, progress has been made insofar as parapsychology is officially recognized as a voluntary additional subject
in new regulations for diploma examinations for students of psychology. Every term the program promises one lecture and one accom-
panying training course. A close collaboration still exists between
the chair and the Institute for Border Areas of Psychology and Mental Hygiene directed by Bender. This independent Institute, the financial backer of which is the Fanny Moser Foundation, has a government paid librarian for its 10, 000 volumes, supported by the
Deutsche Forschungsgemeinschaft (German Research Foundation).

Besides the Freiburg center, a Parapsychological Research Group directed by W. Kugel has been integrated into the Department of Informatics at the Technical University of West Berlin.

Financial support is scarce for the Freiburg chair as well as for the Institute and does not allow more than two assistants for each. Those associated with the chair are only partly engaged in parapsychology. Research funds are so limited that extended programs can only be performed with the financial help of a science foundation. In spite of tax-free arrangements, donors for highly sophisticated and long-term psi research are rare.

The Freiburg Institute would certainly prefer to work in splendid scientific isolation, but the contrary is the case: it has to cope with the ever-growing public interest in psi and its antagonists. By its tradition and its engagement in mental health, it is deeply involved in various, often contradictory, trends in the public "occult wave." In fact, this "occult explosion" gives a more and more ambiguous outlook for parapsychology. Parapsychological "working groups" are emerging everywhere, sponsored by lay initiative and emphasizing subjects which can roughly be denoted as "supernatural beliefs," such as astral projection, contact with beings from other planets, reincarnation, hypnotically-induced regressions, pyramid power, Philippine wonder healers, astrology, and above all, spiritism. It is obvious that this responds to the deep-rooted needs and interests of many people, with hidden religious hopes as the background. In 1976, the so-called Deutsche Gesellschaft für Parapsychologie (German Society for Parapsychology) was founded in Hamburg. The Society presents itself in its journal, Allgemeine Zeitschrift für Parapsychologie (General Journal for Parapsychology) as the representative association for information, research and assistance in problems of life and faith. It has expanded into a network of local groups all over the country. The attitude of this Society is militant spiritism. Sober scientific research becomes a target of animosity which is specially directed against the Freiburg Institute. Mass media, in a sceptical trend, confound parapsychology with these movements and so do the fanatical disbelievers, who continue to organize witch hunts against parapsychology with methods of inquisition the intolerance of which exceeds even that of some members of the American Committee for the Scientific Investigation of Claims of the Paranormal. A considerable amount of the energies of the Freiburg Institute have to be spent in correcting these unreasonable attitudes and in providing the public with balanced information on the present state of psi research and its impact on our understanding of human nature.

An extensive free-of-charge counseling service in regard to personal problems with occultism occupies nearly half of the time of our psychoanalytically-trained collaborator, Dr. Jochen Haas. Widespread activity such as conferences and lectures in the most varied of institutions is conducted by almost all members of the Institute's staff in Germany and surrounding countries.

A special target of the anti-psi witch hunters are poltergeist

cases for the investigation of which the Freiburg Institute is well
known.   After having tried in vain to reduce the Rosenheim case to
influences of defective X-ray equipment, Dr. Schäfer, director of
the Criminal Police in Bremen, recently published in the German
and international press the "confession" of Heiner, the focal person
in the Bremen/Freiburg case (1965-1966) on which J. Mischo, U.
Timm and G. Vilhjalmson reported at the 11th Convention of the PA
in Freiburg in 1968.   Dr. Schäfer succeeded in inducing the now
27-year-old "Bremen boy" to "confess" that he fooled Bender and
his collaborators and to "explain" in detail his alleged tricks.   It
was pure fantasy, what the pseudologue Heiner was shown saying in
a television film.   The Institute could refute his statements point by
point on the basis of original documents, confirmation by the witnesses and experimental checks of the alleged tricks.

We have been engaged once more in investigating a case of
recurrent spontaneous psychokinesis.   Water splashes have appeared--
even in locked rooms--in connection with a 12-year-old girl in a
place in the Black Forest near the Swiss frontier.   Gruber cooperated with electronic engineers to check the phenomena and exclude
trickery.   In collaboration with the University chair, a thorough
psychodiagnostic analysis of the group situation and the individuals
involved was made and presented as an M. A. thesis.

The main accent of research work in the Freiburg Institute
is on psychokinesis.   Physicists Klaus Kornwachs and Walter von
Lucadou, in collaboration with Eberhard Bauer, continue to develop
their theoretical work on quantum theory and theory building in
parapsychology.   Bauer also generously devotes much time to editing
the Zeitschrift für Parapsychologie und Grenzgebiete der Psychologie.

The experimental work with the Berne designer, Silvio M. ,
started by Bender and R. Vandrey in an exploratory phase, was
continued by the physicists to check special hypotheses in collaboration with B. Wälti (Berne), whose records were recently published
in the Zeitschrift.   Kornwachs began a detailed analysis of single
shots obtained on film and videotape of PK moving and deforming of
objects.   A long-term program worked out by von Lucadou currently
awaits financial support to get underway.

Another dominant aspect of the Institute's research is precognition.   The "observation in expectancy" of the dreams of Mrs.
Christine Mylius, which proved partly to be precognitive, has been
continued.   Gruber enlarged this very significant research program
by a new series provided by another person, Mrs. Hella Nagel,
which will be evaluated independently.   An outstanding case of polit-
ical prophecy--two letters written in August 1914 by a Bavarian
soldier to his family which contain exact prophecies of World War I,
Hitler's fascism, and World War II--was thoroughly investigated by
Bender who first reported on his documentation of the authenticity
of the letters at the second Conference of the Society for Psychical
Research in Cambridge, March 1978.

The Freiburg Institute has close relations with French para-psychology and collaborated with Prof. de Argumosa (Madrid), in the establishment of Spanish parapsychology.

FRANCE (Yvonne Duplessis, Paris)

In France parapsychological research is particularly con-cerned with psychokinesis. The effects produced by Jean-Pierre Girard are investigated; new random generators have been built by Yves Lignon of the Faculty of Sciences of Toulouse-le-Mirail and by the engineer, Pierre Janin.

I have engaged in research on dermo-optical perception. This is awareness of non-visual impressions produced by colored stimuli or graphic forms placed close to the subject's palm. The subject is not permitted to look at the stimuli and no guessing or visualization are involved. The first investigation of this phenom-enon was developed in France, in 1920, by Jules Romains.

The best explanation of dermo-optical perception is a physical one. It was first developed in the U.S.S.R. by B. Constantinov, then in the U.S.A. by W. L. Makous. C. B. Nash demonstrated statistically that dermo-optical perception is different from ESP. According to this hypothesis, infra-red emitted by the colors and by the hands produce differential impressions and reac-tions. Systematic investigation of this phenomenon is now being carried out in the U.S.S.R. by A. S. Novomeysky, and in France by me, with the support of the Parapsychology Foundation.

Concerning the methods used I shall deal here only with the measurement of unconscious dermo-optical sensitivity reactions. The procedure, termed passive, is used by Novomeysky for the thermoscopic method. It not only permits objective heat measure-ments of dermo-optical reactions but demonstrates the sensitivity of the hand to colors placed under metallic screens. It demonstrates also that in general reactions produced by colors vary according to lighting conditions: daylight, electric light, dusk or darkness.

The other procedures are termed active. In 1971 I started to use a method adapted from the dynamometric method, developed by the French physiologist, Ch. Féré. The muscular reaction pro-duced by the subject while holding a piece of colored paper in one hand is recorded by a dynamometer held in the other. It is significant that statistical analyses show the pressures induced by red to be greater than those induced by green. However, in electric light the subjects holding the green squeeze the dynamometer harder than do those holding colors at the end of the spectrum, blue and red. These dynamometric curves confirm that we are not dealing with ESP but with a physical phenomenon.

We now come to the regrouping method devised by Novomeysky. It consists of having children regroup squares and rectangles of cardboard on aluminum sheets under which either black or yellow papers have been randomly placed. The average speed of regrouping, by daylight, is slower with black than with yellow paper. These different effects of black and yellow vary according to the "degree of blackness," in the physical sense of the term, and appear to confirm the thermodynamic hypothesis suggested by the thermoscopic and the dynamometric methods.

The thermal exchanges are obvious in the results of my recent tests with liquid crystal sheets. If the sheets are placed over contrasting colors, or over black and white graphic forms, even under thin aluminum sheets, they register differences.

Now we come to the method of writing and reading texts in Braille. I used this method to discover whether blind subjects write or read Braille at different speeds depending upon the color of the papers they punch or read with their hands. It appears that differences in speed not only were due to differences in the colors of the papers used but also were influenced by different types of lighting. For instance, writing speed decreased, in daylight, from green to red; reading speed accelerated maximally, in electric light, on red paper and was slowest on yellow.

Pedagogically the importance of these methods, both in schools and in the rehabilitation of the blind, is obvious.

Some parapsychological aspects are open to question since the domain of dermo-optical perception has been broadened to include the study of stimuli under opaque screens. It appears that some experiments in clairvoyance of guessing hidden stimuli are simply based on dermo-optical exchange reactions between stimuli and subject. Thus, according to the French tradition originated by C. Richet, Nobel prize winner in physiology, phenomena which were first scoffed at have been found to be susceptible to explanations based on the laws of physics and physiology.

SCANDINAVIA (Rolf Ejvegaard, Swedish Society for Psychical
      Research)

Interest in parapsychological research has existed for quite some time in Scandinavia. The Danish Society for Psychical Research (DSPR) was founded in 1905; the Norwegian Society (NSPR), in 1917 and the Swedish (SSPR), in 1947. During the first decade of this century, parapsychology experienced difficult times with constant attacks from almost everyone. Better times were enjoyed during and immediately after World War I. Unfortunately, this encouraging interest gradually waned and difficulties arose anew during the thirties.

World War II did not, as many had thought, stir up new

interest in parapsychology. Not until the end of the forties and
during the fifties did interest begin slowly to grow again. The
development from the fifties continued on into the sixties, a
flourishing period for parapsychology. The seventies culminated
with a boom in interest in the occult. Whether it has been for
better or for worse for parapsychology is a question that cannot
yet be answered.

Scientists of all categories during the sixties appeared to
have a rough idea of what parapsychology was, but one is more
hesitant to make this statement about scientists of today. Persons
involved with astrology, biorhythm, flying saucers and so on often
call themselves parapsychologists. As far as I am concerned,
most of these people are in no way connected with parapsychology.
The societies for psychical research in Scandinavia have tried to
withstand this stream of occultism but they have not been equally
successful. Until recently all three societies had restricted membership policies and a scientific outlook was a requirement for membership. The number of members in each society had always been
around 100.

In 1973 the DSPR could not resist outer pressure any longer.
An alliance was formed with an occult magazine and the membership
was immediately increased by tenfold to 1,000. The NSPR and the
SSPR are still closed, with memberships of slightly more than 100
each.

Because of a lack of resources, very little scientific work
has been carried out in Scandinavia. The societies have mainly had
to follow the research abroad and report back to members and
others interested. Guest speakers to the societies have on many
occasions been from abroad. Noted among them are William Roll,
Montague Ullman, and Stanley Krippner. Krippner spoke to the
SSPR in early 1978. The tenth volume of the proceedings of the
SSPR, containing a study of precognition, was published in 1978.

So far I have talked predominately of the scientific societies
and it was not just by coincidence I did so. It is basically within
these societies and through them that interest in parapsychology has
been channeled. Universities and other institutions have offered few
possibilities for studying parapsychology.

For quite some time the University of Lund was the only
institution of higher learning in Sweden that sponsored work in parapsychology. We have also during the seventies received research
papers presented at the graduate schools of administration and
social work of Örebro and Stockholm. In all these universities it
has been the psychology departments that have opened the doors to
parapsychology.

By and large I have stressed that parapsychology in Sweden
and in all Scandinavia is extremely limited. Only a radical change
in available economic resources will alter this situation.

ICELAND (Erlendur Haraldsson, University of Iceland)

At the present time, as I see it, there is no particular
"European type" of parapsychology. Research methods used in
Europe and topics or problems studied are more or less the same
as in the United States. In Iceland some psychical research was
conducted early this century and then there came a long period of
no activity. My first major project after I started research at the
University of Iceland some five years ago was a national sample
survey of psychic experiences and attitudes toward the paranormal
which I reported on at the PA convention in 1976. This was an
extensive national survey in which over 900 persons (80 per cent
of the sample) returned their questionnaires. I have compared our
results with surveys done in other countries and found that the
frequency of reported psychic experiences differs considerably among
countries.

In Iceland 64 per cent claimed a psychic experience of some
kind. In 1957 only 11 per cent did so in Denmark and only 19 per
cent in Germany. Only a few surveys have been conducted in
Europe but so far all show a much lower frequency of reported
psychic phenomena than we found in Iceland. In the United States,
on the other hand, we also have a high percentage of reported
psychic phenomena as shown in the national survey of Greeley and
McCready and also in the Palmer and Dennis community survey in
Charlottesville, where at least half the sample claimed a psychic
experience. The Icelanders and the Americans have thus a similar
frequency of reported psychic phenomena which is much higher than
percentages so far reported by continental Europeans. Some of the
attitudes show similar national differences. Belief in survival is
shared by the great majority in Iceland and the United States, but
is considerably lower in Europe, at least in northern Europe.
Parapsychological research may not differ much from one country
to another but reported psychic experiences do and also some
attitudes of interest to parapsychologists.

After studying this survey material I have wondered if we
should begin talking about sheep and goat nations, and if this has
perhaps something to do with possibly different rates of significant
and non-significant results of experiments conducted in various
countries.

Since the original survey, I have with some of my students
conducted three follow-up surveys. First of these was an interview
survey of respondents reporting experiences with deceased persons
(apparitions of the dead); a surprising 31 per cent of our original
respondents reported such experiences. In this follow-up study we
wanted to test some hypotheses regarding the nature of these experiences, such as Gardner Murphy's dissociation theory of appari-
tional experiences, the effect of grief on them and also if some
crisis apparitions were to be found among these reported cases.
More or less simultaneously we have worked on two further follow-
up surveys, again with personal interviews based on detailed ques-

tionnaires. These have been on mental healing and out-of-body experiences. The data are in from both these surveys and we are now working on the evaluation.

Apart from these field studies we have conducted a few experiments on dream recall, dream content, the sheep-goat variable and personality variables, all in relation to ESP performance. Last year we replicated successfully Martin Johnson's finding of the rather close relationship between ESP scores and scores on the Defense Mechanism Test (DMT). This relationship has shown a remarkable degree of replicability so far. For this experiment, and one more ESP-DMT experiment not yet evaluated, Martin Johnson was kind enough to come and work with us in Iceland.

Facilities and funding for research in Iceland have been liberal and I have no complaints in that direction. For the last few years I have been able to have a full-time research assistant at least six months of the year.

THE NETHERLANDS (Martin Johnson, University of Utrecht)

Parapsychology has a long history in the Netherlands. The first laboratory for the scientific study of the paranormal was established in Amsterdam in 1907. With some justification it can be said that one of the cradles of experimental parapsychology was at the University of Groningen where pioneering work was carried out by Heymans and Brugmans. The Dutch SPR played an important role in furthering interest in parapsychology and initiating research.

In the early fifties, Utrecht became the natural center for parapsychological research. In 1953, W. H. C. Tenhaeff was nominated "special" professor of parapsychology at the State University of Utrecht, a chair financed by the Dutch SPR, and in the same year the first International Annual Conference for Parapsychological Studies was held in Utrecht, sponsored by the newly-founded Parapsychology Foundation. Tenhaeff has become internationally recognized for his pioneering work with "paragnosts" and on the home front for his active stimulation of public interest in the field.

In 1966 the Psychological Laboratory of the Faculty of Social Sciences appointed a staff member, Sybo A. Schouten, to promote experimental investigations of paranormal phenomena.

In 1974, the Parapsychology Laboratory was established in connection with the inception of the first "regular" chair in parapsychology in Europe. ("Regular" implies that the chair is appointed as well as paid for by the government.) In addition, in April 1978, a continuation of Tenhaeff's chair was secured: the Society appointed H. van Praag, who was approved by the board of the University of Utrecht as a "special professor" of parapsychology.

His appointment is for a limited period of time and present financial limitations dictate that the post is a part-time one.

The task of the Parapsychology Laboratory is to carry out research and to provide a variety of educational programs for Dutch students.   Priority is given to experimental work and long-term planning of research projects.   The development of sophisticated experimental facilities is considered a "must."

The following research programs are in progress: (1) DMT studies, in which the relationship between subliminal processes and ESP is studied; cooperation with E. Haraldsson in Iceland has been established; (2) psychophysiological work, especially centered around the CNV (a surface negative brain wave) in relation to ESP performance; (3) animal research: the effect of drugs such as librium and amphetamines have been studied in anpsi tests; (4) studies with "paragnosts":   studies of alleged "paragnosts" are carried out as a Ph. D. thesis topic, the main aim being to analyze what takes place in a session in which a "paragnost" receives a client and describes the characteristics, behavior or situation either of the client or of a third person in which the client is interested (the study has social and psychological as well as parapsychological aspects);   (5) investigations of the so-called "divergence problem": several members of the Laboratory are taking an interest in the so-called "divergence problem"--studies have been carried out and are under way as well.

Twice a year the Laboratory publishes the European Journal of Parapsychology (EJP).   A hallmark of the EJP is the attempt to avoid selective reporting.   The Laboratory also publishes Research Letters at irregular intervals in which articles that do not fulfill one or more of the requirements of the EJP appear.

Serious research work is also carried out outside Utrecht. In Amsterdam, research is done by the Amsterdamse Parapsychologische Studiekring and by SCEPP (Studiecentrum voor Experimentele Parapsychologie), which cooperates closely with the Utrecht Laboratory in certain areas.   The main emphasis has been on healers, workshops on hypnosis, psychophysiology, and problems related to observational theory.   Leading research workers are D. Bierman and J. Houtkooper.   In Eindhoven, investigations have been reported by H. Breederveld and by J. Jacobs.   Their privately-run center is the Institute for Fundamental Studies.   PK experiments with dice, in which H. Breederveld usually performs as his own subject, have been reported.   Furthermore, studies on a possible influence of birth order on ESP ability have been carried out, as well as studies on ESP in relation to success on a special type of lottery ("Lotto-games").

A proposal has been made to issue an annual project catalog (including listing of useful hardware as well as software) that could be helpful to other research centers, especially in Europe.   The idea has also been advanced to form a European regional branch of the Parapsychological Association.

CHANGING CONCEPTS OF
MIND AND MATTER*

IN DEFENCE OF THE "PSYCHOBIOLOGICAL" PARADIGM

John Beloff (University of Edinburgh)

Recently Rex Stanford has challenged what he calls the
"psychobiological paradigm"--roughly, the traditional view that psi
is some power or faculty of the mind or brain analogous to our
ordinary sensory and motor functions--and in its place has proposed
what he calls "The Conformance Behavior Model." According to
this model all psi phenomena are reducible to PK and PK is basically a property of a "disposed system." What constitutes a "disposed system" is not specified except to say that it exists in a
state of need and that the PK effect is somehow automatically
brought about so as to satisfy that need. Where Stanford's theory
departs most conspicuously from all previous theories of psi is
that the psi source does not necessarily have to be a living system
and its "needs" do not have to be understood in either a biological
or psychological sense. This raises the question of whether a
coiled spring under pressure would constitute a "disposed system"
and whether it could activate a random event generator that would
operate so as gradually to reduce that pressure.

It is a matter for empirical investigation whether psi effects
can be obtained using either inanimate systems as psi sources or
organisms that do not possess a brain but the evidence so far from
work with plants, seedlings, eggs, etc., do not suggest that any
such effects can be demonstrated independently of the human experimenter. It would seem that if this were possible, that if any effect
whatsoever could be produced in this way, then it would be repro-
ducible virtually 100 per cent of the time, since there is no reason
to suppose that one such specimen should differ with respect to its
psi potentialities from any other.

The attraction of a conformance behavior model of psi is
that, if validated, it could be used to explain evolutionary development and perhaps even the emergence of life itself. However, in
the absence of any convincing evidence that psi can occur independently of some human or animal subject, it would be rash to discard
the psychobiological paradigm within which most of our parapsycho-

---

*Chairperson: William G. Roll, Psychical Research Foundation.

logical theorizing has so far been conducted. Nevertheless the conformance behavior model does draw attention to certain important aspects of PK which any theory must henceforth take into account, namely that PK is an inherently teleological process--i. e., given a particular goal the means necessary to attain that goal are automatically brought into play--and also that PK can occur even in the absence of conscious volition on the part of the subject. Thus the earlier and cruder conception of PK, which presupposed a continuous monitoring of the physical processes involved with periodic interventions in the form of PK impulses, has become increasingly hard to reconcile with our knowledge of the experimental evidence on PK, as Stanford, among others, has rightly pointed out.

It is here suggested that, in the light of the new "observational theories" of psi, especially as expounded by E. H. Walker, the traditional psychobiological paradigm can be emended to allow for these peculiarly teleological aspects of the psi process without having to abandon that paradigm altogether in favor of something as questionable as the conformance behavior model.

COMMENTS ON THE QUANTUM THEORY OF PSI PHENOMENA

E. H. Walker (Aberdeen Proving Ground, Md.)

Despite the vigorous growth one sees in the field of physics, particularly in biophysics, there does not exist any reasonable expectation that so unique a thing as would be required to account for psi phenomena could have escaped discovery were the phenomenon the result of some psi energy or a psychic field of force. Indeed it is only in the realm of quantum mechanics that we find problems in physics that correspond so well with the questions raised in parapsychology--observer effects, mind and consciousness, tunneling or translocation of material bodies, non-local transfer of information, statistical effects. It is only the habit of physicists in thinking of quantum processes as microscopic, even though the equations do not say this, and their predisposition to reject with the rest of science the idea of mind that has stood in the way of recognizing parapsychological phenomena as the other side of the quantum mechanical coin. And what has blocked that is the very difficult picture of reality this last step presents to us.

Let us look briefly at the nature of quantum mechanics. The Schrödinger equation is a prescription that allows one to take a set of objects and physical descriptors of those objects--space, time, mass, charge--and compute the "potentialities" of that set of objects. If the physical descriptors are represented by P, then we can calculate the potentialities ψ_1, ψ_2, ψ_3, ..., or as we refer to them collectively, Ψ, by solving the equation

$$P \Psi = 0 \qquad (1)$$

where in the Schrödinger equation P happens to be

$$P = - \frac{\hbar^2}{2m} \nabla^2 - E + V \tag{2}$$

For example, for the problem of the hydrogen atom, the physical description of the problem is that we have a proton and an electron with an attractive force acting between them. Solving equation (1) gives Ψ, that is to say, the large number of solutions for a probability of finding the electron in any particular position in space at any given time.

We can make a measurement, an observation, and determine that the hydrogen atom is in, say, state "5f, 1." It is important to point out that before the measurement, or observation, the hydrogen atom is to be thought of as represented by all the possible states, i.e. by Ψ and not simply an unknown ψ_i, one of the allowed states. Diagrammatically we can represent this by

$$P \rightarrow \{\Psi\} \rightarrow \psi_i \tag{3}$$

Each of these steps represents or embodies a definite amount of information. That is, we could also write

$$\begin{pmatrix} \text{Physical configuration} \\ \text{information} \end{pmatrix} \rightarrow \begin{pmatrix} \text{Information} \\ \text{in the} \\ \text{state} \\ \text{descriptions} \end{pmatrix} \rightarrow \begin{pmatrix} \text{Information} \\ \text{about which} \\ \text{potentiality} \\ \text{was found} \end{pmatrix} \tag{4}$$

What is frequently not appreciated is the fact that the observation is not a passive "finding out" but is a process that changes the physical system in a way that cannot be described by this physical operator P. Each of these steps is required for us to describe physical processes, and each involves changes that are characterized at least in part by information measures.

In other papers the present author has detailed the nature of these quantum mechanical processes as they relate to the brain:

$$\begin{pmatrix} \text{Brain data} \\ \text{processing} \\ \text{functions} \end{pmatrix} \rightarrow \begin{pmatrix} \text{Quantum} \\ \text{mechanical} \\ \text{interaction} \\ \text{of synapses} \end{pmatrix} \rightarrow \begin{pmatrix} \text{Selection of} \\ \text{subsequent} \\ \text{brain state} \end{pmatrix} \tag{5}$$

And the relationship of the various information processes specified using the language

$$\begin{array}{ccc} S & \rightarrow & C & \rightarrow & W \\ \text{(subconscious)} & & \text{(consciousness)} & & \text{(will)} \end{array} \tag{6}$$

Three additional facts should now be introduced into this

picture.   First, if several separate observers carry out independent measurements on a system, quantum mechanics requires the observers to be so constrained that the same state occurs.   Secondly, it is a moot question as to which observer causes the result that several observe.   In some cases the requirements of relativity theory make it clear that we cannot even say which event happened first.   But where we can say which measurement occurred first, it is difficult to say which was the "cause" in the usual physical sense, since there exists no physical causal chain of events connecting the first measurement to the second.   We simply say there is a coupling of observers that does not depend on the physical parameters.

Thirdly, one can specify data rates that characterize the quantum mechanical processes involved in the brain's data processing functions (C), a data rate for the rate at which choices in the quantum mechanical potentialities are selected (W), and a data rate (B) for the brain's total data processing (as though it were a computer). The approximate values this author has obtained are

$$B \approx 10^{12} \text{ hits/sec}$$
$$C \approx 10^{8} \text{ hits/sec} \qquad (7)$$
$$W \approx 10^{4} \text{ hits/sec}$$

These quantities, the coupling of the W channels and relations (3) and (6) lead to a particular picture of the nature of mind as it relates to the physical world and as internally connected.   To illustrate these ideas, picture the physical operator P, somewhat like the laws of physics, acting to generate the potentialities of the world.   The physical system contains strongly coupled quantum mechanical systems.   These are embedded in objects such as brains.   State selection is determined by information carried "in" the W channels constraining all the subordinate consciousnesses C associated with brains B to enter the same state.   The interrelationship of these entities leads us to a picture having a strange similarity to certain Eastern concepts of mind.   One can make the following rather flowery analogy: The "Lotus Blossom" of consciousness "flowers" in the "air" of the physical world and has its "stem" connected to the "roots" of the w_i variables in the "waters" of the collective will which contains neither space nor time as boundaries.   It is only a picture, but it does show graphically how the ideas of quantum mechanics, consciousness theory, and aspects of psi phenomena fit together.

HIDDEN VARIABLES, BOOTSTRAPS AND BRAHMAN

Shivesh C. Thakur (University of Surrey, England)

In two of my recent publications relating to parapsychology,

I have made use of concepts from traditional Indian philosophy in an attempt to provide some sort of theoretical framework for psychic phenomena.   In the course of discussion on the second of these, "Parapsychology in Search of a Paradigm," at the international conference in Copenhagen in August 1976 (published in The Philosophy of Parapsychology, Parapsychology Foundation, 1977), I promised, specifically in response to Beloff's suggestion, that "some time in the future" I might "come back with a bit more" on the possible light that insights from Indian philosophy may shed on psychic phenomena.   This presentation is in partial fulfillment of that promise.

More importantly, I have had time to reflect on the implications of the recent works of two scientists, especially as they relate to my own ideas or, rather, to my interpretation of certain Indian philosophical ideas.   One of them is E. H. Walker who, as is well known, offers to explain various psychic phenomena in terms of the "hidden variables" of quantum theory.   Some of his conclusions seem to be strikingly similar to mine, as they appear in my published works.   For example, in his "Consciousness and Quantum Theory" (in Psychic Exploration, ed. by Mitchell and White [New York: Putnam, 1974]), he dismisses as futile all attempts to explain telepathy as "a transmission on a force-field carrier," and says, "A considerable departure from this mode of thought is required to achieve an understanding of paranormal processes."   Positively, he hypothesizes the operation of a "collective will" and suggests that the meditative state may not be "an experience of things unreal, but a direct channel to an extensive non-physical reality."   Coincidentally, in my "Telepathy, Evolution and Dualism" (Philosophy and Psychical Research, ed. by Thakur [London: Allen & Unwin, 1976]), I suggested that a proper approach to the explanation of telepathy, as I saw it, would require "a revolution within a revolution."   I also said that the notion of the "collective unconscious" (the counterpart of Walker's "collective will"), while making telepathy a more plausible phenomenon, was itself in need of explanation, perhaps in terms of a concept resembling that of brahman, the world-soul--just the sort of "extensive, non-physical reality" Walker seems to be referring to.   Using the model of electricity and the insulated materials along which it flows, I also speculated that telepathy, like hypnosis, trance and meditative states, might be said to represent a temporary failure of the "insulating" function normally performed by the body and the central nervous system.   Sustained failures would then lead to the experience of identity of the self with brahman.

Interesting as these similarities between Walker's ideas and mine are, what is crucial for my present purpose is his argument that quantum theory, on one or another interpretation, can provide an explanatory framework for parapsychological phenomena.   Here the work of the second of the scientists mentioned above becomes significant.   Fritjof Capra, in his essay "Modern Physics and Eastern Philosophy" (in Human Dimensions [Buffalo, N. Y. , 1974]) and in his extremely interesting book, The Tao of Physics [Boulder,

Colo. : Shambhala, 1975]--argues extensively, and reasonably convincingly, in my opinion, the following point. According to him,
the view of reality implicit in modern physics, namely quantum
theory and relativity, and, especially, in the so-called "bootstrap
model" advocated by many eminent contemporary physicists--is much
closer to that encountered in Eastern philosophy and mysticism than
anywhere else. The concept of brahman, the world-soul, its onto-
logical identity with the ātman, the individual soul, and its status
as the ground of the whole universe--consisting of matter and
mind--is, of course, the very essence of Indian mysticism and
perhaps the most influential among Indian philosophical theories.
If all this is correct, then the avowedly metaphysical theory that I
advanced in my "Parapsychology in Search of a Paradigm, " would
seem not to have been so very "speculative" after all. My advocacy of
the brahman-ātman doctrine, with its attendant notions of different levels of reality and the different states of consciousness, and the strikingly
different concepts of matter, mind and their interrelation implicit in it,
appears to receive solid backing from contemporary physics.

PSI STRUCTURES

William G. Roll (Psychical Research Foundation)

According to social behavior theories, personality assessments and changes can better be made in real-life situations than
by personality testing and therapy isolated from where people are
likely to find themselves. Since behavior always occurs in the context of the social and physical environment, our image of personality
has altered from that of a more or less independent structure to that
of a changing interface between organism and environment.

In psychology the focus is on the organism side of the interface and on the dispositions which the organism carries from one
situation to the next, but in parapsychology we can view organism
and environment as one structure.

As science moves from simpler to more complex systems,
say from molecules to living systems, the laws which determine the
simpler structures also apply to the more complex (though the new
system may also exhibit new properties). E. H. Walker and
Shivesh Thakur have shown that the laws of physics may apply to
psi and John Beloff discusses how psychological factors may affect
the psi interactions of an organism with its environment. (On this
point at least he and Rex Stanford would seem to agree.)

I suggest that psi occurrences are the effects of processes
within rather than between structures. If we suppose that psi
structures include not only the physical systems which make up an
organism but also the physical systems which make up its environment, then we may look for the dispositions associated with the

organism also in the physical systems of the environment of that organism.   According to this view, an object with which a person has been in contact remains "psi contiguous" with that person after having been spatially separated.   This idea is basic to the psychological systems of many third-world societies; a physical version is expressed by the Einstein-Podolsky-Rosen thought experiment where two atoms which have once been in contact continue to interact when spatially separated.

The psi structure of which a person is part changes with the physical and social environment of the person.   As the person enters new situations, new physical systems and the dispositions associated with these systems come into play and may reinforce or cancel previous dispositions.

The theory gives us a new handle on a difficult issue, the experimenter effect, and enables us to deal with psi phenomena which cannot be understood in terms of present theories.   If an ESP test comprises not only subject and experimenter, and their dispositions, but also absent persons represented, so to speak, by physical objects in the test situation the absent persons have interacted with in the past, then the dispositions of these absent but psi contiguous persons must be taken into account in designing a test. The "psychometric" objects favored by ESP sensitives to obtain information about persons who have touched the objects; the "inductors" employed by psychic healers to help them affect their patients at a distance; and "haunting" incidents which seem to reflect the lives of persons who once occupied a building suggest that the dispositions of persons are associated with physical objects in their environment and remain associated with them in the physical absence of that person. A PK version of this relationship is suggested by the focussing effect found in RSPK and the linger phenomenon G. Watkins has observed in his PK tests.

Mediumistic communication, including "drop-ins," seem only to succeed when there is a physical link between the deceased person and the experimenter.   Similarly in reincarnation cases there usually is a physical connection between the person who correctly "remembers" past events and the place where the deceased person died who originally experienced these events.   The present theory explains findings of this type since the dispositions of a person remain in the other people and things with which the person has interacted.   The theory is thus a survival hypothesis: If the organism is not the sole seat of a person's psi structure but if this extends to other persons and things, then a person would be expected to survive in these persons or things when the organism has disintegrated.

The theory says that for ESP and PK to occur the "target" must be psi contiguous with the subject.   Since the psi structure of which the subject is part is defined in terms of contiguity, events which are not related to the subject by contiguity or are only remotely connected are not expected to function well as ESP or PK "targets."   It would falsify the theory if, for instance, an ESP subject succeeded as well with events with which he had little such contact as with events with which he had close contact.

PSYCHIC HEALING WITH HUMANS:
FROM ANECDOTE TO EXPERIMENT*

HEALING PRACTICES AROUND THE WORLD

Stanley Krippner (Humanistic Psychology Institute, San Francisco)

"Psychic healing" is a term used to describe the alleviation of physical or psychological problems when the effect appears to be psi-mediated rather than explainable in terms of Western scientific and medical models. The parapsychological literature gives very few examples of "psychic healing"; those mentioned appear to depend, at least in part, upon traditional healing modalities as well.

Psychic healers have no common historical tradition; they have operated throughout history in virtually all parts of the world. They can be divided into four categories, although there is considerable overlap.

Shamans: In the strict sense, shamanism is an historical phenomenon of Siberia and Central Asia, where the term originated. Later, similar developments were observed in the Americas, Indonesia, Oceania and elsewhere. The shaman (according to Eliade) is the "technician of the sacred"--a magician and healer who engages in altered conscious states in which the soul is said to leave the body, ascending to the heavens or descending to the underworld.

Spiritists: Shamans work with their spirit allies without becoming their instruments. Spiritist healers, however, claim to "incorporate" spirits during healing services. The French spiritualist, Allan Kardec, wrote several books in the 19th century which have been influential in Latin America. Spirit incorporation also takes place among various healers in Asia and Africa.

Esoterics: Esoteric healers follow various "hidden" teachings such as alchemy, astrology, the Kabbalah, radionics, tantra and the writings of Alice Bailey. The esoteric oath, "To will, to know, to dare, and to be silent," is said to date back to the healers working with the legendary Hermes Trismegistus. Initiation rites are common practices among esoteric healers.

---

*Chairperson: Gerald F. Solfvin, Psychical Research Foundation.

Intuitives: The intuitive healer undergoes no special training or initiation, but responds to a "call from God." Many simply begin to "lay on hands" or to pray for the ill spontaneously.

The effectiveness of psychic healing appears to depend on how closely it follows the hallmarks of traditional medicine and psychotherapy, some of which are the following. A name is given to the disease or complaint by the healer and the healee accepts the name (or diagnosis, description, etc.). The healee possesses personal qualities which facilitate the healing process (trust, willingness to comply with the healer's advice, etc.). Previous expectations on the part of the healee are met to some degree: Faith is a potentially powerful healing agent and it can be mobilized more easily if the healee's expectations are met. The procedures (medicines, exercises, technology, etc.) are well suited for the healee's disease or complaint. Psychic healers, of course, use a number of procedures not utilized by traditional practicioners--e. g., discarnate entities, divine intervention, the concept of life after death, karma, or reincarnation; "out-of-body" experiences, the "laying-on of hands," subtle bodies and unusual "energies," magic ceremonies, magical remedies (herbs, brews, etc.), and purported psi (clairvoyant diagnosis, psychokinetic healing, etc.).

Recent studies and papers by orthodox physicians and psychotherapists have commented favorably on the potential value of psychic healers. Parapsychologists have treated this area in a spirit of "benign neglect" which now shows signs of changing.

THE HEALING TRADITION IN AMERICA:
PHILOSOPHICAL AND CULTURAL PERSPECTIVES

Russell Moores (Medical College of Georgia, Augusta)

The orthodox healing establishment, be it the AMA, the Navajo healers of the United States Southwest, or the sorcerers of the Azandi in Africa, always reflects the philosophic suppositions and values of its society. To accuse the American allopathic physician of being very proficient technically, but rather impersonal, tending to isolate the patient from his surroundings, not viewing him as a whole person in constant contact with his environment--is merely to say that he is well reflecting the positivist world view of Hume and Comte which rejects a priori knowledge and intuition, making experience the sole source of knowledge and the isolating methods of the empirical sciences the only way to understand our world.

To evaluate the performance of any group of "healers" is most difficult, since so many factors (nutritional, environmental, genetic) influence the health of a people. Probably the individual encounter between an individual physician and any individual patient contributes less to the healing of that patient than we generally suppose.

Historically, the healer has almost always been related to the priesthood. Many feel that this is still true, with orthodox allopathic medicine having become the new state religion. Certainly, deviance in our society is now defined largely in medical rather than theological terms: murderers today are always "sick" rather than "sinful. " With the weakening of tribe, family and church, the professions, by drawing people into common tasks and the common interpretation of life, have become central to the established moral order. This is particularly true of medicine.

Healing has always been an integral part of Catholic-Orthodox Christianity. Following separation of the spiritual from the physical during the Renaissance, spiritual healing has centered in shrines to the Blessed Mother, such as Ste. Anne de Beauprê and Lourdes, and in isolated individuals such as Padre Pio. This was also prominent at the turn of the century in various fundamentalist Protestant sects, and then resurfaced in the Catholic and Anglican churches about a decade ago with the "charismatic renewal. "

Because America is a smelting or transmuting pot rather than a melting pot, with so many coming out "Anglo-Saxon" within a generation or two, we must now look primarily to our non-white population (the black man or the American indian) for non-orthodox healing methods.

In my experience, in the Southern black culture, the healer is typically a female, generally elderly, living alone in a reasonably remote place, using both incantations and medicines, and having a powerful reputation for casting spells and counter-spells as well as for healing. She generally has little formal education, learning her art from her mother or aunt. In addition to these, there are certain large-scale enterprises, such as that in Seminole County, Georgia, where whole bus loads of folk come from all over the East Coast to be healed. These healers are generally black males, better educated and more articulate than the others previously mentioned. These people almost invariably put their healing in a religious context, viewing their powers as a gift of God. K. G. , evaluated at the FRNM in Durham several years ago, claimed that there was a force which she did not understand, which came from God and merely flowed through her when she laid on the hands to heal.

In addition to this "concerned prayer" approach, we also see the "not directly concerned prayer" approach, in the various prayer groups which will pray for anyone whose name is submitted to them.

More recently, we are seeing another phenomenon: the emergence of another group of psychic healers who claim no religious connection whatsoever with their work. They speak only of psychic energy and of altering their state of consciousness through meditation so as to become one with the psyche of the person to be healed. In addition, we now see a plethora of such as acupuncture, chiropractic, sex therapy, natural diet therapy, exercise therapy, massage therapy, and zonal therapy.

Attempts to evaluate these healing methods raise the whole question of the relationship between that which is measurable in the laboratory and that which occurs spontaneously in the "real world." Obviously, the more rigidly we control for every variable, the more artificial "unreal" the situation becomes.

What has happened thus far in the laboratory? It would seem that a psychokinetic effect on living tissue has probably been demonstrated. Also, definite physiologic effects of a cardiopulmonary and metabolic nature have been demonstrated during meditation. Further laboratory evaluation at the animal level can be carried out so long as one keeps in mind the limitations of the isolating properties of the scientific method. The clinical evaluation of healers is rendered difficult by the necessity of removing them from their usual environment. The differences in vocabulary are a further complicating factor.

PSYCHIC HEALING: THE EXPERIMENTAL VIEWPOINT

Graham K. Watkins (Duke University)

Although the literature abounds with cases of "psychic healing," there are only a small number of experimental studies. There are, however, a few laboratory studies dealing with this question. The earliest of these are the studies of Grad and associates which tend to bear out the hypothesis that such an effect exists. Grad used wound-healing in mice as a paradigm, and found that indeed the healing process was apparently facilitated by a human subject's efforts.

Justa Smith, using the same subject as Grad, demonstrated an ability to affect the activity of enzymes in vitro. The effects appear to be similar to those seen when such solutions are exposed to intense electromagnetic fields. While not a demonstration of the subject's healing ability, her studies suggest a possible mediation of the process.

Our own studies used ether anesthesia as the condition from which the experimental animals (mice) were to be "healed." Not only was an apparent effect observed, but quite a strong one; several of the subjects demonstrated an ability to arouse the animal they were concentrating on before the control in some 80 per cent of the cases, usually by a 30 per cent time difference.

In later studies, the physiological state of the subject before, during and after each trial was monitored. Consistent and striking effects were noted in fingertip plethysmogram, EKG, and respiration. No changes were seen in the EEG or GSR. Except for the lack of GSR changes, the observed state is that of general arousal, quite similar to states of fear, anger or sexual arousal.

Two other effects were seen in some of these later studies. The first concerns the apparent "linger effect," that is, the pronounced tendency of mice in the target area to continue to revive faster than animals in the control area though the subject had left the area and was presumably no longer concentrating on the animals. This effect proved to be one of the most reliable in the studies, showing correlations between first halves (subject present) and second halves (subject absent) in excess of 80 per cent, with a high degree of significance.

The second effect is an apparent effect on photographic film sealed in light-tight envelopes and placed under the target animal and at successive distances. This film showed a degree of exposure following a successful experiment which was inversely related to the distance from the subject. The exposure consisted primarily of random patches of light, but on several plates patterns were observed similar to those in exposure due to electrostatic discharge. It has been noted in another laboratory that at least one of our major subjects consistently showed a high level of static charge, and tended to regain that charge rapidly after discharge to ground. This was verified in our laboratory in 1976 in several unreported electrometer studies; we also found the same to be true of one other successful PK subject, and not true of several non-PK subjects. The linger effect and the effects on film were also observed in a brief study involving PK on static objects.

It is not suggested that "healing" processes are solely due to the generation of static fields; however, there are three possibilities worth consideration. One, that the process is mediated via electrostatic or electromagnetic fields; Becker has shown in several studies that DC fields across the body may have a distinct effect on regenerative processes. If this is the case, the problem of the control of such charges remains; it seems obvious that an extraordinary degree of control would be required to affect one mouse only of a pair located not more than six or eight inches apart. If it is true, however, then a possible explanation of the linger effect might lie in induced (and re-induced) charges due to an effective capacitance between the animal (as one plate), and the table parts as the effective dielectric and second plate. The difficulty with this hypothesis, of course, is that the induced charges would be very small.

The second possibility is that electrostatic phenomena are merely correlates of the PK process, not directly involved with it. If this is the case, then electrostatic measures could be used as indicators; attempts in our laboratory to do this have not, however, been successful.

A third possibility is that we are dealing with a form of energy not identical to an electrical charge, but which behaves in the same manner under some circumstances. If this is true, then the explanation of the linger effect above might still apply, but other characteristics of the field would be impossible to predict.

Finally, it must be remembered that these speculations are quite tenuous, based as they are on mere suggestions from the data. We do not know of any limits to the psi process, and the possibility of the subjects' continuing to concentrate on the mice in the linger experiments, even though not present, is certainly real, as is the possibility of experimenter effects. Expectations of the subjects, also, make determinations of this sort difficult. Most of the subjects in the mouse-ether study believed, as determined from interview, that the PK process involved some nebulous "electrical" field, and it is not out of the question that they produced results coherent with their own prejudices. These difficulties arise in almost any parapsychological study and they can only be resolved with further study to determine the limits within which psi processes can be expected to occur.

EXPERIMENTAL DESIGNS FOR REAL-LIFE HEALING SITUATIONS

Gerald F. Solfvin (Psychical Research Foundation)

Why have research parapsychologists virtually ignored the area of psychic healing for so long? The answer to this is in large part methodological. Early studies of psychic healing, reminiscent of the British SPR's early work with mediums, focussed on painstaking collection of facts to document the phenomena. The results, exemplified by West's "Eleven Lourdes Miracles," always seem to fall short of "proof." Indeed, people are sometimes relieved of their symptoms, but there are always alternative explanations, such as the possible misdiagnosis of disease or that the cure was psychosomatic. It would be nice, of course, to isolate our phenomena by systematically eliminating all of the confounding variables, as we have done by sensory isolation in laboratory tests of psi, but it is here that an important (and usually implicit) decision must be made. If our goal is to prove that psychic healing exists, the isolation of it is our logical choice, but if we would ask questions of how it operates in its natural environment (including how it may interact with other variables) our approach to it would be along other lines.

The isolation approach has so far been the predominant force in parapsychology and therefore in psychic healing research. This may explain the paucity of research with healing in humans since some of the major variables that need to be eliminated are products of human interaction: suggestibility, belief and placebo effects. And here we see one of the limitations of this approach--while these studies represent the strongest scientific evidence we have of the existence of a paranormal healing effect, they give the practicing physician little guidance for what he might do to incorporate these findings into his or her everyday world of patients with cancer, glaucoma and cardiac arrests.

An example of the other approach, exploring the phenomenon as it naturally occurs, is found in Dolores Krieger's experiments where she found significant increases in blood hemoglobin values after the laying on of hands. No such differences were found in the control groups. Here human patients with real illnesses were her subjects. It is of interest to note here that her research design is right out of a clinical research textbook. Only with continued experimentation, with replications and variations, can this effect be established as a parapsychological one, a process much less efficient than the isolation approach. Meanwhile, medicine has a new tool, and Dr. Krieger has an experimental design which has produced consistent results of a possibly parapsychological nature.

Parapsychologists interested in exploring the laying on of hands should seriously consider Krieger's research model--the measurement of a physiological indicator of health before and after the treatment. There are many such indicators that are commonly used in medical diagnostics. Obviously, there are problems that need to be carefully worked out by a skilled and creative researcher (or group) to turn this into a rigorous experiment, but the potential gain seems to be large. Krieger, for example, has expanded her investigations into the characteristics of the receptive patient and the training of healers, using the change in hemoglobin values as a criterion variable.

Another research opportunity with psychic healing is suggested by the fact that many healers work at a distance from their patients. Lawrence LeShan has trained people throughout the U.S. in his Type I distant healing technique, many of whom are willing to collaborate in healing research. At the Psychical Research Foundation we have developed a simple yet rigorous design in which: (1) the subjects are real patients with real medical complaints who seek the services of a physician for its relief; (2) the healers are trained or gifted healers who are requested to perform distant healing in the way they normally do; and (3) the physician continues normal medical treatments on all of the patients involved in this project. Half of the patients, randomly selected, are "treated" by distant healing while the remaining half are controls. A double blind is maintained between the physician and patient, neither one knowing whether the patient is a healee or control. Accurate records of each patient's progress are maintained by the physician.

We need more research in the area of psychic healing--much more. While I would encourage continued efforts to isolate, and establish, a psychic healing effect, I would also advocate equal time for naturalistic designs. With this latter approach, the researcher should be willing at the outset to de-emphasize proving the phenomena, in favor of exploring the interaction of variables in a real-life setting. This is the inevitable trade off we deal with in research, where the question that is asked defines the range of possible answers.

Part 2:   Roundtables

WOMEN IN PARAPSYCHOLOGY*

ELEANOR M. SIDGWICK

Janet Lee Mitchell (City College, City University of New York)

Many women have made significant contributions to the field of parapsychology.   In this presentation three women are discussed who devoted their lives to parapsychological investigations, in different ways.   They are Eleanor M. Sidgwick, Louisa E. Rhine, and Eileen J. Garrett.

Eleanor Mildred Sidgwick was born in England on March 11, 1845, and lived to be nearly 91.   She grew up in an aristocratic setting and became interested in psychical research in her late twenties.   She was the only woman in a group of friends who sat with mediums who purported to produce physical phenomena.   To give you an idea of the level of her friendships at that time, the group consisted of her brother, who became prime minister of England; Lord Rayleigh, who won the Nobel prize in physics; and Henry Sidgwick, a Cambridge University professor, who later became her husband.   She probably sat with more physical mediums than any of the early investigators and her keen scientific mind never totally accepted the reality of physical phenomena.   However, she did think that probably such things did occur even if she had not witnessed them, and this sustained her interest in continuing to search for solid evidence of these occurrences.

She was not a founder of the Society for Psychical Research in 1882, possibly because of her many duties at Newnhamn College, Cambridge.   Newnhamn was a women's college which owed its existence mainly to her husband.   Eleanor was a brilliant mathematician, as well as psychical researcher.   She was college treasurer from 1876 to 1919 and became the second principal of Newnhamn in 1892, holding that position for 18 years.   She played an important part in promoting the higher education of women and stood for equality of opportunity for women in the 19th century.   She was so highly thought of that the Encyclopaedia Britannica, published in 1887, invited her to write a comprehensive history of spiritualism for their ninth edition.

Sidgwick did become an official member of the Society in 1884, two years after its founding, and her most industrious psychic

---

*Chairperson: Janet Lee Mitchell, City College, CUNY.

work extended over the next 50 years.   She was president of the
Society in 1908-9 and again joint president of honor with Sir Oliver
Lodge in 1932.   Her opinion as to the value of evidence was highly
respected because she paid close attention to detail and sought
accuracy and precision in her judgments.   She then expressed herself with absolute candor after her thorough analysis of the data.

She helped compile two of the classics of psychical research:
Phantasms of the Living and the Census of Hallucinations.   She was
early convinced of the reality of telepathy as an established fact.
She felt that clairvoyance would have to be dealt with in the future
as a possibility.   This opinion came about as a result of her studies
and report on the famous book tests in sittings with Gladys Osborne
Leonard.

For six years after her husband's death in 1900, she worked
faithfully in his memory.   She brought out new editions of three of
his philosophical works, with four volumes of unpublished material
left by him.   She also coauthored a Memoir of him.

Sidgwick was extremely critical of evidence for survival and
communication between the living and dead for many years.   The
work with Piper swayed her opinion somewhat towards survival but
she did not find it satisfactory as proof.   She openly admitted that
she had uniformly failed, whether as agent or percipient in thought-
transference experiments, or as sitter with Piper and other mediums.   She felt that the sitter, the deceased and the medium were
in some sort of telepathic rapport and if the sitter was not very
telepathic, it could distort, impair and sometimes exclude messages
from getting through intact.

The cross correspondences seemed to contain better evidence
for survival in Sidgwick's estimation and she began tentatively in
1908 to suggest that there may be "intelligent cooperation between
other than embodied human minds."   Her last report, in 1932 at
the age of 87, stated that, based on the evidence before her, she
was a firm believer both in survival and in the reality of communication between the living and dead.

It does not appear that Sidgwick was discriminated against by
her male peers.   This could possibly be accounted for by her aristocratic birth, her marriage to Henry Sidgwick and her work at
Cambridge, or simply because she was a brilliant woman of excep-
tional character and therefore her opinion was considered important
and valuable.   It is not surprising that when the editor of the SPR
Journal asked for a series of short biographies of the great men
and women of the early decades of the British Society, the first in
that series was an article on Eleanor Mildred Sidgwick.

LOUISA E. RHINE

Athena Anne Drewes (Maimonides Medical Center, New York)

Louisa Ella Rhine, born on November 9, 1891, in Sanford, New York, is a noted parapsychologist, writer, as well as associate and wife to J. B. Rhine. From 1948 to 1962 she was a staff member of the Parapsychology Laboratory at Duke University and until recently she was research director of the Institute for Parapsychology. She was coeditor of the Journal of Parapsychology and is currently its acting consultant. Louisa Rhine is a charter member of the Parapsychological Association. Aside from her many research articles, she has authored Hidden Channels of the Mind (1961), ESP in Life and Lab (1967), Mind Over Matter (1970), and PSI: What Is It? (1975).

Rhine's major research interests and contributions to the field of parapsychology are in spontaneous cases of psi phenomena and in PK. As seen in her numerous journal articles, she has particularly specialized in the collection and analysis of personal experiences in ESP, attempting to further the understanding of the mental processes involved and thereby to help in the creation of experimental hypotheses for laboratory work.

A brief summary of Rhine's major contributions are in order. Out of over 15,000 cases accumulated over the last 30 years, Rhine has roughly designated the types of spontaneous experiences as either contemporary (telepathic or clairvoyant) or precognitive. The largest single classification of all spontaneous cases were found to be precognitive with an estimate of 40 per cent out of one collection of 3290 cases. Rhine's assessment from her extensive survey was that all of the ESP experiences could be processed into one of four forms: realistic, unrealistic, intuitive and hallucinatory (with the addition of a few PK experiences). Dreams, being either realistic or unrealistic, were viewed as major media for psi experiences. Next would come waking spontaneous ESP consisting of full-blown hallucinations, intuitions or impressions. Rhine also included spontaneous psychokinesis as a form of spontaneous ESP. This was based on a section of cases where physical manifestations such as inexplicable clock stoppings were simultaneously linked to a death or accident.

Another outstanding conclusion arrived at from the analysis of spontaneous cases is that it is often the percipient who is the active partner in the ESP experience, be it clairvoyance, precognition, psychokinesis or telepathy. This view radically upsets the commonly held notion that in telepathy an agent is necessary for sending the information which is received by the percipient.

Louisa Rhine's latest finding based on her review of cases is that psychological processes of the individual affect the complete or incomplete transference of psi information from the unconscious

to consciousness.   She states that in each form of psi (realistic,
unrealistic, intuitive, hallucinatory and psychokinetic), the types of
incompleteness of psi information was linked to the process that
produced the psi form.   The amount of conviction people had regarding their experiences also played an important role.   Rhine
found that the conviction element of an individual did not appear to
result from any conscious decision, but rather was an item from
the unconscious that was frequently able to cross independently into
consciousness even when the factual information regarding the psi
experience was incomplete.

Through these outstanding contributions of Louisa Rhine,
researchers have been able to build laboratory experiments to explore further the many hypotheses that her works have stimulated.
We are grateful for the opportunity to be able to pay tribute to such
an outstanding woman in our field.

EILEEN J. GARRETT

Sally Ann Drucker (University of Buffalo, N. Y.)

Eileen Janette Garrett was born on March 17, 1893, in
County Meath, Ireland, and was raised on a farm by her aunt and
uncle.   Eileen had childhood playmates no one else saw, precognitive and telepathic experiences, and visions of the life force
spiraling elsewhere as farm animals died.   Punished severely by
her aunt when she told about her experiences, it was not until adult-
hood, after training at the College of Psychic Science in London,
that her psychic gifts truly flowered.

One of the greatest mediums of the century, by the end of
her life in 1970, she was known all over the world.   As a medium,
her visitors included movie magnates and prime ministers.   As a
psychic, she was investigated by scientists wherever serious research was taking place.   To the end, she retained a skepticism
about her gifts that made her a gifted psychic who was also a valuable coresearcher in experiments.

She was tested with cards at Duke by J. B. Rhine, through
dreams by the Maimonides staff, and in countless other ways, often
achieving spectacular results.   In addition, she went through weari-
some rounds of physiological and psychological testing to determine
the nature of the control spirits who spoke while she was in a
trance.   She was as curious about what they were as the investigators.

Because of this curiosity, Eileen Garrett established the
Parapsychology Foundation in 1951.   She wanted to support, finan-
cially and emotionally, the best scientific investigations of the paranormal.   But too much parapsychology was a bore, she said, and
she sought relief in running a restaurant, a hostel, a book publish-

ing firm and a literary magazine.   Just the same, in 1953 she and
the Foundation organized and sponsored the First International
Annual Conference of Parapsychological Studies in Utrecht, the
Netherlands.   The conferences continued, and the Parapsychology
Foundation issues an annual Proceedings of the meetings.

As a medium and a psychic, Eileen Garrett will always be
remembered as someone who not only cooperated with, but basically
co-experimented with investigators.   Despite her international reputation, she was detached, skeptical and objective about her trance
personalities.   Nevertheless, she helped thousands who were grief
stricken and wished for contact with loved ones through these trance
personalities.   Her talent and generosity of spirit alone ensure her
a memorable place in this century's history of parapsychological
research.

But in addition, she helped to develop parapsychology as a
field of science at a time when researchers were scattered and
funding minimal.   She provided the connecting links and organization that now, too, make it possible for much of the research going
on today to take place.

Eileen Garrett was a woman who did not let difficult marriages,
children's deaths, financial difficulties, or social criticism stop her
from developing her abilities and accomplishing what she set out to
do.   All of us in this room, to the degree that we, too, regard
parapsychological investigation as a very important human endeavor,
are in her debt.

RESEARCH ON NEAR DEATH EXPERIENCES*

A NEW LOOK

Karlis Osis (American Society for Psychical Research)

I am indeed happy to present a panel of researchers made up of those who are not identified with parapsychology along with those who are. Parapsychologists or not, we all share a common interest in near death experiences (NDEs) and all have empirical data, gathered and analyzed with scientific methods, to be presented. The samples mainly consist of interviews and observations of re- suscitated patients. This panel includes not only "insiders" and "outsiders" of parapsychology, but represents various disciplines, such as psychiatry, social psychology, and cardiology. In my opinion, the pluralistic approach, which brings to bear various disciplines and viewpoints, is essential in such a newly established field of inquiry. Science does not grow best in isolated pockets-- percolation of information and ideas is needed, and that is why this panel is here.

Work with NDEs is growing rapidly. Beside the panel mem- bers and the clinical approaches of Elisabeth Kübler-Ross and Raymond Moody, there are also systematic surveys being conducted by Garfield, Noyes and Kletti. Back in 1958, I felt very lonely when we started our first survey. The Zeitgeist then had no ears for listening to the dying. Nevertheless, our first survey of doc- tors and nurses found rich phenomena in the 190 cases. On the basis of this pilot survey, we developed our methods. A bipolar model was constructed by Erlendur Haraldsson and myself, which contrasted the two basic viewpoints: death as transition to post- mortem existence and death as ultimate destruction of personality. Each pole of the model consists of groups of hypotheses describing how the phenomena--and their interactions with medical, demograph- ical, psychological and cultural factors--are expected to be, if post- mortem survival is the case, and how they should look, in case the destruction hypothesis obtains. Subsequently, we tested the model with the data of two surveys (877 cases), one conducted in the United States and one in India.

The panel members will introduce their own methods and data. We may expect that an open exchange between researchers

---

*Chairperson: Karlis Osis. [See also pp. 49-50--editor.]

of various disciplines, like those on the panel here, will sharpen our methods and develop further models for the phenomena. Integration of medical, psychological and parapsychological viewpoints, in turn, might bring a new realism to survival research. I hope that new data and a fresh examination of the issues will be more fruitful than decades of theoretical arguments pro and con the "super ESP" hypothesis--that strange invention which shies like a mouse from being tested in the laboratory but, in rampant speculations, acts like a ferocious lion devouring survival evidence. My warmest appreciation to the panel members of other disciplines for their willingness to share their data with us.

SOME DETERMINANTS OF THE CORE NEAR DEATH EXPERIENCE

Kenneth Ring (University of Connecticut)

In a recent study, 102 persons who recovered from near death experiences (NDEs) were interviewed, the majority of them within two years of their near death incident. The main purpose of the study was to gather evidence relevant to Raymond Moody's conclusion (expressed in Life After Life) that there is, on coming close to death, a core NDE made up of certain common elements (e.g., floating out of one's body, traveling down a dark tunnel, seeing a light, etc.) which tends to unfold in a particular way. There were other questions this study was also designed to answer: Does it make a difference how one almost dies? This involved a comparison among illness victims, accident victims and suicide attempt victims. Does degree of prior religiosity influence the likelihood or the depth of the core NDE? What aftereffects can be traced to NDEs? This report is a summary of the data bearing on the first two questions; the last will be discussed elsewhere.

Forty-eight per cent of the respondents reported experiences which accorded with the basic pattern outlined by Moody. Overall, there were no sex differences in this regard (with one exception, to be noted below). Nevertheless, certain features of the core NDE more commonly appeared than others. In this regard, five stages of the core experience were distinguished. They are a feeling of indescribable peace, a sense of being out of one's body, a movement into a dark void, seeing a brilliant light, and entering into that light. The earlier stages were more common than the later ones and the frequency pattern was, in fact, monotonic over stages. The percentages ranged from 60 for Stage 1 to 10 per cent for Stage 5. Of those reporting a Moody-type experience, fully one third had a subjectively real out-of-body experience. Other features of the Moody pattern not mentioned above (e.g., the life review, encountering an "unseen presence," being greeted by deceased relatives, etc.) also occurred in significant numbers.

Near death experiences tended to be disproportionately as-

sociated with illnesses for women and with accidents and suicide
attempts for men.   The reasons for this unexpected and statistically
significant effect are not clear and require further examination.
The experiences of suicide attempt victims appear to be qualitatively
somewhat different from non-intentional near death experients in
that the pattern tends to be abridged and damped down; the highest
proportion of no recall cases is also found in this category.   The
data on suicide attempt victims, however, need to be interpreted
cautiously at this point.   Various measures showed that there was
absolutely no relationship between prior religiosity and the likelihood of having a Moody-type experience on coming close to death.

RECOLLECTIONS OF PATIENTS
WHILE UNCONSCIOUS AND NEAR DEATH

Michael B. Sabom and Sarah A. Kreutziger (Emory University and
     Veterans Administration Hospital, Decatur, Ga.)

        Numerous reports have appeared in the non-medical literature
of unique experiences of people near death.   To document the existence, nature and clinical implications of these experiences, 100
patients (68 prospective, 32 referred) who had been unconscious and
near death were interviewed.   At the time of unconsciousness, 39
patients experienced amnesia while 61 encountered a near death experience (NDE).   Of these latter, 32 experienced the passage of
consciousness into a foreign region or dimension of great beauty,
often encountering deceased relatives or friends (transcendence), 16
viewed their body and physical surroundings from a detached position of height, often clearly observing details of their resuscitation
by others (autoscopy), and 13 experienced both autoscopy and transcendence.   A feeling of great calm and peace pervaded all NDE
irrespective of the type or intensity of physical crisis causing unconsciousness and nearness to death.

        When patients with and without a NDE were compared, no
significant difference in age, sex, race, education, occupation,
formal religious involvement, or knowledge of similar events from
other sources were noted.   A definite decrease in death anxiety
occurred in most patients encountering a NDE (a response different
from patients without a NDE, $p < .001$).   In addition, most patients
with a NDE felt that the experience itself greatly assisted them in
coping with the day-to-day uncertainties of a disabling or terminal
physical condition.   Adequate medical explanation of these phenomena
is not presently available.   Further investigation is needed into the
cause of NDE and the implications these experiences may have for
personal and social concepts of death and dying.

THE CONTRIBUTION OF NEAR DEATH
EXPERIENCES TO THE EVIDENCE OF
SURVIVAL AFTER DEATH

Bruce Greyson and Ian Stevenson (University of Virginia)

The recent reawakening of interest among physicians and
psychologists in death and dying has led to a number of investigations of near death experiences (NDEs). However, few of these
investigators have been familiar with the scientific parapsychological
literature, which includes almost 100 years of convergent evidence
from a variety of sources suggestive of survival after death. By
virtue of this background, parapsychologists may be able to offer
suggestions for discriminating between NDEs that suggest postmor-
tem survival and those that are better explained otherwise. The
frequency with which certain features of NDEs are reported among
mystics and among users of hallucinogenic drugs is an important
factor in their interpretation. Corroborative evidence such as from
medical records may be of value in interpreting NDEs, as well as
psychological profiles of those reporting these experiences. It may
also be helpful to discriminate between primary aspects of NDEs
and their secondary effects, the attitudinal and behavioral changes
that often follow them. Methodological differences in investigating
NDEs can influence the amount and type of data reported. Though
cultural factors influence NDE reports, they do not fully explain
the veridical paranormal features often found in NDEs.

RESEARCH ON NEAR DEATH EXPERIENCES

Ian Stevenson (University of Virginia)

Widely divergent interpretations of near death experiences
(NDEs) show the need for research in this area; indeed, they show
that research in it has barely begun. Noyes and Kletti subsume
these experiences under "depersonalization" and regard them as a
particular type of adaptation to the stress of dying or the fear that
one is about to die. On the other hand, recent popular writings on
this subject have either explicitly said, or allowed readers to
believe, that near death experiences provide substantial evidence
for man's survival of death. Most persons who have had such experiences become convinced by them, if they were not already,
that they will survive death. The word "depersonalization" (originally a term in psychopathology) implies a diminution of personhood,
but the patients who have had these experiences almost invariably
later report that, at a time when they were thought to be dead or
nearly dead, they felt more alive and were in a sense more
"personalized" than ever before. The task of researchers is to
use the scientific method in order to learn whether those who have
not had such experiences are justified in sharing the beliefs of
those who have.

In this research, medical training--either on the part of the parapsychologist or that of a parapsychologist's collaborator--is absolutely essential. Only medical data and their analysis can clarify certain variations that have appeared in cases already studied. I shall mention two of these.

First, wide variations occur in the frequency with which patients who have had ostensibly similar physical conditions, such as cardiac arrests, report experiences during their physical crises that they can afterward remember. Some of these variations may derive from psychological factors--both on the part of the patient and on that of the interviewers eliciting information from them-- but it is at least possible that some of them are due to hitherto unnoticed physiological factors. We should also note that some patients who believe themselves to have been close to death during their crises were not in fact so, at least according to the indications of their medical records. Even if we attribute these discrepancies to exaggeration on the part of the patients or to deficiencies in the medical records, the possibility remains that important and hitherto unrecognized physical factors influence the occurrence of memorable experiences during NDEs.

Second, certain features of the experiences occur more commonly with some types of physical crises than with others. Unexpectedness of the crisis, as in falls during mountain climbing and near drownings, appears to be associated with a high incidence of the "life review" or panoramic memory. Yet panoramic memory occurs also in other types of cases such as in patients with severe physical illnesses. Understanding of these variations requires an investigation that combines observations of both physiological changes and psychological features.

Despite the importance of medical observations, however, they alone will not suffice to clarify the contribution of NDEs to the evidence of survival after death. For this we shall need the techniques that parapsychologists use in the study of other types of spontaneous cases. When patients claim to have had paranormal perceptions--such as of events at a distance from their bodies-- during their experiences, we should try as often as possible to obtain corroborations and verifications of their statements. Cases of this type seem to occur rarely among all reported NDEs, but one of them may be worth a hundred others that lack such apparent paranormal processes. Other types of experiences, such as those in which the patient later reports he looked down on his inert body from a position above it, or that he met deceased members of his family or religious figures, may not provide objective evidence of a paranormal process. Yet from the analysis of large numbers of cases with and without these features, we may gradually assemble evidence that justifies an interpretation of at least some of these cases as providing evidence for survival after death.

Part 3: Research Briefs

PSI AND PSYCHOPHYSIOLOGY*

THE EFFECT OF SHORT-TERM STIMULUS UPON E S P PROCESS

Soji Otani (The Japanese Society for Parapsychology)

The purpose of this investigation was to produce a transitional change in the ESP process by giving a short-term sensory stimulus during ESP tests. The subjects were asked to make their calls at a regular pace and a sensory stimulus, sound or light flash, was given at an unexpected time in the run. There were two series. The first series consisted of a preliminary experiment and a confirmatory one, in which the subjects made their calls by writing the ESP symbols. In the second series they were asked to press a key, guessing a target which was generated by a random number generator. The stimuli interposed during the test consisted of pleasant and unpleasant ones.

The result of the preliminary experiment showed that the sound stimulus given during the ESP test had a passing effect on ESP scoring. There was a decline of score in the two trials just after the stimulus (CR = 2.55, p = .02, two-tailed) and a rise in the third trial. After this the score approached the chance level.

In the confirmatory experiment, four kinds of sounds, 125 Hz, 250 Hz, 2000 Hz and 4000 Hz, were used as the interposed stirzuli. The ESP test proceeded at the rate of two seconds a trial. Each subject engaged in eight sessions, each of which consisted of four runs of ESP tests. The sound was given at a random place in the run, for a duration of two seconds, synchronized with the subject's calls. There was a decline in the trial just after the stimulus, a rise in the second and then an approach to the chance level. The positive deviation for the second trial was significant (CR = 2.94, p = .007, two-tailed).

In the second series, two kinds of sounds, 125 and 250 Hz, and a 10-Hz light flash were used as the interposed stimuli. The targets were the four digits 0 to 3, which were generated by a random number generator. The interval between calls was five seconds and the duration of the stimulus was 3.5 seconds. The subjects were given three units, consisting of about 100 trials each, and eight stimuli were interposed randomly in each unit. There was a difference in the change of ESP score after stimulation by the two kinds

---

*Chairperson: William Braud, Mind Science Foundation.

of stimuli.   When a sound was interposed, the change of score was
similar to the previous experiments, but when a light flash was
used, there was no change.   In the former condition, there was a
decline of score in the trial just after the stimulation (CR = 2.61,
p = .01, one-tailed), a rise to the chance level in the second trial,
and again a decline in the following two trials (CR = 3.01, p = .005,
two-tailed), followed by an approach to the chance level.

The results of these three experiments suggest that a short-
term stimulus interposed during ESP performance has a transitional
effect, inhibitory and excitatory, on the ESP process.   The method
used in this investigation makes it possible to observe a change in
the psi process for short periods and the method can be used as a
tool to gather or condense psi effects within a small area.

PSI CORRELATES OF VOLITION: A PRELIMINARY
TEST OF ECCLES' "NEUROPHYSIOLOGICAL HYPOTHESIS"
OF MIND-BRAIN INTERACTION

C. Honorton[†] and L. Tremmel (Maimonides Medical Center)

In John Eccles' solution to the problem of mind-brain interaction, the brain is a detector rather than a generator of mind:
"weak mind influences" psychokinetically modify the pattern of discharge of large neural networks.   This suggests that a primary
function of psi is mind-brain communication.

Two pilot studies were conducted to test the hypothesis that
there is a psi component to volition.   A binary noise-driven random
generator (RNG) served to detect PK activity in relation to the subjects' efforts to influence their ongoing EEG activity through biofeedback.   RNG output was sampled and gated ("triggered") by the
subjects' success/failure in meeting preset EEG feedback conditions.
If Eccles' hypothesis is correct, significant PK effects (deviations
from randomness) should coincide with periods in which the subjects
succeed in the volitional task, i.e., when they meet the specified
EEG feedback conditions.   This was our only prediction in Experiment 1.

Ten volunteer subjects each contributed a single session.
The subject was seated in a reclining chair in an IAC Sound-
Isolation Room and was placed in Ganzfeld.   EEG recording was
monopolar with the active electrode on the left occipital area,
referenced to the opposite earlobe.   The subject was informed that
the presence of EEG alpha rhythm activity would be associated with
an audible tone.   The subject's volitional task during the session
was to keep the tone ON as much as possible.

---

†Dagger will indicate speaker.

EEG activity was recorded on a Beckman Type R Dynograph. Alpha detection and feedback was provided via a digital frequency discriminator.   The RNG was run at 10 trials per second, with the target bit logically complemented on each trial.   Each run consisted of 100 EEG alpha gated trials.   Ten runs were taken in each session.

PK scores were obtained by squaring the Z-scores for each run and summing across runs to obtain a chi-square with 10 df. The overall PK results were significant with X^2 (100 df) = 145. 7 and p = . 002, two-tailed.   However, the results are ambiguous with regard to Eccles' hypothesis.   Since we did not monitor ungated RNG output (i. e. , when the subject's EEG was outside the feedback range), it is possible that the observed PK effect was unrelated to the subject's EEG.

We addressed this and other issues in Experiment 2.   We monitored both gated (alpha) and ungated (nonalpha) RNG output and added a no feedback "baseline" condition.   The baseline condition was identical to the EEG feedback condition except that the subjects were asked simply to relax and were not given EEG feedback or volitional instructions.   This provided a basis for discriminating between the intrinsic alpha-PK hypothesis and the hypothesis that there is a PK component to volition.

Several other changes were made: (1) EEG electrode placement was C_z to linked earlobes; (2) EEG recording and feedback was from an Autogenic Systems 120a EEG Analyzer; (3) total RNG trials per run (gated plus ungated) were increased to 500; (4) soft music was provided by headphones, with EEG feedback (during feedback trials) superimposed over music; and (5) the subject's EEG feedback was shaped by the experimenter (L. T.) by increasing the minimal amplitude threshold to maintain EEG alpha feedback approximately 20 to 30 per cent of the time during feedback runs.

We tested the following predictions in Experiment 2. (1) The significant PK result of Experiment 1 would be replicated in the gated feedback condition; (2) gated feedback PK scores would be significantly larger than ungated feedback scores; (3) gated feedback PK scores would be significantly larger than gated baseline PK scores; and (4) for the gated feedback condition, there would be a significant relationship between EEG frequency and amplitude changes within the session and overall PK scores.

Seven subjects contributed 12 sessions under these conditions. In each session the subject completed 10 runs of 500 RNG trials in the baseline and EEG feedback conditions.

For the gated feedback condition, PK results are significant with X^2 (120 df) = 159. 2 and p = . 005, one-tailed.   Thus the alpha gated PK results of Experiment 1 are replicated, confirming our first prediction.   PK results for the remaining three conditions (feedback ungated, baseline gated and ungated) are nonsignificant.

Predictions 2 and 3 were examined by t tests for uncorrelated means.   PK scores for gated EEG feedback trials are significantly higher (p = . 01, one-tailed) than the ungated feedback PK scores. This indicates that the PK result is related to the subjects' EEG alpha activity, thus confirming prediction 2.   Moreover, and very importantly with regard to Eccles' hypothesis, the gated EEG feedback PK scores are significantly higher (p = . 034, one-tailed) than gated baseline PK scores, suggesting a relationship between PK and EEG feedback rather than an intrinsic relationship between PK and EEG alpha activity (prediction 3).   These latter two findings isolate the PK activity in this experiment to the gated EEG feedback condition.

Prediction 4 was not confirmed.   Although in the expected direction, the degrees of change in EEG frequency and amplitude were nonsignificantly related to PK scores.

SKIN POTENTIAL ACTIVITY AND GUESSING PERFORMANCE OF HIGH VS. LOW DEFENSIVE SUBJECTS IN A GESP TASK

M. Johnson, [†] J. Hartwell and W. van den Brink (University of Utrecht)

A GESP test was given to 27 university students selected according to their scores on the Defense Mechanism Test (DMT). One group of subjects was composed of those with higher degrees of preconscious defensive organization; the other group was composed of those with lower degrees.

A subject chose from a set of seven color slides the one he found most appealing.   He rated two qualities of this slide along scales of semantic differential (unpleasant to pleasant, and makes me feel tense to relaxed).   The chosen picture was used as the "pleasant" stimulus upon which the agent concentrated during the experiment.

A polaroid photograph was taken of the subject and placed in a binder along with a group of unpleasant (frightening) pictures. They were observed together by the agent (M. J.) when attempting to transmit an "unpleasant" feeling to the subject.

The subject was then led to the experimental room, a few rooms away from the agent's room, and seated in a comfortable chair.   He was instructed in the procedures and told to relax.   The room was dimly lit and white noise was provided.   After a five-minute period for habituation the study commenced.   The subject's skin potential was recorded during trials of 20 seconds while the agent viewed the pleasant or unpleasant pictures and attempted to communicate his feeling or impression to the subject.   At the conclusion of each trial, the subject registered a guess about the kind

of stimulus by pressing one of two buttons.   A total of 30 trials
were given to each subject separated by 15-second intervals.

The stimulus selection, trial timing and data collection was
under the programmed control of the laboratory computer.   The
target was chosen randomly for each trial by a noise-driven random
number generator (RNG).   It was communicated to the agent by a
pair of small lights.   Tones from a loudspeaker to agent and subject marked the onset and end of each trial.

Three hypotheses were assessed: (1) the subjects in the low
defensive group would guess more accurately than those in the high
defensive group; (2) the skin responses during trials with unpleasant
stimuli would differ significantly from those during trials with
pleasant stimuli; and (3) the subjects in the low defensive group
would manifest stronger skin potential activity toward the unpleasant
stimuli than those in the high defensive group.

In addition to these formal hypotheses it was agreed to study
the data for the presence of PK upon the selection of stimuli by the
RNG and to examine the accuracy of guessing for dependence upon
reaction time and types of stimuli.

None of the hypotheses was confirmed by the results.
Specifically, (1) the "higher defensive" subjects guessed somewhat
more accurately than the "less defensive" subjects although not
significantly so (t = 0.93).   (2) No consistent differences in the
magnitude of skin potential activity to the two types of stimuli were
observed (CR = 0.29).   And (3) although low defensive subjects
showed somewhat higher skin potential activity than high defensives
to unpleasant stimuli, the difference was not significant (t = 0.65).

The RNG selected more pleasant stimuli than expected.   On
17 of the 27 runs (there were three ties) an excess of pleasant
stimuli was chosen.   The result is suggestive of PK but not significant.   Guessing accuracy was assessed for dependence upon type of
stimulus and response time by a four-cell chi-square test.   Subjects
were slightly more accurate in their guessing when they responded
slowly to pleasant stimuli and quickly to unpleasant ones.   The effect
was not significant (p = 0.1).   No evidence was found for a correlation between guessing accuracy and skin potential activity.

One should notice that the DMT was used as an instrument
for prediction of ESP scoring as well as for skin potential activity.
The hypotheses related to the DMT were not supported.   However,
one should observe that the population did not represent extreme
groups.   The subjects were simply divided into a "less" and "more"
defensive group.

As a strategy for future work in which time-consuming and
complicated electrophysiological techniques are used, we would
recommend a preliminary screening procedure for selection of subjects.

PHYSIOLOGICAL RESPONSE DURING PSI AND
SENSORY PRESENTATION OF AN AROUSING STIMULUS

Michael Thorne Kelly, [†] Mario Varvoglis and Patrice Keane
(Maimonides Medical Center)

Several researchers have worked from the assumption that
psi interactions can be detected as changes in physiology at the
level of the autonomic nervous system whether or not the subjects
consciously experience any interaction.   In 1933, L. L. Vasiliev
successfully used a measure of galvanic skin response to establish
when his subjects responded to telepathic instructions to go into
and come out of hypnotic sleep.   Since then, Douglas Dean has used
the plethysmograph--an instrument for measuring changes in digital
blood volume--to monitor autonomic response to remote stimuli.
As of this writing, only a few studies of autonomic response have
been done.   So that in spite of the support for a correlation between psi stimulation and autonomic response provided by Vasiliev,
Dean, Tart and by Braud [RIP 1977, pp. 123-134], the failures to
confirm by Beloff et al. , Barron and Mordkoff, and Woodruff and
Dale leave the issue open.

The most extensive work has been done on the basic issue
by Douglas Dean.   While no one has attempted a literal replication
of his work, several researchers have cited it as a conceptual
model in their use of other measures than the plethysmograph.   In
recent research, excepting Dean's, the preferred measure of
autonomic activity has been electrodermal.   Measures of electrodermal activity (EDA) are felt to be more reliable and more sensitive than those obtainable with the plethysmograph.   The research
using electrodermal activity, perhaps because it has been attempted
by different experimenters with a wide variety of equipment, experience, and experimental design, is contradictory.   Some of the
studies which failed to confirm suffered from flaws in design or
execution which may have been responsible for their failure to con-
test the null hypothesis.   With this in mind, we decided that sufficient advances in instrumentation and in psi-conducive techniques
had taken place since the most recent prior study to warrant again
exploring EDA as an independent measure of psi activity.

In a double-blind study with automatic data recording, nine
sessions were completed.   In each session, the subject was put
into a psi conducive environment using Ganzfeld stimulation and
sensory isolation in an IAC sound-shielded room.   Each session
was composed of a psi module immediately followed by a sensory
module.   Each module was made up of a 15-minute relaxation
period followed by four consecutive potential stimulus periods each
of which was five minutes long.

The stimulus period was chosen randomly with an electronic
noise-driven random number generator.   During the psi stimulus
period, the subject's sender--usually someone he or she brought

along--was shown a five-minute film of a child's birth.   During the
sensory stimulus period (which had the same sequential position
within the four potential stimulus periods as the psi stimulus period
had among the four potential psi stimulus periods), the subject saw
the film.

The receiver's skin conductance level (SCL) was monitored
with an Autogenic Systems 3400 Feedback Dermograph, as was his
skin conductance response.   Skin temperature was monitored with
an Autogenic Systems 2000b Feedback Thermometer (TMP), and his
muscle activity was monitored with an Autogentic Systems 1700
Myograph (EMG).   All data recording was done with an Autogenic
Systems 5600 Computing Multichannel Data Acquisition Center.

We predicted that the subject would show arousal specifically
in the skin conductance response (SCR) for both conditions.   No
predictions were made for the other three measures.   The data were
analyzed by comparing the level of arousal in the stimulus period
with the average arousal of the other three (potential, now baseline)
periods.   This was done for all four physiological measures with a
pairwise t-test.   The results for both psi and sensory conditions
were significant.

LEFT-RIGHT HEMISPHERIC DIFFERENCES
BETWEEN A PSI AND NON-PSI GROUP

Ken Kobayashi, James C. Terry[†] and William D. Thompson (San
Antonio, Texas)

Research has provided evidence that psi is associated with
the right hemisphere of the brain.   To better understand the processing of psi and the functioning of the hemispheres in relation to
psi, it is necessary to record the EEG of each hemisphere.   Galin
and Ornstein have reported that the appearance of alpha rhythm
indicated a "turning off" of information processing in the area involved.   We hypothesized that there would be a significant difference
in alpha level between a "psi group" and "non-psi group" (as determined by a CR measure beforehand) in the right hemisphere.   We
also hypothesized that the right hemisphere would be highly active
(little or no alpha activity) during a successful psi task and the left
hemisphere would be highly inactive (large amounts of alpha activity)
during the task.   We hypothesized for successful psi subjects that
there would be less alpha activity in the right hemisphere during
the psi task period than during the relaxation period.

Subjects were 50 student volunteers.   All but five were left-
hemisphere dominant (and right-handed).   The subjects' task was to
obtain an impression of a Zener card concealed in an opaque envelope.

Experimenters and subjects were unaware of the symbol within each envelope. Envelopes were divided into sets of 50 and placed in containers. The containers were returned to the experimenter who administered the task. Before each experimental session began, the experimenter randomly numbered each envelope. During the task period, the experimenter recorded the subject's call. Each subject received 50 trials per session.

An assistant recorded each target symbol according to the number on the envelope. The assistant kept the recorded target symbols and the experimenter kept the recorded subject's calls until the experiment was completed. The records were scored for matching target symbols and subject calls. The scoring was done by the experimenter and an assistant.

Once the subjects had met the criteria for selection, a brief description of the experimental procedure was presented. The subjects were told about the ESP task and were shown the five ESP symbols.

Autogen System Incorporated standard EEG electrodes were placed according to the 10-20 System of Electrode Placement; left and right occipital lobes (O_1 and O_2), temporal lobes (T_3 and T_4) and frontal poles (Fp_1 and Fp_2). The frontal poles were used as the reference.

Subjects were seated in an anechoic chamber and in a reclining chair. A Ganzfeld procedure was then followed. EEG activity was imputed to two autogen 120 EEG analyzers, one for each hemisphere. Total time spent in alpha was measured.

Subjects were given recorded experimental instructions through headphones. After 30 minutes, white noise was presented for five minutes and then a relaxation period for five minutes. After this, the task period was initiated when the experimenter laid an envelope with a target card in it on the back of the subject's right hand. When the subject vocalized a (self-paced) call, the experimenter recorded the response, removed the envelope from the subject's hand, and replaced it with the next envelope. This procedure continued for 50 trials. Total time spent in alpha for the task and relaxation period was measured.

Using a CR measure, subjects were placed into one of three groups. Subjects with an absolute CR of 2.00 or greater constituted the psi group. Subjects with a CR not greater than .5 constituted the non-psi group. All other subjects were not used. The cross-dominant subjects had a CR of 3.00, $p < .002$, the other subjects had a CR of 3.95, $p < .00004$. Fifteen subjects were independently significant. The psi group contained 13 subjects and the non-psi group 17. Further data analysis was conducted on these two groups only.

The percentage of time spent in alpha for each hemisphere

was determined by dividing the total time spent in a period into the amount of time the hemisphere spent in the alpha frequency during that period. The percentage of time spent in alpha for each hemisphere during the two periods was not calculated until the entire experiment was completed. These calculations were carried out by an experimenter independent of the ESP protocol scoring.

The means and standard deviations of the dependent variable (percentage of time spent in alpha) were worked out. There was a significant difference between the right hemisphere from the relaxation period to the task period for the psi group (t = 3.16; 12 df; p < .01). As expected, there was more alpha in the relaxed condition, but less alpha during the task period for the right hemisphere. In the left hemisphere, there was no difference from the relaxed to the task period for the psi group. The non-psi group showed just the opposite effect, with significantly more activity in the right and also the left hemisphere from the relaxed period to the task period (t = 2.94; 16 df; p < .01).

Our first hypothesis, that there would be a significant difference between alpha level in the right hemisphere between the psi and non-psi groups, was not confirmed.

Our second hypothesis, that there would be a significant difference between the hemispheric activity as measured by percentage of time spent in alpha during the psi task period, was also not confirmed. Our third prediction, that there would be significantly more activity for the psi group in the right hemisphere from the relaxed to the task period, was confirmed. The non-psi group had a significant opposite effect, with the left hemisphere becoming active during the task period. It appears that the right hemisphere became active too with a significant change at the .05 level of significance (t = 2.32, 16 df) from the relaxed to the task period. These findings seem to suggest that successful subjects were able to quiet down both hemispheres in the relaxation period; then activate the right hemisphere in the task period while continuing to keep the left hemisphere relaxed. For the unsuccessful subjects, when they went from the relaxation period to the task period both hemispheres became active. This seems to support the possibility that the left hemisphere may be adding competitive noise to the system, confusing subjects in the kind of responses to make.

STUDY OF RELAXATION TECHNIQUES WHEN USING
PLETHYSMOGRAPHIC RECORDINGS AS INDICATORS OF ESP

Erlendur Haraldsson (University of Iceland)

In a previous experiment by the author, vasomotor reactions to emotional stimuli were used as a sole indicator of ESP. In a telepathy experiment, pairs of subjects were used, one member of

each pair first serving as a receiver and the other as a sender.
In a session immediately following, members of the pair changed
roles. The person who had first served as a receiver now became
a (second) sender, and the first sender became a second receiver.
In three experiments involving 182 subjects an unexpected effect
emerged.   That person of the pair who first served as receiver
tended towards psi-missing whereas the second receiver, who before
had acted as sender, tended towards psi-hitting.   This difference in
psi performance was significant.

One can speculate on the reasons for this difference in psi
performance between the first and second receivers.   Possibly the
first receiver had not come sufficiently to rest physiologically,
causing psi-missing in the first session.   If this explanation is
correct, a longer period of rest for the first perceiver, before his
ESP session, may eliminate the psi-missing.

The purposes of the experiment to be reported are three:
to try to replicate the difference in scoring direction between the
first and second receivers; to test the hypothesis that the psi-missing
of the first receivers can be eliminated by longer rest before the
ESP session; and to test the effect of the Ganzfeld technique, claimed
to enhance psi performance, on the first and second receivers.

Seventy-eight subjects participated in the experiment; of these
three were dropped because of the low quality of their plethysmograms.
Eight senior students of psychology served as experimenters, each
participating in 18 to 20 sessions, in half of them as a chief experimenter and in the other half as assistant experimenter.

The same basic procedure was used as in a previously reported experiment by the author; and is similar to that used by
Dean in his experiments with the plethysmograph.   The vasomotor
reaction which served as an indicator of ESP was measured by a
photoelectric plethysmograph.   Two subjects took part in each session, each only serving once in the experiment as a receiver.   By
a random procedure one of each pair was allotted the role of receiver and rested on a reclining chair.   Two experimenters participated in each session.   One of them stayed with the sender and
handed him the targets at predetermined times, while the chief experimenter attended to the receiver and took the plethysmographic
measurements.   The receiver and the chief experimenter were in
separate rooms during the session.   The sender and the assistant
experimenter were in a third room some distance from the other
two rooms.   One-way communication from the chief experimenter
attending to the polygraph allowed him to signal the assistant experimenter that he should start the ESP session.   For use as targets,
names were supplied by the receiver of persons who recently had an
emotional effect on him.   In each session 10 names were "sent,"
each for 20 seconds.   Ten equally long periods in which no names
were sent were used as controls.

This basic procedure was used throughout the experiment,

but two new variables were introduced. First, the length of rest given to each receiver before the start of the ESP session was 25 minutes for half the subjects and five minutes for the other half; and second, a Ganzfeld technique was administered to half of the subjects (visual and auditory). Thus each subject might get one of the four treatments: short rest and Ganzfeld, short rest and no Ganzfeld, long rest and Ganzfeld, and long rest and no Ganzfeld. Each of four pairs of experimenters handled the subjects in only one of these four treatments. Experimenters were randomly selected for each of the four treatments but subjects were not randomized.

The 37 first receivers obtained a mean Z score of -.19 and the 38 second receivers a mean Z score of +.33. The difference between them is significant (t = 2.26, p = .03, two-tailed). This result confirmed our previous finding of the difference in the scoring direction of the first and second receiver. Our first hypothesis was confirmed, first receivers showing psi-missing and second receivers psi-hitting.

Longer rest did not effect the psi-missing of the first re- ceivers. The Ganzfeld technique also had no effect on the psi performance of the first receivers nor on the subjects as a whole. In this experiment the subjects had no task but to relax. There was no free association as in most previous experiments using the Ganzfeld technique. In our long rest period with Ganzfeld, many subjects complained about difficulties staying awake and some dozed off.

Post hoc we analyzed what effect the different experimenters might have had on the psi performance of the subjects. There was a significant effect for the chief experimenters (F = 2.32, df = 7,74, p = .04).

SPONTANEOUS CASE STUDIES AND SURVEYS*

SPONTANEOUS PSI EXPERIENCES AMONG UNSELECTED HIGH SCHOOL SUBJECTS

JoMarie Haight, [†] J. E. Kennedy and H. Kanthamani (Institute for Parapsychology, FRNM, Durham, N. C.)

Spontaneous cases are instances of psi operating in a natural setting. From a study of these cases, one could possibly gain some insight into the psi process. The Duke collection and the study of it by L. E. Rhine stands as the most thorough attempt to study spontaneous cases with this objective. Recently an opportunity arose for us to initiate a similar project using our most common subject population: unselected high school students.

Students from five psychology classes of one high school were administered a standard personality questionnaire (Cattell's HSPQ), an ESP test (12 runs of standard ESP symbols), and an "ESP experience" questionnaire constructed to tap variables such as attitude, frequency of dream recall, luckiness and so on. One item on this questionnaire asked for the students to indicate if they had had any psi experience, and if so, to describe the experience in as much detail as possible. A total of 113 students out of 257 described some type of experience. We have collected these data for two years, 1977 and 1978. We presented parts of the first year's data at the fifth SERPA meeting.

The experiences written by the students were divided into five categories: (1) good cases--experiences that clearly fit the criteria of spontaneous cases; (2) borderline cases--experiences that, for one reason or another, were not clearly classifiable as likely psi experiences; (3) déjà vu cases; (4) non-psi experiences; and (5) experiences which happened to someone else.

The 46 cases classed as "good psi cases" were separated into the forms suggested by L. E. Rhine. All of the cases, except one, fell into either dreams (43 per cent) or intuitive (54 per cent). One case suggestive of PK was reported.

Rhine found a relationship between the form of the experience and completeness of information contained in the experience. The

---

*Chairperson: Ian Stevenson, University of Virginia.

present cases showed the same pattern with 90 per cent of the dreams and 52 per cent of the intuitive cases containing complete information. In addition, these cases showed a pattern of more conviction in intuitive experiences as reported by Rhine.

Regarding the relationship between completeness of information and the presence or absence of conviction, 69 per cent of the complete intuitive cases also had conviction, while only 22 per cent of the complete dream cases had conviction. A similar trend was found by Rhine.

Our sample came from a specific age group, namely teenagers between 16 and 18 years old. However, we find the patterns in their reported experiences similar to those in a larger, more heterogeneous and older group.

The close similarity of the results to previous work is very encouraging as it suggests that our sample has characteristics comparable to the large body of cases collected by L. E. Rhine. This suggests that Rhine's classification patterns have general applicability. Of course, the small number of cases in our sample dictates that any conclusions would be decidedly premature.

Of our total sample, about 44 per cent provided further information about a specific experience. About a third of these experiences were clearly suggestive of psi. Thus, while this type of screening project is susceptible to selection of case bias, it does provide some information about the type and amount of selection occurring.

Telephone interviews are currently being conducted with all students from the 1978 group who described a possible psi experience. This will give more detailed information about the experience and make classification clearer.

PERSONALITY AND SPONTANEOUS EXPERIENCES:
AN EXPLORATORY STUDY

H. Kanthamani, JoMarie Haight[†] and J. E. Kennedy (Institute for Parapsychology, FRNM)

While there is abundant literature on personality variables and lab test performance, there is very little that can be related to spontaneous psi experiences. Previous investigators working with case studies, could hardly worry about personality variables, since their foremost interest was first to identify the forms and types of experiences. Early in her studies Louisa E. Rhine noted that spontaneous experiences may be influenced by the basic personality type of the experimenter. We were able to explore this issue in our project.

As mentioned in the previous paper, for two years we have collected data on spontaneous experiences, attitude, personality and other relevant aspects from a large group of unselected high school students. Personality comparisons were made between those reporting some experience and those who did not report any. Also, comparisons between people reporting different types of experiences were examined.

The "experience report group" was compared with those not reporting an experience on the 12 items of the ESP experience questionnaire. On the question "Do you believe you have ESP?," the experience group reported significantly more positive attitudes than the no-experience group. On the remaining 10 items of this questionnaire, seven showed significant differences between the two groups, with the experience group showing greater acceptance of psi and related phenomena than those having no experience. A similar analysis was done with Cattell's HSPQ factors. Only one of the 24 factors was marginally significant. From these results one possible interpretation emerges. There does not seem to be any relevant personality difference between those who report psychic experiences from those who do not. Nevertheless, there seems to be wide attitudinal differences between them as can be noticed from the ESP experience questionnaire.

Next those subjects whose cases were classified as good cases were compared with those whose cases were classified as non-psi experiences on all the factors as before. None of the differences for the ESP questionnaire showed striking significance. On the HSPQ factors, the two groups differed somewhat more. On factor B, which is a measure of "general intelligence," subjects reporting good cases obtained significantly greater scores than those reporting non-psi cases. Considering the secondary factors, school achievement (SA) and neuroticism (N) show interesting differences. The good cases have lower N scores and higher SA scores than the non-psi cases. It should be noted that the school achievement factor is a measure of intelligence plus a number of other personality variables from the HSPQ and is not based on the actual achievement in the school (e. g. , grades). These three factors together (B, SA and N) might suggest that the good case group are well adjusted, with greater motivation and potential for school achievement. More detailed analysis showed that the school achievement and neuroticism differences were primarily due to the high N and low SA scores of the non-psi group.

The next level of analysis divided the good cases into those with complete versus incomplete information. We were particularly interested in this classification as L. E. Rhine had hypothesized that lack of complete information may be related to some aspect of personality which may block or inhibit some information from reaching conscious awareness. The school achievement factor was again found to be related to whether the subject reported complete information. Those reporting complete information scored higher on this factor than those reporting incomplete information. A particularly interesting relationship between completeness of information and a sheep-goat question was found. For the question "Do you believe you have ESP?" a majority of the complete cases said either yes or uncertain. However, none among the incomplete cases said yes for this question; most were uncertain about it.

Further analysis could be done as we develop specific hypotheses. We hope to continue this project and as more cases are collected the relationship with personality aspects should become more meaningful.

A PHENOMENOLOGICAL ANALYSIS
OF NEAR DEATH EXPERIENCES

Bruce Greyson and Ian Stevenson (University of Virginia)

Contributions to the evidence of man's survival of physical death may come from visions, or other experiences that may be paranormal, reported by persons close to death in three distinct situations. Persons who actually die may, in the brief period before death, have and report such experiences; persons who seem to be at the point of death, or are even formally declared dead but then recover, may report such experiences during their "near death" period; and persons who narrowly escape death, as in an automobile accident, without being seriously injured, may report such experiences during their "close brush" with death.

The first type of situation, frequently referred to as "deathbed visions," has been extensively studied by Barrett, Osis, and Osis and Haraldsson. The two remaining types of situations, frequently referred to collectively as "near death experiences" (NDEs) have received much attention in the popular press in recent years. However, they have yet to be explored intensively, despite a growing number of case collections of various subgroups of these types in the scientific literature.

We and others are planning prevalence studies of near death experiences. Through detailed interviews of all persons in a specified population that have come close to death (e.g., in a hospital coronary care unit or emergency room), we hope to ascertain the incidence, the characteristics and the effects of NDEs on people. This strategy would eliminate the biases engendered by the selection or self-selection of subjects which has characterized most of the studies published to date.

Prior to attempting such a controlled study, however, it is necessary to establish the range and expected varieties of experiences to be included in the prevalence study. This paper will report the results of a phenomenological analysis of the frequencies and cross-correlations of characteristic features of an unselected sample of approximately 100 NDEs.

Cases were obtained from a variety of solicited sources, and consisted of firsthand accounts written or tape-recorded by the subjects, supplemented in most cases by detailed questionnaires, in-depth interviews, and/or relevant medical records of the events. From these data, each case was coded along approximately 200 parameters, which included:

subject's familial and sociodemographic backgrounds;

extent of subject's prior knowledge of or experience with transcendental or paranormal phenomena;

medical, psychological and social circumstances surrounding the NDE;

actual actions or events experienced while near death;

sensory and perceptual aspects of the NDE;

cognitive and intellectual functioning during the NDE;

affective quality and emotional content of the NDE; and

subsequent effects of the NDE on the subject's attitudes and behavior.

These variables are currently being analyzed with the aid of the Statistical Package for the Social Sciences (SPSS), a Fortran computer program. Major results of the frequency analysis of these variables will be described, as well as specific cross-tabulations of these variables, selected to explore hypothesized interactions. Contingency coefficients will be used as a measure of strength of association for these interactions and the significance of the correlations will be assessed by chi-square tests.

The frequencies of various elements of NDEs found in this collection of cases will be contrasted with anecdotal reports and previous surveys reported in the literature. The implications of the significant cross-correlations among various factors will be explored in terms of research strategies for proposed prevalence studies and the interpretation of results as possible evidence of survival of physical death or of paranormal occurrences at the threshold of death.

INSIDERS' VIEWS OF THE OBE:
A QUESTIONNAIRE SURVEY

Karlis Osis (American Society for Psychical Research)

Out-of-body experiences (OBEs) appear to be molded considerably by the beliefs and expectations characteristic of the experient's subculture. Researchers, in turn, tend to select aspects of the OBE that are highly specific to their own subcultures. We attempted to counteract biases by developing a questionnaire in close cooperation with the experients themselves.

Our questionnaire consists of 96 items, including free descriptions of the OBE, as well as a combination of open-ended and alternate-choice questions. Appeals were made via media, through newsletters of interested groups and to teachers of parapsychology. We intended to study phenomenology intrinsic in our OBE sample; because of a lack of sufficient resources, we were unable to aim at a representative sample of the United States population.

So far we have performed frequency analyses on 304 questionnaires. Age and sex were rather evenly distributed, while educational level was unusually high: 79 per cent attended college. Religious affiliations were somewhat biased toward the non-traditional groups. To most respondents, the OBE seemed to come naturally as an unexpected surprise: 58 per cent read nothing about the OBE and only 13 per cent read a book about this phenomenon prior to the experience. After the experience, 92 per cent read up on it, but only 3 per cent said that their personal experience was the same as one or more found in the literature they had covered.

In parapsychological interpretations, the OBE is often reduced to fantasies of flying coupled with ESP. Fully 86 per cent of our respondents stressed dissimilarity between the OBE and ESP; 81 per cent said that OB perception differs from that of customary ESP. The reasons behind these observations varied. Although 68 per cent said they maintained a continuous visual environment, only 12 per cent reported "seeing" in brief, few-second snatches, and the rest reported that vision fluctuated: sometimes continuous, at other times impressionistic. The majority of respondents claimed to "see" in a normal perspective; however, 40 per cent stated that the usual perceptual habits periodically broke down: seeing around corners, 360-degree vision, etc. One-third (34 per cent) of our respondents reported a kind of fusion occasionally occurring between themselves and the objects they perceived, e. g., "being intimately close," or "engulfing" them. To 44 per cent of our respondents, the objects themselves seemed to be more intrinsically related than in normal vision; yet, 79 per cent said they saw them as sharply accentuated and detailed. At times, 52 per cent "see" objects as transparent, glowing with inner light or having auras around them. They sometimes "look alive," change shapes, move or vibrate for 24 per cent of our respondents. However, things are still experienced as percepts independent from personal volition.

OBEs have often been interpreted as dreams or daydreams, but for various reasons respondents disagree. For example, only 4 per cent found dream imagery similar to OB "seeing."

Experients frequently claimed that they were noticed when visiting via OB. We obtained only 16 verifications through witnesses (6 per cent) that the OB individual was indeed perceived; in one case, the apparition was collectively seen.

A large majority (82 per cent) of experients find their OB existence describable by size, that is, they perceive it within spatial dimensions. More than half (54 per cent) believed themselves to be of normal body size, while others felt either smaller (just a "point in space") or larger; 6 per cent said that they could change from small to very large.

The form of the perceived self varied more than size: 36 per cent spoke of a second body, while 22 per cent reported spaceless consciousness. Fourteen per cent reported such highly localized, bodiless self images as a point in space, light and a ball of energy. The most illuminating finding was that 23 per cent reported varying self images within the same individual, e. g. , at times a ball of light, while at other times a second body. Either we are faced with a bewildering variety of OBEs or with a variety of images in which basically similar phenomena are represented.

A wide range of beneficial changes were claimed by 88 per cent of the respondents, while 11 per cent reported no changes and 1 per cent spoke of negative ones. Philosophical outlook on life and death was deepened, broadened and new meaning revealed (73 per cent); day-to-day functioning improved (60 per cent); fear of death was reduced or lost altogether (67 per cent); social relationships were said to have improved (45 per cent). Mental health was felt to have improved in 50 per cent of our respondents; 44 per cent reported no change, 3 per cent felt worse and 3 per cent thought it a mixed blessing--some gains and some losses.

One other question might sum up the value of the OBE for our respondents: "If you could, would you like to have another OBE?" Ninety-five per cent answered yes, and 5 per cent said no. Apparently the OBE was reported as a major experience which, unlike fantasies, changed the lives of most respondents.

PSI PHENOMENA IN TIBETAN CULTURE

David Read Barker (University of Virginia)

Tibetan culture serves as an example of a radical alternative to Western scientific understanding of psi. Tibetans are popularly thought to place great importance on the paranormal, and during my fieldwork from 1970 to 1973 with Tibetan refugees in Nepal and northern India, I heard many accounts of allegedly paranormal events. In an apparent paradox, however, the Tibetan language has no word or concept which corresponds to the Western notion of the "supernatural" or the "paranormal, " and Tibetan philosophy and ethos steadfastly avoid the dichotomy between matter and spirit, between mind and body, which makes the Western idea of the paranormal appropriate or relevant. From the Tibetans' own viewpoint, there simply is no such thing as psi. But at the level of personal ex-

perience, Tibetans seem to experience many of the same sorts of
"psi" phenomena which people in the West experience, and the ESP
and PK phenomena described in the literature of parapsychology find
ready analogs in Tibet.

Tibetans look upon ESP as the natural byproduct of spiritual
advancement, the common but not universal result of concentrating
and pacifying the mind through meditation in this or in past life-
times. Successful meditation requires the guidance of a personal
spiritual master with whom a meditator establishes an intimate
psychological and psychic relationship. The overwhelming majority
of the telepathic communications which are reported anecdotally
occurred in the setting of the master-disciple relationship. This
situation corresponds in some respects to the interpersonal relationships in the West in which spontaneous telepathic communications
have been reported, inasmuch as there is commonly a powerful
emotional link between sender and percipient in both cultures.

Divination is an important source of personal guidance for
Tibetans. Some divinations may involve precognition: my own
monastic preceptor once performed a rosary divination in connection with a pilgrimage he was organizing, and some of the situations he described to me in detail actually occurred. Successful
divination, he said, demands mental quiescence and concentration,
both of which are acquired through meditation. These states of
consciousness are common to both telepathy and precognition in
Tibetan thought.

Powers which are comparable to precognition and clairvoyance
are also said to be evidenced in the utterances of the oracles who
were to be found in every large village and town in Tibet. For a
fee, and in a controlled setting, oracles became possessed, nearly
always by an indigenous, pre-Buddhist Tibetan divinity, and func-
tioned as a medium. I have not heard of deceased humans speak-
ing through Tibetan mediums; the spiritualist mode seemed unknown
to the Tibetans I interviewed.

The concept of PK held by parapsychologists has relatively
little meaning for Tibetans because they understand the world to be
primarily psychokinetic, the creation of form by consciousness.
Within their over-arching system of understanding of PK, Tibetans
have developed several specific cultural expressions of what appears
to be similar to our more limited concept.

Probably the most dramatic expression of apparent PK in
Tibet is weather control. I witnessed what appeared to be a demonstration of this in Dharamsala, India, on March 10, 1973, when
a revered shaman-priest named Gunsang Rinzing was employed by
the Dalai Lama to stop a huge storm long enough to permit a
festival of mourning for the collapse in 1959 of the ancient Tibetan
state. About 8:00 p.m. in the evening before the festival, the
shaman arrived at the grounds and built a large fire which he
struggled to keep burning in the downpour. He was in a state of

intense concentration and recited mantras and a sadhana.   Early
the following morning the rain had diminished to a drizzle, and by
10:00 o'clock it had become only a cold fog over a circle with a
radius of about 150 meters.   Everywhere else in the area it continued to pour, but the crowd of several thousand refugees was
never rained on during the six hours it was assembled.   At one
point a huge hailstorm caused a tremendous clatter on the tin-
roofed buildings adjoining the festival grounds, but only a few dozen
hailstones fell on the crowd.   The atmosphere at the grounds seemed
to have an "airless" quality, and the whole experience produced in
me a feeling of distress and disorientation which persisted for
weeks.   The shaman, who had steadily tended his fire and recited
his mantras for 20 hours, was heartily congratulated by individuals
in the crowd for his fine performance.

A SURVEY OF EXPERT OPINION ON
POTENTIALLY NEGATIVE USES OF PSI,
UNITED STATES GOVERNMENT INTEREST IN PSI,
AND THE LEVEL OF RESEARCH FUNDING OF THE FIELD

Charles T. Tart (University of California, Davis)

          A questionnaire was mailed to the heads of the 14 active
parapsychological research centers in the United States to sample
expert opinion in several areas.   All were headed by full members
of the PA, and 13 of the 14 replied, so the results are representative of mainstream scientific research in parapsychology.

          To the question, "How strongly do you believe that psi
abilities might potentially be used in the future in a practically
useful way for espionage and military intelligence activities?   Assume that very large amounts of money and scientific manpower
would be used to study and develop these activities in making your
estimate," no respondent considered espionage use of psi impossible
or unlikely, four considered it possible, five likely, and the remaining four, certain.

          To the question, "How strongly do you believe that psi
abilities might potentially be used in the future in a practically useful way for the military to physically harm, sicken, or kill individuals?   Again assume enormous resources devoted to such development," no respondent considered this impossible, two thought it
unlikely, seven possible, three likely, and one certain.   To a similar question about the potential use of psi to interfere with equipment like computers, observation instruments, etc., no respondent
thought this impossible, one thought it unlikely, seven possible,
four likely, and one certain.

          In response to the question, "Have you or one of your labo-
ratory staff been approached by agents or officials of the U.S.

government, acting in an official capacity, in the last five years, in order to gather information on parapsychology for any government agency?," the bulk (eight of 13) of the respondents had never been approached, one had been approached once, and four had been approached several times.

The respondents also provided a confidential figure on their center's average yearly budget over the past five years for funds devoted to parapsychological research. This included all funds for research, such as salaries, equipment, etc., but excluded non-research activities like education and the value of volunteer help. I would estimate that the 13 centers probably account for 80 to 90 per cent of the scientific research in parapsychology in the United States, so the following figures represent the field.

The total funds for all the centers responding was $552,000 per year over the last five years. The distribution of funds was quite uneven, ranging from zero to $150,000 per year. The median budget was $17,000 per year, so half the research centers had budgets of less than $17,000 per year. A general comparison figure for United States industries to support a single research scientist is $75,000. I could not find a field of conventional science small enough to compare this parapsychological figure against. There was no relationship between annual budget and estimates of overall military potential for psi, nor between estimated military potential and frequency of government visits. There was a suggestion (p < .10, two-tailed) of a positive correlation between frequency of government visits and budget level, probably because of the higher visibility of larger centers.

OBSERVER EFFECTS AND RSPK*

THE OBSERVER EFFECT AS A TOOL IN PARAPSYCHOLOGICAL ANIMAL RESEARCH

James W. Davis[†] and Dick J. Bierman (Institute for Parapsychology, FRNM, and University of Amsterdam)

Experimenter effects have become a problem in parapsychology to the point where one branch, research with animals, is at a stand-still because of the inability to define the source of the effect. A new design methodology has become necessary and the experiment described here is a developmental attempt at separating experimenter effects from the effects of a single variable, namely whether or not rats get food pellets as feedback of the outcome of a trial determined by a random number generator. In the feedback or "real rat" condition, the data are first observed by the rat involved, then by one or two designated human observers (Joseph Sandford and Dick Bierman) with different expectancies of outcome, then by a human analyzer (J. E. Kennedy) who prepared statistical summaries, which are then checked by a second analyzer (James W. Davis). In the nonfeedback or "pseudo rat" condition, the same steps occur, only the data are not observed by the rats. The observations by the designated observers (called O_1 and O_2) are made in two stages. First, the combined "rat" and "pseudo rat" data are presented in such a manner that they are indistinguishable, and in four groups. The first group is observed only by O_1. The second group is observed by O_1 followed by O_2 and the third group by O_2 followed by O_1. The fourth and last group is observed only by O_2. Each group consisted of 10 sessions, each session comprising 1000 "real rat" trials and 1000 "pseudo rat" trials, the score to be analyzed being the first-half versus second-half run difference as in previous similar animal work. In the second round of observations, the same data are presented with the "real rat" condition and the "pseudo rat" condition separated.

The strategy of analysis was to use the different observer conditions in the first (combined data) observations to construct a model of how multiple sequential observations would combine, interact or constrain each other. This model would then be applied to the second (separated data) observations to evaluate separately the contribution of the first observers, namely the rats in the "real

---

*Chairperson: Helmut Schmidt, Mind Science Foundation.

rat" condition.   No psi effects were noted in the data, however, neither observer effects from which to construct a model, nor any interaction between observer expectancies and animal effects.   As such, it is not only a failure to produce animal psi, but also a failure to produce human psi.   The results are therefore not interpretable in terms of questions of experimenter effects versus animal effects, nor do they tell us much with regard to the useful-ness of the design employed.   Further work is planned using what is hoped to be a more robust independent variable than the "rat-pseudo rat" condition employed here.

AN OBSERVER EFFECT IN DATA ANALYSIS?

Debra H. Weiner[†] and Dick J. Bierman (Institute for Parapsychol-
    ogy, FRNM, and University of Amsterdam)

The data used in this "study" came from a pilot experiment previously conducted by D. H. W. in which subjects participated in a computerized PK task.   At the beginning of a run, four zeroes would be displayed on the terminal.   To each zero either a one or a zero (depending on a random number generator [RNG] output) would be added and the sum displayed below it.   This process was repeated eight times per second, creating columns of numbers underneath these four initial zeroes that "counted" upward.   The independent counts of the four columns could vary at any time de-pending upon the RNG outputs that had gone into the series.   The subject was to select one of the four columns and cause that column to finish the 50-trial run with the highest count (MCE = 25).

In the pilot, a planned secondary analysis found a significant difference between the number of hits (the final count of the selected column) of individually-tested (IT) and group-tested (GT) subjects ($p < .005$, two-tailed) with higher scoring in the IT condition. Clinical observations of a subtle interpersonal conflict in the GT condition (if the subject's partner disagreed with the column choice but had no way to input his own preference) were offered as a possible explanation of this result.   D. J. B. suggested that if this hypothesis were true, the second person might have used PK to influence his preferred column, in which case one would expect that the total number of hits for all four columns would be higher in the GT than in the IT condition (reflecting this influence on one of the three columns not chosen by the subject).   D. J. B. suggested making this comparison; furthermore, he suggested dividing the data into two parts--one to be analyzed by himself and the other to be analyzed by D. H. W. --to test for observer/analyzer effects as pre-dicted by observational theories and found in parapsychological re-search.   The present study consists of these analyses.

Nineteen subjects (11 tested individually, eight in groups)

had completed 10 runs each.   D. H. W. compared the subjects' four-
column scores for the two conditions using their odd-numbered runs
and D. J. B. performed the same analysis using the even-numbered
runs.   The ad hoc hypothesis was not confirmed; on the contrary,
the total scores of the IT subjects were higher than that of the GT
subjects.   The observer/analyzer effect investigation led to the
following results.   While there was no significant difference between conditions for D. H. W. 's data, D. J. B. 's data did show a
significant difference (t = 3. 74 corrected for nonhomogeneity of
variance; 17 df; p < . 01, two-tailed).   The difference between the
analyses of the two experimenters was due to a significant difference in their IT scores (t = 4. 37; 10 df; p < . 01, two-tailed)
caused by highly significant positive scoring in this condition for
D. J. B. 's data (t = 7. 38, 10 df; p < . 001, two-tailed).   This last
result was due in part to a significantly low empirical variance in
the IT condition overall (p < . 05, two-tailed) that was particularly
strong in D. J. B. 's data (p < . 01, two-tailed).   It is interesting to
note that significantly low variances do not appear in the original
experiment, in which only the scores of the subjects' chosen
columns entered into the comparison of testing conditions.

A replication study was attempted to determine whether the
difference between the experimenters' results was due to an observer effect or to some psychological or parapsychological distinction on the part of IT subjects between odd and even runs that
would bear on their psi influence on all four columns (although no
such effect was found in the subjects' chosen columns).   During the
original experiment certain persons who did not fulfill the pre-set
subject requirements had asked to participate in the task.   Their
data were not included in the reported analyses, but D. H. W. had
analyzed their scores in order informally to assess the subject
protocol.   Hence, for the purpose of the observer/analyzer test,
these data were comparable to those of the first study in terms of
how and when the scores were obtained and the prior analyses conducted on them.   Since there were few GT scores, the experimenters attempted to replicate the significant difference between their
IT scores.   The data of the seven IT subjects were divided on the
basis of a scheme derived empirically from the first study to yield
two nearly-equal sets of scores (under the assumption of similar
scoring patterns between the two sets of subjects).   There was no
significant difference between the scores analyzed by the two experimenters; however, there was also no evidence of an odd- versus
even-run effect.   The small n and changes in the experimenters'
attitude toward the analyses may have contributed to this failure to
replicate.

To the extent that the results of the first study represent an
observer effect, they suggest that such an effect may occur with
data that have been previously observed and analyzed.

AN RSPK CASE IN PHILADELPHIA

Joan Krieger, [†] Daniel Dal Corso and Gerald F. Solfvin (Psychical Research Foundation)

On January 15, 1978, a series of apparent RSPK disturbances began in the home of the Z family in Philadelphia, Pa. Three PRF investigators visited the home on January 29, staying until February 1.

The initial occurrences began on January 15 after the Z family, Mr. Z (75), Mrs. Z (65) and their granddaughter, Joyce (15), had gone to bed. Joyce had recently been ill and was sharing a bed with Mrs. Z. While lying in bed, they heard a knocking sound apparently coming from the night table beside the bed. They also experienced a vibrating sensation from the mattress, but dismissed both incidents as nothing abnormal. The following night, however, the noises were much louder and more persistent. Joyce and Mrs. Z joined Mr. Z in his bedroom. The disturbance then moved into that room with a lamp falling off a night table. This happened repeatedly until Mrs. Z left the lamp where it was. After that, the night table on the opposite side of the bed opened and spewed forth Mr. Z's socks. After a picture fell from the wall, the family decided to sleep downstairs. The rest of the night was quiet. The activity resumed the following day and continued sporadically up to and including the time of our visit.

On the evening of our first encounter with the Z family, we were greeted by a number of overturned pieces of furniture, knick-knacks and clothing lying about, dresser drawers on the floor and broken objects (we had asked the Z's to leave things as they were).

The poltergeist activity continued while we were in the house during the first evening and the next morning, but was never directly observed by any of us. During the next three days the activity diminished. Though we did not witness any of the occurrences ourselves, statements by visitors and the family suggested this may have been a genuine RSPK case.

We interviewed Ms. F, a Catholic parish worker, and Mr. and Mrs. T, neighbors, independently about an occurrence which had happened in their presence. On January 20, at 2 p.m., Ms. F was standing with Joyce and Mr. and Mrs. T around the dining room table. Joyce and Mrs. T were standing at one of the narrow ends of the table and Mr. T and Ms. F were standing next to them at one of the long ends when they saw the protective padding covering that half of the table slide several inches off the top of the table towards Mr. T and Ms. F. Then the end of the padding nearest Joyce rose rapidly, approximately one foot in the air and moved entirely off the table, striking Mr. T in the stomach. The cover then fell on the floor. Ms. F and Mr. and Mrs. T said they were watching Joyce and that she did not touch the padding or cause it to move normally in any other way.

Because the incidents happened so close to Joyce, in most cases it could not be determined whether she caused some of them normally, perhaps in a dissociated state.   These included a number of slapping incidents and reports that she had been hit in the face by the phone receiver when she went to answer it.

The morning after our arrival, the occurrences subsided and we left 48 hours later.   The evening after we left, there was a renewal of activity, but only for that evening.   We remained in contact with the family, but they reported no further activity.

There was strong evidence for attenuation, with most of the movements originating within one or two feet from Joyce and decreasing with increasing distance.   There was evidence of focussing which seemed independent of the proximity factor.   For instance, the night table lamp moved repeatedly though there were many other objects near Joyce during the active periods which were not affected.

At 15, Joyce was close to the median age of 14 for RSPK agents.   As with many RSPK children, she was not living with her natural parents but with older people.   As in other RSPK cases, the home life was stressful.   Mr. Z was a heavy drinker and the family income very modest.   Mrs. Z had a mastectomy in December, and a relative who was close to Joyce had died then.   Joyce herself was recovering from bronchitis and had also recently seen a doctor for a nervous condition.

Some RSPK cases seem to be triggered by recent situations likely to be stressful, including illness and death as in this case.

AN RSPK CASE IN COLUMBUS, OHIO

M. J. Luthman[†] and Gerald F. Solfvin (Psychical Research Foundation)

An apparent case of RSPK occurred in Columbus, Ohio, during October and November 1976.   It received local newspaper coverage, which brought it to the attention of David Blissenbach, a student at Ohio State, graduate in biochemistry.   He contacted G. F. S. at the Psychical Research Foundation; later M. J. L., a PRF field reporter, followed up the investigation in Columbus.

Mrs. W had lived in a two-story duplex with her two daughters, Rita Marie, 5, and Debbie, 11, for a year and-a-half. For several months, Vern, a friend of Mrs. W, had lived with them.   He had emphysema, and Mrs. W sent him to a nursing home where he died on September 30.

On October 13 Mrs. W said that a broken dustpan hit her in the back five or six times, until she grasped it.   After further in-

cidents, she called the housing inspector and Ohio State to no avail.
She called the police twice. The first time they accused the children of trickery, since one movement occurred near them, and the
second time they took Mrs. W to the hospital for a mental checkup.

On October 20, a neighbor, Mr. A, who had come to investigate, saw a salt shaker land on the middle of the floor, then a light
bookcase fell over and a lamp fell off the table. As Mr. A and the
entire family left the house, Mr. A being the last one out, a house
slipper came from the empty house and hit him in the head.

Newspaper articles appeared on October 22 and 23, 1976, and
David Blissenbach visited the house the following week. He saw a
kitchen chair fall over on its side with a quick movement when no
one was near. He also saw a vase move across the room from a
table to the floor, along a horizontal trajectory from the right to
the left side of his peripheral vision; he could not fixate it since it
moved too fast. It made a noise when it landed, but did not break,
and stopped immediately upon impact. Again no one was near it,
although everyone was in the room. Because of the ruckus, the
family moved in with friends on October 21 and planned to move
permanently.

Some local ministers suggested getting rid of everything be-
longing to Vern. This Mrs. W did, with the exception of the television. The incidents continued as before.

When Mrs. W and Blissenbach visited the house without the
children, nothing happened. After that Mrs. W did not want Blissenbach to come to the house while the children were there, because
if movements occurred again, then she might have to conclude that
the children were associated with them. Mrs. W did not believe in
spirits and thought that the problem had something to do with the
house since nothing happened away from it. The family sometimes
heard noises, which Mrs. W said sounded like Vern.

In mid-November the family moved back to the house until
they could move to a new place a block away. They reported fear-
ful voices coming from the walls and a couple of incidents. Blissenbach made one visit and M. J. L. three, but neither was convinced
the RSPK incidents had resumed.

The events which most resist a common physical explanation
are the house slipper blow to Mr. A, as he left the house, and the
movements of the chair and the vase seen by David Blissenbach.
The most reasonable explanation for these occurrences seems to be
RSPK. Though there was no evidence of trickery, some of the
other incidents could be explained as normally-made movements and
sounds.

We are unable to decide whether Mrs. W, Debbie, or both
was (were) the agent(s) of the RSPK activity. Though Debbie was
at a more typical age for RSPK agents (the median age is 14 years

according to Roll's survey at last year's convention) Mrs. W may
for other reasons be the more likely agent.   She had medical problems, suffering from spinal arthritis and dental problems which
caused recurrent pains.   She also expressed regret at having to
send Vern to the nursing home and his death there may have accentuated these feelings.   This event may have acted as a precipi-
tating factor and provides a link to some previous cases in which a
death preceded the activity.

FREE RESPONSE STUDIES*

A PRELIMINARY EXPLORATION OF SOME TECHNIQUES
REPUTED TO IMPROVE FREE RESPONSE E S P

Robert L. Morris[†] and Kathleen Bailey (University of California,
Santa Barbara)

The present study is an attempt to apply some specific
"mental development" techniques in a free response procedure without an active agent. Our subjects were 18 students enrolled in an
introductory parapsychology class at UCSB. Targets were slides
drawn from the Maimonides slide pool, and projected on the wall of
a locked room adjacent to the subject, via a remote-controlled
carousel slide projector. All targets and target judging pools were
prepared in advance by an assistant not otherwise involved in the
study. There were two targets per session. To determine each
target, the assistant randomly (using a noise-diode random number
generator or RNG) selected two slides from a large group judged to
be similar in visual complexity by outside judges. These two slides
became the target judging pool for the first trial, and were placed
in a marked envelope. One of the two was then randomly selected
as the actual target, and its exact duplicate (we have two sets of
Maimonides slides) was loaded into the appropriate position on the
carousel projector. In this way all the targets and target pools for
a day were prepared.

When the subject arrived for the preliminary session, the
procedure was described in detail by K. B. or R. L. M. The subject
was shown the target room briefly, with the square of light projected
on the wall, and was told that the target slide would be there during
the session. The subject was then ushered into an adjoining semi-
darkened room and made comfortable in an easy chair facing the
same direction the projector was facing.

Then the subject was verbally given a 10-minute progressive
relaxation procedure followed by a brief mind-clearing exercise.
The subject then generated images for exactly four minutes. Following this the subject drew each image roughly as the experimenter
read back the imagery. After this, the drawing sheet was turned
over, revealing two parallel lines running left to right through the
middle, dividing the page in two, top and bottom. The subject was

---

*Chairperson: John Beloff, University of Edinburgh.

then shown one slide in that trial's target pool for five seconds and
was asked to draw it, using verbal labels, in the space above the
lines.   Then the subject was shown the second slide in the target
pool and asked to draw it in the space below the double lines.   Next
the subject was allowed to see each slide as long as was needed,
rated the correspondence of the imagery with each slide by placing
a slash at the appropriate place across the line corresponding to
each slide drawing, and selected which one was most likely to be
the target.   Following this, the experimenter went next door to see
which slide was the actual target, returned, and projected the correct slide on the wall to give the subject feedback.   Then the subject was given a couple of minutes to relax and clear out the imagery from the first trial.   A new target slide was projected on the
wall and the process was repeated.

Each subject participated in one preliminary session plus
four follow-up sessions using the same procedure.   After the first
follow-up session, the subjects were asked to practice progressive
relaxation and mind-clearing exercises once a day, at home.   After
the second follow-up session, half the subjects were given a simple
visualization enhancement technique to practice each day at home;
the other half were given a simple concentration enhancement technique.

Overall, these 18 subjects showed no evidence of ESP.   They
made 70 correct choices out of 142 trials, which is one below
chance.   On a scale from zero to 200, subjects assigned the target
picture a mean rating of 56.58 and the non-target picture a mean
rating of 56.80, an insignificant difference (t = 0.05, p = ns).   We
had hypothesized that the subjects' ESP scores would improve from
the first two sessions to the last two.   The subjects showed an insignificant decline from the first two sessions to the second two
sessions for both correct choices and for ratings of target versus
non-target (t diff. = 0.50, p = ns).

We also hypothesized that the subjects' imagery abundance
would increase.   The subjects' imagery abundance, as rated by two
blind judges on a 200-point scale, had a mean rating of 98.81 for
the first two sessions and 101.4 for the last two sessions.   This
increase in imagery abundance, although in the expected direction,
falls short of statistical significance (t diff. = 0.46, p = ns).   Subjects who received visualization instructions showed the effect more
strongly, as we expected, but not to a significant extent.   Their
imagery was rated as more abundant during the second half by an
average of 8.44 points; the imagery of those given the concentration
instructions was rated as more abundant during the first half by an
average of 3.97 points (t diff. = 1.36, .20 > p > .10, ns).
Although the trends were in the expected directions, our hypotheses
about imagery abundance were not confirmed.

We also hypothesized that subjects would rate their imagery
as corresponding more in general to each slide during the second
two sessions.   Subjects rated the correspondence between their

imagery and each of the slides a mean of 58. 66 for the second half
as opposed to 54. 73 for the first half.   This difference, although in
the expected direction, was also not significant (t diff. = 1. 10,
p = ns).

Thus the "mental development" techniques employed by the
subjects in our study did not have a statistically detected influence
upon their behavior.

A GANZFELD EXPERIMENT WITH TRANSCENDENTAL MEDITATORS

John Palmer, [†] Karen Khamashta, and Kathy Israelson (John F.
    Kennedy University)

The purpose of this experiment was to assess the performance
of a group of practitioners of Transcendental Meditation (TM) on a
free-response ESP test in the Ganzfeld.   A secondary purpose was
to explore further the relationship between ESP scores and subjective
reports of experience in the Ganzfeld.

The subjects were 20 volunteer TM graduates recruited by
K. I. from the TM center in Davis, California.   There were 10 subjects of each sex ranging in age from 22 to 57 years, with from
one to eight years of meditation experience.

When the subject arrived for the Ganzfeld session, he or she
was seated in a comfortable reclining chair and the eyes covered
with halved ping-pong balls.   During the actual session, a spot
reflector lamp of adjustable distance from the subject shone into
the ping-pong balls, and moderately loud white-noise, adjustable by
the subject, was played through headphones.   The session lasted 35
minutes during which time, K. I. , seated beside the subject, transcribed his or her mentation report.   The session was preceded by
brief autogenic (relaxation) suggestions.

While K. K. and K. I. were preparing the subject, J. P.
entered a random number table to select a set of four magazine
pictures from a pool of 10 such sets.   A second random number
determined which picture in the set was to be the target.   An independent selection was made for each subject.   J. P. removed the
target picture from its packet, placed it inside a manila envelope,
and deposited the latter on a desk in the agent's room.   Shortly
thereafter, K. K. (the agent) left the subject and went to the agent's
room (which was several rooms down the hall from the subject's
room).   Fifteen minutes after the Ganzfeld period began, K. K. removed the picture from its envelope, concentrated on "sending" it
for five minutes, and then replaced it in its envelope.

At the end of the Ganzfeld period, K. K. brought the envelope
to J. P. , who replaced the target picture in its packet in proper

sequential order and deposited the packet on the deck in the agent's room. Meanwhile, the subject filled out a rating scale describing the Ganzfeld experience. K. I. then took the subject to the agent's room (since vacated by J. P. and K. K.) where the subject rated each of the four pictures in the set on a 31-point scale according to its correspondence to his or her imagery. In contrast to the author's previous research, the subject was not given a detailed set of judging instructions but was simply told to rate each picture independently.

Several months later, two independent judges each rated each subject's transcript against the four pictures in the appropriate set. Both the subjects' ratings and the ratings of each judge were converted to Z-scores for analysis. The Z-scores of the two judges, which correlated +. 42, were averaged. These composite Z-scores (hereafter called "judges' ESP scores") correlated +. 68 with the Z-scores based upon subjects' ratings (hereafter called "subjects' ESP scores").

The mean of the subjects' ESP scores was in the psi-missing direction (-. 34) while the mean of the judges' ESP scores was in the psi-hitting direction (+. 37). Although neither of these means differed significantly from zero by a two-tailed test, they differed from each other to a highly significant degree by Wilcoxon Test (T = 15, CR = -3. 36, p < . 001). These results illustrate rather dramatically the effect that judging can have on free-response ESP scores.

The rating scale of subjects' experiential reports was factor-analyzed to yield five mutually independent subscales. In Palmer's previous Ganzfeld experiment [RIP 1976, pp. 45-8], one factor clearly emerged that reflected the degree to which the subject reported experiencing an altered state of consciousness (ASC) during the session. In the present experiment, this subscale in effect split in two, resulting in two independent ASC subscales.

None of the Spearman correlations between subjects' ESP scores and the five subscales was significant. The correlations with the two ASC subscales were both in the positive direction (+. 16, +. 29). There was one significant Spearman correlation with the judges' ESP scores, the effective predictor being one of the two ASC subscales (r_s = +. 54, p < . 02, two-tailed). The correlation with the other ASC subscale was -. 00.

The one significant correlation above supports Palmer's hypothesis, stated elsewhere, that there should be a positive relationship between ESP scores and ASC reports when the overall ESP mean is positive. The particular ASC subscale involved in this correlation reflects more clearly than its counterpart the presence of a hypnagogic-like ASC, the significant loadings reflecting auditory imagery, regressive imagery and loss of body awareness.

More generally, the hypothesis tended to be supported for judges' ESP scores but not subjects' ESP scores. The authors have more confidence in the judges' scores because (1) they have more desirable psychometric properties (as noted in a paper presented by Palmer [RIP 1977, p. 22] before the present data had been independently judged), (2) subjects did not receive detailed judging instructions, and (3) the procedure for subject judging left a remote possibility of sensory cues, since the physical target picture just handled by the agent was among the pictures rated by the subjects.

The significant negative correlation between ESP scores and subjects' time estimates of the Ganzfeld's duration, found in two previous experiments, was not confirmed for either subjects' (+.12) or judges' ESP scores (+.17). However, the factor analysis suggested that the time contraction item may have reflected different things in this experiment than in at least one of these two previous experiments.

APPARENT PSI-MISSING WITH A FREE-RESPONSE PROCEDURE

Irvin L. Child[†] and Ariel Levi (Yale University)

We report here an instance of apparent psi-missing with free-response procedures. The conditions are ones which might often recur in educational settings, permitting a test of whether they do with some consistency give rise to psi-missing.

The subjects were all students enrolled for credit in the course in parapsychology given as one of the courses offered in Yale College by the Department of Psychology. The course meets the requirement that all psychology majors must take at least one course involving collection and analysis of data (a requirement many majors do not like). One of the exercises representing this aspect of the course was participation in a Ganzfeld demonstration, generating data for class analysis and discussion.

Students signed up in pairs, each pair participating in one Ganzfeld session. Just prior to a session, the two student participants were shown the two rooms to be used, and the procedures were described. The instructor and the teaching assistant took turns serving as agent's experimenter and percipient's experimenter. Target pools had been made up in advance; each consisted of five colored slides from the Maimonides series, selected by a table of random numbers. Each pool was enclosed in an opaque envelope; the agent picked an envelope, and then shook a die which the experimenter read to determine which slide would be the target. The experimenter turned on and focussed the projector, and then left the room to sit in the hall outside. The agent had been instructed that for 30 minutes he should concentrate on the picture and attempt to send it telepathically to the percipient.

Meanwhile, the percipient and the second experimenter had

gone to a well-separated room where the percipient was in a reclining chair, with Ganzfeld and white-noise stimulation, for the
same 30-minute period. The percipient's experimenter sat at a
table in this room writing down the percipient's imagery descriptions.   At the end of the period, the agent's experimenter brought
the projector and slides to an intermediate room (altering the position of the several slides). The percipient's experimenter brought
these into the percipient's room and projected the slides as often
and as long as needed for the percipient to make and revise ratings
on a 100-point scale (with no ties) of the similarity of each slide to
his imagery. When the rating was completed, agent and agent's
experimenter were called in to identify the target and join in discussion of the outcome. The participants were asked not to reveal
the outcome to other students, and so far as we know none did.
There were 14 sessions, each with a different target pool.   The
percipient was different for each session, and so was the agent
(except that for two sessions only one student was present and procedures were altered by having the teaching assistant act in the
double role of agent and agent's experimenter).

   The mean rating of the actual targets (30, on a 100-point
scale) was significantly lower than that of the non-targets (55, with
$t = 3.27$, 52 df, $p < .002$).

   When the quantitative results suggestive of psi-missing were
presented in class, students were asked to write about what motives
might have occasioned psi-missing, if indeed it occurred.   Eight
students who had acted as percipients were present, and six of
them mentioned the relation between teacher and student as pertinent
to the possible motivation; nine students who had acted as agent
were present, and only two of them mentioned the same point.   This
difference, which is significant at the 5 per cent level (one-tailed)
by Fisher's exact test, suggests that the percipients felt some strain
in attempting psi-performance.   Likely scores of strain include the
presence of instructor or assistant, fantasies of vulnerability and
conflict about possible evidence of psi in oneself.   More subjects
had expressed a preference for being agent than percipient; two
who did wish to be percipients were the only ones who ranked the
true target in second place among the five slides.   (No percipient
ranked the true target first, and eight ranked it last.)

LONG DISTANCE PRECOGNITIVE REMOTE VIEWING

Brenda J. Dunne and J. P. Bisaha[†] (University of Chicago and
   Mundelein College, Chicago)

   A series of five precognitive remote-viewing trials were
conducted between northern Wisconsin and various locations in
Eastern Europe (approximate distance more than 5000 miles) over
a five-consecutive-day period, with an average of 24 hours separating

the percipient's description and the agent's presence at the target site. The agent's whereabouts during the trial period were unknown to either agent (J. P. B.) or percipient (B. J. D.) at the time the experiment was arranged.

Before J. P. B. left on a trip to Eastern Europe in August 1976, it was agreed that each morning for five consecutive days between 8:30 and 8:45 (central daylight-savings time) B. J. D. would attempt to describe the geographical location where the agent would be at 3:00 p. m. (European time) the following day. The descriptions were tape-recorded each morning and subsequently transcribed. The agent was to spend the 15-minute period between 3:00 and 3:15 p. m. attempting to concentrate on his surroundings and to take a photograph which could later be compared against the percipient's description.

Upon the agent's return, the five photographs and the agent's brief descriptions of the target sites along with one of the transcripts were presented to each of five independent judges for rank ordering. In this way each one of five judges ranked one transcript against the five targets. The sum of the assigned ranks was nine, resulting in a p value of . 041, one-tailed.

A brief description of each trial will provide an indication of the degree of accuracy obtained in the descriptions.

Trial 1 (rank: 1). The target was a "flying-saucer" restaurant on the Danube River, Bratislava, Czechoslovakia. The building was circular, raised on pillars high into the air above a footbridge near the bank of the river. The percipient described the agent as being "near water ... a very large expanse of water ... boats ... vertical lines like poles ... a circular shape like a merry-go-round ... it seems to have height, maybe with poles ... a dark fence along a walk ... like a path or walkway ... a boardwalk and there's a fence along it. "

Trial 2 (rank: 3). The target was St. Michael's Church, Bratislava. The agent was inside the old church and described stained glass windows in beautiful colors, and an altar with large benches on each side with carved animals. The transcript read: "a lot of glass windows ... a great many colors ... some object, rectangular shaped, like a table or cabinet. There seem to be several small items of various shapes and sizes on it ... some kind of an arch ... feeling this is indoors ... some sort of statue ... gray stone. "

Trial 3 (rank: 2). The target was the Ukrainia Hotel, Moscow, U. S. S. R. During most of the experimental period the agent was riding from the airport to the target in a cab. The hotel was rectangular with a statue on a pedestal and park in front. The percipient described "some kind of path or road leading off into the distance ... no continuity. I have the feeling he's moving ... a large open space ... rectangular shapes ... some kind of large, maybe stone, pedestal or monument. "

Trial 4 (rank: 2). The target was the Tretyakov Gallery, Moscow, an art gallery in a large red brick building with pointed arches around the doors and windows and a small dome on top. The percipient described "some kind of building ... round balls that seem to be on top of something that's of a generally square shape ... windows with like arches. They may not be exactly arched, the arches come to a point on top almost ... great big double doors. "

Trial 5 (rank: 1). The target was the Exhibition of Economic Achievement of the U. S. S. R. , Moscow. The photograph showed a huge iron gate within a stone archway, ornate and carved. The agent described "building after building inside. A Museum of Science and Industry based on a Disneyland format. " The percipient described "a busy, urban sort of site. Busyness, movement. Different shapes and activity. Buildings ... some sort of gate or fence ... made of metal of some sort--it's high for a gate ... dark metal ... something like a doorway or a row of doorways. "

The positive findings of these experimental trials support our earlier findings that the remote-viewing protocol is a reliable instrument for ongoing research in extrasensory perception and communication in spite of large space and time differentials. The participation of the experimenters as percipient and agent has also provided an opportunity to observe the nature and quality of the remote viewing experience firsthand, permitting a comparison of the quality of descriptions obtained under varying environmental and internal influences. These observations have provided insights which can be explored and utilized in future research and subject training.

"PSI ON THE TIP OF THE TONGUE" REVISITED:
A FURTHER INVESTIGATION OF THE INFLUENCE OF
AN INCUBATION PERIOD ON FREE RESPONSE G E S P

William Braud, [†] Gary Davis and Robert Wood (Mind Science Foundation, San Antonio, Texas)

At the 1975 convention, we presented a study of the influence of an "incubation period" on GESP performance [RIP 1975, pp. 167-71]. Unselected volunteers attempted to retrieve psi impressions of target pictures both immediately and following a 15-minute incubation period during which the volunteer's attention was occupied by a non-demanding task. It was hypothesized that psi retrieval would be more effective following the incubation period. We obtained evidence for psi but not for our hypothesis. We concluded this may have been due to our use of a within-subjects design and of an incubation period which was too brief. These two factors resulted in our having to request volunteers to make a decision about which of four alternatives was the correct target picture and then make another decision shortly thereafter. It is understandable that a volunteer would be reluctant to change his decision under these circumstances; a change might imply that he had not exercised sufficient care in making his first decision.

In the present experiment we employed a longer incubation period (24 hours) and used a between-subject design. The longer incubation period would be expected to provide an opportunity for additional target information to rise into consciousness, and the "single measurement" procedure does not necessitate any decision change based on this new information.

Sixteen males and 16 females, ranging in age from 18 to 74, participated. Each subject was seated in a recliner chair in the testing room, given headphones and instructed in the use of a slide viewer. In their office 20 meters away, the experimenters turned on a tape recording which could be heard by the volunteer via head-phones. The 20-minute recording contained suggestions for relaxation, mental stillness and successful ESP performance.

After starting the tape, the experimenter opened one of 32 numbered envelopes containing information detailing which one of the 10 target packages would be used, which of the four 35 mm. slides inside of the package would serve as the target slide for that session, and whether the session would be a control or treatment session. The 10 packages containing the target slides were located in the experimenter's room and a duplicate set of 10 was located in the room in which the volunteer was seated. Each of the 10 packages contained four slides which had been selected so as to be as different from one another as possible in terms of colors, shapes, themes, etc.

Fifteen minutes into the tape recording, the target slide was removed from its package and projected onto a screen. For the next five minutes the tape recording was silent and the experimenters attended to the projected picture.

At the end of the impression period, the volunteer retrieved an envelope from beneath the closed door of his room, one of two envelopes, depending on whether the session was a treatment or control session. If the session was a control session, the volunteer retrieved the appropriate target package, opened it and removed the four slides contained inside. Using the slide viewer, the volunteer examined each of the four slides, and then rank-ordered them from one through four.

If the session was a treatment session, the volunteer con-tacted the receptionist and made an appointment to return 24 hours later. Upon returning the following day, the volunteer again sat in the recliner chair and listened to the 20-minute tape recording. However, during the impression period portion of the tape, no one viewed the target slide. At the end of the impression period, the volunteer followed a procedure identical to that of the control group as described above.

        Two predictions had been made about the outcome
of the experiment: that psi would be evidenced in each of the two
groups and in the experiment as a whole, and that the group tested
after the incubation period would score significantly higher than the
group tested immediately after target exposure. Neither of these
predictions was confirmed. Both groups scored insignificantly
positively. Since there was no between-group difference, the
scores were pooled to test for the presence of a psi effect in the
experiment as a whole. Overall, there were 21 hits and 11 misses.
This 66 per cent hit rate did not quite reach significance (binomial
$p = .056$, one-tailed, corrected for continuity).

        We can offer two interpretations of our present findings.
The first is that an incubation period does not facilitate psi retrieval.
The second is that an incubation period is useful, but in this study,
there was no psi to retrieve. The absence of extra-chance scoring
is consistent with this second interpretation.

AN EXAMINATION OF THE MENSTRUAL CYCLE AS A HORMONE
RELATED PHYSIOLOGICAL CONCOMITANT OF PSI PERFORMANCE

Patrice Keane[†] and Risa Wells (Maimonides Medical Center)

        Preliminary evidence reported by M. Schmitt and R. Stanford
suggests that the hormonal rhythm of the menstrual cycle and its
consequent physiological fluctuations play a role in enabling a woman
to achieve a psi-conducive state. In a free response Ganzfeld ESP
experiment, these authors proposed that the first half of the menstrual cycle, i. e. , when the hormone estrogen is circulating through
the bloodstream in increasing quantities, and progesterone is present
in minimal quantities, may have a facilitating effect on psi ability.
Whereas the latter half of the cycle, when both progesterone and
estrogen are present in large quantities, may have an inhibitory
effect.

        The ovarian hormones (estrogen and progesterone), in addi-
tion to their effect on the reproductive system, are known to be
absorbed by cells of the limbic system of the brain. These may be
the more likely candidates for any hormone related physiological
concomitant of psi ability, whereas the anterior pituitary hormones
act mainly upon the ovaries.

        In an attempt to replicate and extend the work of Schmitt
and Stanford, we conducted a clairvoyant experiment at three different points of the menstrual cycle. In addition to the pre-ovulatory
and post-ovulatory points we selected a third point within 24 hours
from the onset of menstruation. This point might have proven to
be a psi-conducive time perhaps by some rebound effect since the
production of progesterone and estrogen is suddenly greatly reduced
to allow menstruation to begin.

As our primary hypothesis, we predicted that sessions conducted at the time determined for the pre-ovulatory and menstrual points would yield psi-hitting. Furthermore, for sessions completed during the post-ovulatory phase, we expected significantly lower psi scores. This was tested by a single mean t-test and by a one-way analysis of variance treating percipients' scores by phase of cycle.

In addition, we used two methods of target selection. All targets were generated using a noise-driven random event generator in May 1975. Half of the percipients were given a remote control switch that enabled them to initiate the trial runs, which were later converted into a target number. They were also given auditory feedback from the random event, a brief introduction to the machine, and the instructions to affect the duration of the tone in whatever way they chose. The other half of the percipients received no feedback and utilized targets that were randomly generated by a second experimenter. We hypothesized that the percipients given feedback from the ongoing event would produce more significant psi scores.

Skin conductance levels, skin conductance responses, absolute temperature and derivative temperature were also monitored. Since these measures would be expected to vary rhythmically during the course of the monthly cycle, we were interested in determining whether there were any specific correlation between these autonomic fluctuations and psi ability.

Eighteen women with regularly occurring cycles completed the study, participating on a voluntary basis. Each experimenter was blind to the phase of the cycle of the percipients with whom she worked.

During the experiment the percipient was in a sound-isolated room, seated in a reclining chair with halved ping pong balls over her eyes. Uniform red light and white noise provided Ganzfeld stimulation.

The target pool consisted of eight sets of four art prints. After the target number selection a 15-minute progressive relaxation instruction was presented. The percipient then continued listening to music for five minutes while the second experimenter placed the target (sealed in a manila envelope) on the wall of another room. Ganzfeld instructions were presented and the percipient was asked to begin her mentation. During the 20-minute mentation the primary experimenter recorded the percipient's imagery.

The percipient was then shown and asked to rate each picture on a 0 to 10 scale after which the experimenter ranked the pictures. The second experimenter was then summoned to identify the target. Our primary hypothesis that sessions completed at the pre-ovulatory and menstrual points would yield significant psi-hitting was not confirmed. The overall result for the percipients' psi scores, combining the three phases, was psi-missing ($t(53) = -2.24$, $p = .029$). Sessions completed in the pre-ovulatory phase showed significant psi-missing ($t(17) = -2.27$, $p = .037$). The menstrual phase yielded nonsignificant below chance scores ($t(17) = -1.19$, $p = .25$). The post-ovulatory was also below chance and nonsignificant ($t(17) = -.50$, $p = .62$). A one-way analysis of variance treating subjects' psi scores by phase of cycle revealed no significant variation among groups ($F(2, 51) < 1$). Experimenters' ratings in the pre-ovulatory phase ($t(17) = -1.11$, $p = .28$), menstrual phase ($t(16) = -.76$, $p = .46$), and post-ovulatory phase ($t(16) = -.55$, $p = .59$) were nonsignificant.

No difference was found between the psi scores for percipients who generated their targets and experimenter generated targets ($t(26) = -1.11$, $p = .28$). Therefore our hypothesis, that percipients involved in the generation of their own targets would score more significantly, was not confirmed.

Post-hoc analysis correlating psi scores and autonomic variables revealed a significant relationship in the pre-ovulatory phase for derivative temperature ($r = -.517$, $t(14) = -2.26$, $p = .040$), with near significance in that phase for skin conductance level ($r = -.447$, $t(17) = -2.00$, $p = .062$), and for absolute temperature ($r = -.409$, $t(16) = -1.80$, $p = .091$). No significant relationship was found in the post-ovulatory or menstrual phase. A one-way analysis of variance of physiological measures by phase of cycle revealed no significant physiological differences among the three phases.

MISCELLANEOUS STUDIES I*

PSI AND PHYSICAL FIELDS

Victor G. Adamenko (Moscow, U. S. S. R.)[†]

I have worked with Alla Vinogradova since 1970 and she has repeatedly demonstrated the ability to move small objects at a distance. Previous investigations by Soviet scientists into similar effects have revealed that an electric field may develop between the object and a grounded subject. This field has been detected around the object by means of high impedance volt meters and neon voltage indicators. It was also found that the surface on which the objects move becomes electrically charged.

In my experiments, I used a 60-cm. glass cube as a surface on which to place the objects to be moved. The cube, made of non-conducting glass, was intended to conserve or accumulate electrical charge, and to provide a suitable distribution of the electrical field. In 1970, I attempted to imitate Nina Kulagina's PK by electrically charging the dielectric glass by friction of my hand in a rubber glove. Matches were then attracted to the glass plate. It was found that Vinogradova could charge the glass plate without wearing the rubber glove, indicating that the electrical properties of her hand may be similar to those of a rubber glove. The intensity of the electrostatic field she induced on objects in experiments varied, sometimes reaching 10^4 volts per centimeter.

In training Vinogradova, I used an electronic device of my own invention which operated like a galvanic skin response (GSR) biofeedback instrument. She was trained to change the electrical conductivity of acupuncture points on her fingertips by effort of will. I used very small electrodes, three mm. in diameter, to obtain a better signal-to-noise ratio. Vinogradova also studied hatha yoga, and still practices some simple asanas.

After training, Vinogradova was able to move objects weighing six to eight grams by rolling, and two to three grams by sliding. Initially she had to charge the cube with her hand by light friction (four to five touches). After further training, she could induce electrical charge in the objects without using friction. She would

---

*Chairperson: J. G. Pratt, University of Virginia.
†Presented by Stanley Krippner.

hold the object in her hand for about 30 seconds and then put it on
the surface of the cube.   Drawing her hand near to the object, she
was able to induce an electrical charge in the motionless object by
an effort of will.   She would then move the object by means of motion of her hand at a distance (approximately five centimeters).
She is able, upon demand, to move objects forward and backward,
and to stop, start and accelerate their motion.

When Vinogradova was grounded by bracelets (on each arm
and leg) connected to earth, the PK effect increased slightly.   Her
physiological condition was measured during attempted PK and an
increased heart rate and disturbance of heart rhythm was found.
The same physiological disturbances take place when she only thinks
about or imagines moving the object by PK.

I have also studied Vinogradova's psychological conditions.
She needs to overcome an inner barrier by an effort of will in
order to produce PK.   She reaches an altered state of consciousness by overcoming the barrier.   After overcoming it, it is not
necessary for her to make an effort of will to move the object.
She then becomes able to move objects weighing eight to 50 grams
by rolling and eight to 10 grams by sliding.

Her PK abilities are amplified by emotional stimulation, such
as performing for movies or television.   In this case, she can
move heavier objects, and better control their movement.   Afterwards, she remains in a state of intense excitement, is unable to
sleep normally and has dreams in color.

After psychic stimulation, Vinogradova has been able to
rotate the angle of polarization of a light beam in an instrument by
four to five degrees without moving any part of the instrument.   A
control instrument of the same type present at the same time showed
the absence of a rotating plane of polarization.   In other experiments, it was found that photographic film in a black envelope can
be affected by Vinogradova.   These experiments and others conducted
using photomultiplier tubes confirm that PK is accompanied by some
physical effects such as an electrostatic field and ultraviolet light
emission.   Nevertheless, these effects are not the substance of PK,
but accompany it in the way that EEG currents accompany mental
activity.

The quantum theory of psychic energy assumes that there is
a whole set of fundamental particles generated by the psychic field.
It is proposed that besides the network structuring of the brain, there
is also the field structuring of its functioning.   In this hypothesis,
the neuron network generates a sort of psychic field; when pulses
are transferred from the synapses to the neurons proper, corresponding particles and anti-particles can originate, multiply, vanish
by way of transition to a vacuum, and reappear.   It should be noted
that a holographic model of brain function assumes that a field is
present.

Thus, we can interpret the brain's transformation of psychic into physico-chemical energy as "miniature" PK over the neurons proper; the neurons, in turn, set muscles into motion. Sometimes a very strong field is generated which produces an extra-motor influence on target objects, as in the experiments described above. The difference between the two types of brain function appears to be a quantitative rather than a qualitative one in the transformation of psychic energy into physico-chemical energy. This transformation can be assumed to be one of the basic phenomena of life.

SEARCH FOR PSI FLUCTUATIONS IN A PK TEST WITH COCKROACHES

Helmut Schmidt (Mind Science Foundation)

In 1970, I reported significant PK results in a situation where cockroaches were connected to an "electronic coinflipper" so that the animals received an electric shock for every generated "head. "

The basic idea in the cockroach experiments was that for PK effects to occur, we may not need conscious human intelligence, but that PK may rather be a general principle of nature which could act, even though in a weak form, at all levels of animate nature. Then certainly, experiments with primitive animals would appear most interesting: the basic psi principle should be more easily visible if we deal with simple systems.

A weak point of the mentioned cockroach experiment may be that in real life cockroaches do not encounter electric shocks and therefore nature's PK mechanisms may not be prepared to deal with the situation.

In an attempt to test a simple organism under more natural conditions, I did, with the help of Lee Pantas, tests with algae (chlorella) exposed to light which was randomly turned on and off. A binary random generator was automatically activated at the rate of about once per minute so that each head would turn on (or keep on) the light while each tail would turn off (or keep off) the light. These tests were done under a variety of light and food conditions and showed no PK effects. It seemed that the chlorella did not activate a PK mechanism in order to obtain more of the growth-favoring light.

In another similar experiment, I used a random generator to vary the temperature of yeast cultures. These very extended experiments, done in different temperature ranges, also gave no indication of PK effects. The experiments with the yeast and chlorella were fully automated so the experimenter had only to set up the experiment and to read the final score.

More experimenter involvement was present in a later experiment with wingless fruit flies. In this experiment, I selected 4000
fruit flies, one by one, and decided, with an electronic coinflipper,
whether to kill or release each particular fly. But "heads," which
led to release, did not occur with significantly different frequency
from "tails" which led to the animals' deaths, i. e. , there was no
PK effect in favor of the animal's survival.

Some further interesting animal PK work by William Braud
and by Graham Watkins showed initially promising results, but there
also effects could not be reproduced indefinitely. A recent attempt
to observe PK effects in animals was based on a theoretical paper
which suggests that one might be able to detect short-term fluctuations of psi by comparing the scoring on random processes with two
different hit probabilities, and that furthermore the repeated feedback of the same recorded event should make the detection method
for such fluctuations more sensitive.

Therefore, this experiment compares a possible PK effect
on random events with hit probabilities of 1/4 and 3/4. Furthermore, some of the random events are recorded and presented 32
times.

The binary events were displayed to a pair of cockroaches
as electric shocks or non-shocks, at the rate of 10 events per
second. In view of the high trial speed, the shocks were provided
by voltage pulses of only 10^{-4} seconds' duration with an amplitude
of 25 volts, adjusted so that the animals showed a slight reaction
to the shocks.

The total experiment comprised 32 sessions with different
animals. Each session lasted about 27 minutes and contained 2^{14}
(i. e. , 16, 384) binary random events. The results showed no evidence for PK effects either in the form of a constant bias or in the
form of psi fluctuations.

A FOLLOW-UP STUDY OF 30 POSSIBLE P K CASES

H. H. J. Keil (University of Utrecht)

In 1974 the Institut für Grenzgebiete in Freiburg, Germany,
obtained a grant to carry out a sociological survey of persons who
reported PK phenomena in connection with the media coverage of
Uri Geller. In addition to sociological data a number of questions
were included which were of direct interest to parapsychologists.
Approximately 800 questionnaires were returned. About 80 personal
interviews were conducted and a number of cases which were of
particular interest to members of the Freiburg Institut were investigated [RIP 1974, pp. 141-4].

During my study leave at the University of Utrecht I was interested in trying procedures which might register PK among relatively unselected persons. It seemed desirable, though, to test these procedures by working initially with persons who presumably had a higher ability or expectancy to produce PK phenomena. With the kind assistance of the Freiburg Institut, approximately 150 of the more promising respondents were selected by E. Gruber and asked (by letter) for their cooperation. Approximately 40 positive replies were received, a fair number if one takes into account that more than 40 letters were returned because the people concerned did not live any longer at the previous address and others who replied were ill, not available at the time and so on. Only 10 actually claimed that they had bent metal themselves by paranormal means. In some of the cases only watches were involved and in others the respondents had reported about children or other members in the household who were no longer available.

For the 1978 study, the following procedure was used. Discussion of the 1974 phenomena led to an introduction of the Kulagina investigation and a screening of the film. I suggested that even with less-developed abilities it should be possible to move a compass needle, and I introduced a set-up with a compass needle (or non-magnetic needle) shielded from air movements but constructed in such a way that the needle could be viewed directly. A movie camera could also be attached and a stopwatch and counter assisted in the identification of trials.

Needle movements of approximately 30 to 90 degrees were observed in connection with one family in Biel under conditions where intentional or unintentional manipulation can be ruled out with virtual certainty. The possibility that external normal magnetic changes might be responsible for the movements has been examined during a further visit to Biel. Magnetometer recordings in Biel seem to support the psi hypothesis even though some uncertainty remains with respect to external magnetic changes. During their first visit to the Freiburg Institut, the family did not succeed in a comparable way. Further visits and investigations in Biel and Freiburg are planned.

With the exception of the first four respondents (because at that stage the device was not available) a strain gauge was also used. This device, constructed by Brian Millar, was glued with epoxy to a 15-cm. strip of 1 x 10 mm. stainless steel. It will register minute variations in the tension of the steel long before any visible distortion takes place. The gauge consists essentially of a special wire which changes its resistance as a result of minute compressions or elongations. With the aid of a small amplifier, the changes in the resistance can be clearly observed on a meter and filmed if required. With such a sensitive device, relatively uniform changes occur because of temperature variations and other not clearly identifiable but undoubtedly normal reasons. In spite of these normal changes in the system itself, it is possible to extract certain indicators of paranormal influence. One such indicator for paranormality is the speed with which these changes occur.   A second indicator is the differential rate of change (even if relatively slow) if attempts are made to bend the metal in opposite directions.

In two cases relatively fast changes were observed which did not seem to be due to general normal changes in the system.   However, after three such changes no further variations of this kind could be observed, and it must remain somewhat doubtful whether psi was involved.   In four other cases differences in the rate of change (of the order three to one) were observed depending on the direction in which the metal was supposed to move.   Similar differences were observed in a number of other cases but were less marked.   It is hoped this situation may be clarified by further visits and possible laboratory investigations in Freiburg or Utrecht.

A TEST OF EXPERIMENTER EFFECT
IN AN ANIMAL PSI EXPERIMENT

William Eisler (New York, N. Y.)

The role of the experimenter in parapsychological research has recently come under scrutiny.   One area of importance is animal research, where experimenter effects are an uncontrolled variable that could affect the outcome of an experiment.   Much of the evidence for experimenter effects in this context is of a hypothetical nature; the following experiments were designed explicitly to examine experimenter effects in an anpsi experiment.

Two pieces of equipment were used: a Grason-Stadler Animal Chest, commonly known as a Skinner box; and a Grason-Stadler series 1200 modular programming system serving as a random target generator (RTG).   The Skinner box was connected to the RTG.   This device was programmed to generate targets randomly--the right or left bar in the Skinner box--and deliver a food reward to the animal when it pressed the correct lever.   The RTG was on a moveable cart and was towed into an adjoining room during the experiment.   The Skinner box and the RTG were separated by about five feet with a wall between them.

Two experimenters were involved.   Our subjects were six white laboratory rats, four male and two female, all three to four months old.   The rats were trained by W. E. to bar-press before the experiment started.

To start the experiment a rat was placed in the Skinner box. Because the RTG had already been turned on, a target bar had been chosen.   Thus the first correct press the rat made would deliver a food pellet, but we did not count this as an experimental trial. As soon as the animal made this correct bar-press, it triggered

the first trial.   The RTG selected a target bar, which was observable by the lighting of one of two lights on the RTG corresponding
to the right or left bar.   The first experimenter recorded this
choice.   On half the trials he was trying to influence the rat to
press the correct bar, on the other half he recorded the target but
did not try to influence the rat.   There was a 10-second inter-trial
interval (ITI) during which the first experimenter was "sending."
During the ITI the rat's behavior was not rewarded or recorded,
but at the end of 10 seconds a light went on in the Skinner box.
This signalled the second experimenter, who did not know the target, that the ITI was up and that the rat's next response was to be
recorded.   This first response after the ITI was the one we were
interested in, and was the only one recorded.   This response was
either correct or incorrect.   If the animal pressed the bar selected
by the RTG, it received a pellet of food.   This was a correct
response.   If the rat pressed the wrong lever, it was allowed to
continue bar-pressing until it pressed the correct lever, at which
time a food reward was delivered and a new trial started.   When
an animal had done 40 trials, it was taken out of the box and the
two experimenters met to compare results.   The sequence of sending and control (not sending) trials in a session was varied in
blocks of 10 or 20 trials.   The animals were each run for 10 sessions of 40 trials.

A chi-square analysis showed the target sequence to be random to the sixth order, allowing us to assume a $p = .5$ for a correct bar press by the rats.

The total score was 1365 correct presses in 2400 trials
(dev. $+65$, CR = 6.75, $p = 2.0 \times 10^{-9}$, two-tailed).   There were
675 correct responses on 1200 control trials (dev. $+75$, CR = 4.30,
$p = .00006$, two-tailed) and 690 correct presses on sending trials
(dev. $+90$, CR = 5.23, $p = 5.7 \times 10^{-7}$, two-tailed).   With only one
exception, under both control and sending conditions all scores for
individual rats showed a positive deviation.   Three rats scored
significantly overall.

There was not a significant difference between sending and
control trials (CR = 0.46).

In the spring of 1978 a confirmatory experiment was carried
out.   This experiment was identical to the first one except: a
"sending-incorrect" condition was added; the order of the three conditions was determined by the first experimenter's rolling a die
immediately before each run; the control trials were more effective
controls because the target lights on the RTG were covered so that
the first experimenter did not know what the correct target was;
the first five days of the experiment used a 10-second ITI, days
6-10 five seconds; during control trials the first experimenter was
also recording the animals' responses to serve as a check on the
accuracy of the second experimenter's scoring.

Five rats were used, with 10 experimental sessions.   Each

rat was run for 60 trials per session, containing 20 trials of each
of the three conditions.

A chi-square test showed the targets for each rat to be
randomly generated.   On the control runs only one rat's score
reached significance but the total score for all rats combined was
significant (dev. +35, CR = 2.18, p = .01, one-tailed).   All five
rats scored positively on the sending-correct runs, with two rats'
scores reaching significant levels.   The total score here for all
rats combined was significant (dev. +72, CR = 4.50, p = .00003,
one-tailed).   Four of the five rats scored significantly negatively
on the sending-incorrect trials (meaning they pressed the correct
bar leading to a food reward more often).   The total score here
was also significant (dev. -48, CR = 3.00, p = .02, two-tailed).
The total results for all three conditions combined was significant
(dev. +59, CR = 2.14, p = .016, one-tailed).

Comparisons of the scoring rates under each condition
reached significance in each case.   We had greater success with
the five-second ITI than with the 10-second one.   The difference was
significant in all three conditions.

An examination of the records kept by the two experimenters
on the control trials showed that what discrepancies there were
went against us as often as they were for us, so recording errors
do not seem to have been a factor.

PSI PHENOMENA IN LOW COMPLEXITY SYSTEMS:
CONFORMANCE BEHAVIOR USING SEEDS

Donald McCarthy, [†] Patrice Keane and Lawrence Tremmel (New
    York University and Maimonides Medical Center)

Rex Stanford has developed a conceptual approach to psi
phenomena which regards them as instances of what he terms conformance behavior.   The conformance behavior model predicts that
when the outcomes of a random event generator (REG) are contingently linked to the future states of a suitably disposed system,
the behavior of the generator will tend to conform to the needs of
the system--in the sense that the REG will become biased towards
outcomes favorable to the system.   This prediction was put to an
experimental test by Charles Fox, using systems of low complexity:
mung bean seeds.   In essence, his experiment was as follows.

The future state of the individual bean seeds was determined
by the outcome of an electronic random number generator.   Specifically, he used the generator PSIFI located at the Maimonides
Medical Center [RIP 1975, pp. 20-2].   For each seed the generator
made a fixed number of binary trials, with a "hit" or a "miss"
being equally likely.   If the number of hits was below mean chance

expectation, the seed was destroyed; if above, it was nourished. The procedure was applied to a large number of seeds, half of which had been sterilized in advance. It was hypothesized that fewer potent seeds would be destroyed than sterile seeds. This hypothesis was strongly supported by the data obtained; indeed, Fox's experimental results were highly significant.

The present experiment represents an attempt to replicate and extend this initial work. The principal objective was to test the primary hypothesis of Fox's experiment: a random event generator will display conformance behavior when a disposed system of low complexity is contingently linked to the REG for fulfillment of its disposition. A secondary objective was to examine the role of the experimenter in contributing to such effects. This was done in two ways, by varying the experimenter as a parameter, and by varying the degree of experimenter involvement.

The basic approach was a refinement of that used by Fox. Prior to the experiment, 1000 mung bean seeds (half of which had been sterilized by baking in an oven at 450° F for 15 minutes) were sealed in individually numbered envelopes, with numbers being previously assigned to potent and sterilized states by a pseudo-random procedure. This was carried out by D. McC. who was never present during the assignment of seeds to the favorable or unfavorable conditions. The experimenter operating the REG and recording the outcomes was always blind as to the state of the individual seeds in the sealed opaque envelopes. Two such experimenters, P. K. and L. T., were employed, so that a subsequent analysis could be made for possible differences in the data obtained by them.

The envelopes were processed individually, using PSIFI to generate a sequence of 50 binary trials, at a rate of 10 trials per second; scores above 25 were classed as Hi, those below 25 as Lo. P. K. and L. T. each completed 10 sessions, working with 50 envelopes per session. Prior to the experiment, D. McC. used a pseudo-random procedure to decide the contingency for each session--i. e., which of the two REG outcomes (Hi or Lo) would correspond, for all trials in that session, to the favorable consequence (nourish the seed) and which to the unfavorable condition (destroy the seed). On half the sessions, this information was made available to the two experimenters, and for the remaining sessions it was withheld. This provided the basis for varying the degree of experimenter involvement. In those sessions in which the experimenter was blind as to contingency, his or her role was that of a passive data collector. In the other sessions, not only was he or she aware of the contingency which had been selected, but at the end of the session those seeds which had been assigned to the unfavorable condition were to be personally destroyed by the experimenter by crushing the seed with a pliers while it remained concealed within the envelope. All seeds assigned to the favorable condition were nourished by a person not otherwise connected with the experiment and potent seeds in this category were sprouted and eaten. All analysis of data was deferred until this final stage was completed.

The planned analyses included (1) a chi-square test of the frequency counts in a two-by-two table for Fate of Seed (Nourish/ Destroy) versus State of Seed (Potent/Sterile); (2) comparison of the data obtained by P. K. and L. T. using a Mann-Whitney test; (3) a three-factor analysis of variance for State of Seed versus Experimenter versus Degree of Involvement; (4) an analysis which essentially ignores the presence of the seeds: a chi-square test on frequency of Hi outcomes for Experimenter versus Contingency; and (5) goodness-of-fit tests on the output of PSIFI during experimental sessions and on control runs.

None of these analyses yielded statistically significant results at the . 05 level. The results obtained were just those expected by chance and provide no evidence whatsoever for a conformance behavior effect involving seeds.

A SERIES OF MEDIUMISTIC EXPERIMENTS USING AUTOMATIC WRITING

William Eisler (New York, N. Y.)

In September 1976, when I lived in St. Louis, I was introduced to a local sensitive named Marjorie Melker. Her psychic ability lies in her automatic writing, which she has been producing since 1970. Her material has generally been well received and seemed to contain information she could only have arrived at through psychic means, but nothing had been done under controlled scientific conditions. I wish to describe here a series of experiments we have carried out over the past two years to test her mediumistic ability.

Experiment 1: One type of reading Mrs. Melker does is what she terms a "superconscious" reading. These are messages ostensibly relating to an individual's personality, state of mind or situation at the time. Our first experiment was a test of these messages.

I collected the names of 16 people (hereafter referred to as subjects), wrote them on slips of paper, and put them in a paper bag, which I kept. Once a week when Mrs. Melker and I got together, she would pull a name from the bag and immediately afterwards do a reading. Between two and five messages were done each session. The experiment started September 26, 1976, and all readings were completed by November 1, 1976. The readings were typed up and randomly numbered, and each subject was given four transcripts, one of which had been done for him or her and the other three selected from among the other transcripts by a random procedure. Subjects were asked to rank the four transcripts in order according to how closely they thought the transcripts corresponded to the subjects' circumstances. There were seven males and nine females participating in the study; males were given only

male transcripts and females, female readings. On November 8
the transcripts were mailed or given to the subjects with the request that all rankings be returned in two weeks' time. When all
results were in, subjects were told which reading had been for
them and given a copy of it.

Results were at chance. There were four correct first
choices, three people picked their reading as second choice, four
picked it third and five fourth.

Experiment 2: Our next experiment I considered a pilot
study in that it only involved three persons. This was an attempt
to receive communications from dead persons for living persons,
something Mrs. Melker had also previously had success with. All
three subjects were widows, and we tried to get messages from
their dead husbands. The same basic design was used as in the
previous experiment. All readings were done on February 13,
1977. Each participant was mailed all three numbered transcripts
and asked to rank them. When all were returned, each received a
copy of the correct one.

Two of the women correctly picked their reading as the first
choice, and the third woman picked it last (for whatever it is worth,
she later told me there was evidential material in her message).

Experiment 3: This result seemed encouraging, so we next
tried a confirmatory experiment with a parapsychology class I was
teaching at St. Louis Community College at Forest Park. Nine
persons gave me names of deceased persons they had known. The
procedure for this experiment was the same as for the previous
ones. On the next-to-last class, the subjects were given three
transcripts, one of which was theirs, asked to rank them, and
bring them to the next class (one week later). Results were insignificant: there were three correct first choices, three second,
and two third (there was one no response). Participants were
given their message at this class.

Experiment 4: Our fourth experiment was done in March
and April 1978, again attempting to receive communication from the
dead. A notice was placed in the journal Theta, requesting readers
to send me the name of a deceased person they wished to receive
an ostensible message from, along with their own name. It was
emphasized that this was the only information I wanted. Thirty-nine
responses were received by March 14, 1978, at which time the
names were put on slips of paper, randomly numbered and given to
Mrs. Melker. In a departure from previous procedure, in this
experiment Mrs. Melker was given all the names and left at her
leisure to do the readings (in contrast to the other experiments
where all readings were done in my presence on the night we got
together). There was no danger in this since respondents came
from all over the U.S. and Mrs. Melker did not have any information regarding their addresses.

Results did not reach significance.   There were nine correct first choices, four second, and eight third.

Along with the transcripts subjects were sent a seven-item questionnaire.   The only trend to emerge from this questionnaire was the fact that those who spent the most time making their decision (over one hour) tended to make the correct choice more often than those who made their choices quickly.   This supported the author's hypothesis that the raters are an important factor in this kind of free-response experiment; it is not simply a matter of the medium's getting or not getting a correct message.   A statistical assessment of these experiments may be misleading.   Several people commented that there was material in their readings which was correct, and which Mrs. Melker could not have known.   There may not have been enough of these hits to reach statistical significance, but they do suggest the use of psi.

ESP IN LIFE AND LAB:
AN INVESTIGATION OF INTUITION AND CARD-CALLING

Judith Taddonio O'Brien, [†] Steven MacDonald and Janet Bibeau
   (University of Lowell)

The relationship between incidents of psi in everyday life and their occurrence in the laboratory has been discussed extensively by L. E. Rhine.   In her outline of the forms in consciousness through which psi manifests, Rhine suggests that an intuitive experience may be similar to card-calling in its mode of operation.   Card-calling seems to involve the reception of information in quick succession, and subjects often report having hunches about certain cards, or gaining incomplete images of the target.   The following study was designed to investigate the relationship between intuitive psi experiences and card-calling in the laboratory.   It is part of a line of research currently being conducted at Lowell concerned with the relationship between ESP in life and lab.

Impetus for the research stems not only from Rhine's work, but also from literature concerning the relationship between the subject and the target in an ESP task.   This research has suggested that matching the target (or task) with a subject's preferences, or structuring the task to fit the subject's perceptions of how ESP operates often increases the likelihood of successful psi results. It is reasonable to assume that when faced with a given psi task, the subject forms an impression of whether the task is something he can or cannot do.   Structuring the task to fit the subject may result in two things: belief that he can perform well may be heightened in the subject, or the dynamics of psi operation might, in fact, be similar to his spontaneous experiences, and so result in better performance.

Forty-one college students from an introductory psychology class served as paid subjects, and were chosen on the basis of their responses to a questionnaire that had been circulated during class. The questionnaire provided information regarding the subject's age and sex, belief in ESP and whether he or she had ever had an ESP experience in everyday life. The forms that psi takes in consciousness were explained and illustrated on the questionnaire, and subjects were asked to indicate whether they had experienced any of them and how often they had occurred.

Subjects were then divided into three groups: those who had had intuitive psi experiences, those who had had psi experiences which were not intuitive, and those who had never had a psi experience. The subjects were then assembled as a group and were asked to complete four runs of clairvoyant card-calling. Targets for the test were generated individually for each subject by the Institute for Parapsychology, and were contained in a large opaque envelope in the front of the testing room. When the subjects had completed the task, the record sheets were collected, and they were debriefed about the study. The data were then scored by S. M. and J. B. without knowledge of the particular group into which a subject had been assigned. J. O. then divided the data into the three groups and double-checked the scoring with S. M. and J. B.

Initial analyses were conducted without respect to age, sex, belief or frequency of reported experience. An analysis of variance showed signficiant differences among the groups ($F_{2, 38}$ = 7. 33, p. < . 01). The results showed significant hitting for subjects who had had intuitive experiences (scoring rate = 23. 03%, MCE = 20. 00%, CR = +2. 58, p. < . 01), chance scoring for the subjects with no psi experience (scoring rate = 18. 38%, CR = -1. 42) and significant missing for the subjects who had had ESP experiences, but not intuitive ones (scoring rate = 17. 81%, CR = -2. 15, p. < . 02). Additional tests conducted on the variables of age, sex, belief in ESP and frequency of occurrence were not significant.

These results suggest that there may be a relationship between psi manifestation in intuitive experiences and psi operation in card-calling. No determination can be made as yet as to whether the relationship is psychological in nature or whether the dynamics of psi in the two instances are really similar. Further research to explore these two alternatives is now being conducted.

MISCELLANEOUS STUDIES II*

A NON-VERBAL G E S P STUDY WITH CONTINUOUS RECORDING

Joseph H. Rush (Boulder, Colo.)

This study employed a technique that allows a subject to seek a target and register a decision by continuous manual manipulation. The search is recorded, so that individual peculiarities can be observed and various criteria of success applied. The purpose was to explore the potentialities of the instrument for revealing psi performance.

The apparatus at the experimenter's station was a rectangular chart recorder (Heath Model IR-18M) and a signal light and switch. The target for each trial was a point on the recorder scale designated by a movable arrowhead symbol. The subject's station was a box bearing a large knob, signal light and switch. The knob operated a potentiometer, so connected to a dry battery as to supply to the recorder a voltage proportional to the rotation of the knob. Either signal switch would turn both lights on or off.

Nineteen subjects participated in one to five sessions each. Twelve were student volunteers from university parapsychology classes; the others were four housewives, two young children and J. H. R. The experimenter in almost all runs was J. H. R.

An appointment usually was for one hour, of which the experimental run occupied 30 to 45 minutes. At the first session, the experimenter explained the apparatus and experimental procedure, and encouraged the subject to operate the knob while watching the response of the recorder. The subject and the apparatus then were moved to another room, and the doors closed.

The experimenter turned on the signal lights while setting up the target for a trial. Two consecutive digits from a random series (Rand Corporation table), rounded to the nearest multiple of 5 to simplify evaluation, determined the target position on the recorder scale. The experimenter then started the paper drive and turned off the lights to signal the subject to begin turning the knob, trying to "find" the target and set the recording pen near it. No time limit was prescribed; trials ranged from a few seconds to two

---

*Chairperson: Gertrude Schmeider, City College, CUNY.

minutes. When satisfied with a setting, the subject turned on the signal lights, and the experimenter then marked the target location on the chart and prepared the next trial.

Most subjects found frequent reports on their performance distracting. The experimenter intervened only between trials, usually to reinforce success or to suggest a different subjective approach when the subject was not doing well. The subject was invited to examine the chart record after each run. Usually a run was ended by expiration of the hour or by the subject's decision to stop. In a few instances, when the subject appeared tired or bored, the experimenter stopped the session.

Results were evaluated by a binomial method. In one mode, the circular range represented by the recorder scale is treated as six discrete $60°$ sectors, one being centered on target. The probability for a hit in the target sector is then $1/6$, and statistical significance is determined by computing the CR as in discrete-choice tests. In a second mode, two $180°$ sectors are treated, with $p = 1/2$.

Forty-six runs yielded 960 trials. Of these, 165 were hits within the $60°$ target sector, a non-significant score. Two subjects achieved marginally significant scores: $29/120$, $p = .028$; and $12/40$, $p = .034$ (all p values are two-tailed).

Inspection of the records suggested certain position effects, particularly an excess of hits on first trials of runs and a deficit on second and on last trials. Before this tendency was evaluated, five runs that involved noncomparable conditions were excluded. The 41 remaining runs yielded 11 hits in the $60°$ target sector on first trials and three on second and on last trials of runs. By Fisher's test of this difference, $p = .015$. Fifteen runs by the six subjects whose total scores each exceeded MCE yielded six hits on first trials and one each on second and last; $p = .037$. The difference for the remaining subjects was not significant; $p = 0.16$. Similar evaluations on the basis of opposed $180°$ sectors yielded no significant results.

These quantifications give only a bare-bones intimation of the tantalizing and sometimes exciting incidents that emerged in this study: e. g. , the utterly casual four-year-old girl who stopped a few degrees from target, repeatedly; or the young man who converged on target as if tuning a radio. The record of each trial contains much more information than merely the terminal point.

This method is not adapted to rapid accumulation of great numbers of trials, but rather to detailed investigation of the process by which ostensibly blind groping is biased toward (or sometimes away from) the target. However, more elaborate equipment, including computer readout and processing, is needed to explore more fully the potentialities of the method.

LANGUAGE ESP TESTS WITH A SINGLE SUBJECT
UNDER NORMAL AND RELAXED CONDITIONS

K. Ramakrishna Rao (Institute for Parapsychology, FRNM)

Using words in two languages, Telugu and English, Rao
found evidence of consistent differential response as well as a consistent sex difference among his subjects.   His male subjects obtained significantly more hits on Telugu targets than on English
words.   Female subjects did the opposite.   Later studies by
Kanthamani, Sailaja, and Rao and Davis suggest among other things
that experimenter variables as well as subject variables influence
the manifestation of the differential effect.

The present exploratory study attempts to test how the differential effect between the words of two languages would manifest,
when a single subject is repeatedly tested under normal waking and
relaxed conditions.

A female subject in her twenties participated in this experiment, which stretched over a period of about four months.   It was
decided in advance to test her in 10 sessions.   Half of these sessions were carried out under normal waking conditions and the other
half followed immediately after the subject had gone through a period
of relaxation induced through suggestion.

Of the five sessions in each condition, two sessions consisted
of three runs in each session.   One of these employed the mixed
deck of 50 English and 50 Telugu target cards.   Of the other two,
one run was with English cards alone and the other with Telugu
targets.   Two sessions had two runs.   In one of these sessions both
the runs were carried out with English cards and in the other only
Telugu cards were used.   In the final session there were two runs
with the deck of 100 mixed cards.   In one run only English key
cards and in the other only Telugu key cards were used.

The procedure used was the standard blind matching technique.
The test consisted in the subject's attempting to match the target
cards against a set of key cards enclosed in black opaque envelopes.
The target words were ball, fish, love, peace and tree, and their
Telugu equivalents.

For the relaxation session, the subject was asked to stretch
herself and relax on a couch.   The experimenter spent a few minutes talking about relaxation and its benefits to the human mind and
how it could possibly help the subject obtain better ESP scores.
This talk was periodically punctuated by the suggestion that the subject was going into a more and more relaxed state of mind.   In a
couple of minutes the subject entered into a "relaxed" state.   After
remaining two minutes in this state, the experimenter woke her up
and administered the planned test.

The results were analyzed in terms of language under the two conditions. The subject obtained 78 hits in 400 trials on English targets in the normal condition. She obtained 55 hits in the same number of trials on the Telugu targets. In the relaxed condition she obtained 73 hits and 92 hits respectively on English and Telugu targets. A two-by-two chi-square of this distribution is not significant. Also the difference in scoring rate between the normal and relaxed conditions is not significant. However, the difference in the rate of scoring on Telugu targets in normal and relaxed conditions gives a chi-square of 4.929 (1 df) p < .05. It may be mentioned that in Rao's previous studies also the differential effect in language tests found in the data of female subjects was largely due to psi-missing on Telugu targets.

Since there is some evidence of differential scoring only on Telugu targets between normal and relaxed conditions, a secondary analysis was done to see how the subject's scoring on Telugu targets in these two conditions compared for the results obtained with mixed decks and those obtained with separate decks. It was observed that the differential scoring is more marked with mixed decks than with separate decks, while the difference in the rate of scoring on Telugu targets in the mixed decks between waking and relaxed conditions is marginally significant with a Z = 2.25, p < .05. Such a difference is not significant with separate decks.

As in Rao's previous studies with female subjects, the present subject also showed a tendency to psi-miss on Telugu targets in the normal condition. What is of special interest is that she tended to reverse this trend in those sessions in which she had gone through the process of relaxation prior to taking the ESP tests. If this tendency is something not peculiar to the subject or the particular set up of this experiment, this finding could have important implications.

The fact that a significant difference in the rate of scoring on Telugu targets in the normal and relaxed conditions occurred with mixed cards and not with the separate language cards supports the assumption that presenting the two sets of language cards together may facilitate differential scoring. Further work is therefore planned to test the hypothesis that the differential scoring would occur only when the contrast between targets is in the subject's focus, and not otherwise.

DEALING WITH DIVERGENCE

Brian Millar and John Hartwell[†] (University of Utrecht)

There is currently a major problem (the "experimental control dilemma") in the observation-based theories. All concur that psi is not limited by space or time. Each observer of the data, no matter how remote, may contribute to the result to the same extent. Because the relevant factors in the future are outside our control, it would seem that a repeatable experiment would necessarily be impossible.

Instead of the above situation, Schmidt and others have examined the case where a large number of weak psi sources observe the data: the variance increases and the subject's contribution is washed out. While this minor "many subjects paradox" shares common features with the experimental control dilemma, the two "divergence problems" are, nonetheless, quite distinct.

Schmidt has proposed that the paradox may be cured by taking subject-selection into account: successful subjects select themselves into psi experiments by PK. Schmidt shows that in an experiment where each subject performs only a single trial, the many subjects paradox disappears. However, this has little relevance to the important question, experimental control. Furthermore we can show that his solution fails when each subject does more than one trial. Mathematically the cause of this failure is Schmidt's multiplicative theorem for the combination of psi sources.

While developed independently, our ideas share much common ground with Schmidt's. We too have found problems arising from the combination hypothesis. We propose that the rule of multiplying individual theta's be replaced by taking the mean, this immediately removes the variance increase, the source of many of the difficulties. Other than this we require no new assumptions. We are primarily concerned with the question of experimental control and resolve the above paradox only as a side effect.

The observation theories assert that one normal physical condition must be satisfied for psi to occur: the subject must get feedback. The crux of our approach lies in the realization that feedback pathways are not perfect but contain some corrupting noise. The further removed an observer is from an experiment, the more degraded the feedback signal will (usually) be. Thus, while psi may be of its own nature completely space-time independent, the characteristics of the feedback pathways introduce well-defined limitations into its otherwise anarchic manifestation. Formally we represent the noisy feedback channel as itself a random number generator, with probability P_{ext} of transmitting a valid "hit" signal. The rest of the universe is connected to the experiment only via this channel. In practice the "noise" will run the gamut from equipment malfunction to journal publication policy.

We find that the contribution of a single external psi source (θ_1) is attenuated by the factor P_{ext} as compared to the subject (θ_0) within the experiment. However, we can remove the external observer's influence virtually entirely by adding more randomly selected observers θ_2, θ_3, $\ldots$ θ_n. If we have, say, 100 external observers with no psi ability, on average the contribution the external observer θ_1 can make to the result is divided by about 100. If the experimental subject (θ_0) were not partly "insulated" by the noisy channel, his or her psi too would similarly be cancelled out by the rest of the universe.

If our treatment is correct, we can ensure that the only effects are due to those involved in the experiment by the simple expedient of allowing only a fraction of the data to be seen by the rest of the world.   Fortuitously this happens to be the typical situation in psi experiments.

The important point is that we have demonstrated that the postulate of space-time independence is by no means incompatible with the possibility of full experimental control.   Within the enchanted boundary, however, subject, experimenter, data-checkers, etc., all have virtually unrestricted feedback; thus we would expect them all to contribute to the psi effect.

We have pointed out that it may be possible to control psi by controlling the feedback.   Our results hinge critically on the truth of the observational hypothesis: if feedback should prove to be unnecessary for psi, then our results immediately collapse.

We do not provide answers.   Our work only establishes some of the questions that are worth experimental testing.   A high priority for research should be given to the general question of feedback, bit by bit and partial and the effects of various feedback manipulations to subject and experimenter.   The other main area of enquiry indicated for examination is how psi sources combine.

If we should prove to be extremely good at guessing and the picture presented above is true, then deliberate use of the "insulation" principle should allow us to partition a total psi effect into subject and experimenter contributions, thus resolving the continuing controversy over the role of experimenter psi.

THE EFFECT OF SINGLE VERSUS MULTIPLE
TRIALS PER TARGET ON ESP PERFORMANCE

Ephraim T. Schechter (University of Pittsburgh, Johnstown)

The idea that psi-mediated information is subject to interference from other sources of information seems common to recent parapsychological research and theories on such topics as psi-conducive states and the effects of response biases.   Information-processing concepts suggest that message repetition, or redundancy, should be effective in offsetting the effects of interference from background noise much as the repeated transmission of a radio message can help the listeners distinguish between true message content and random static by "averaging out" the effects of the interfering static.   This suggests that repeated psi trials with the

same target should make it easier to identify the target than if only
one guess at each target was allowed.   This hypothesis was tested
in a pair of repeated-measures clairvoyance studies using an automated four-choice testing apparatus.   Each percipient took two psi
tests; each test consisted of four 24-trial runs.   In one test, a
random number generator (RNG) selected a new target for each
trial, so that the percipient had only one guess at each target.   In
the other test, the RNG was turned off and the same geometrical
symbol served as the target for all 96 trials.   Test order and the
single-target symbol were counterbalanced across subjects; the
percipients were not told which test they were to take first nor
which symbol was to be used in the single target test.

Psi performance was measured in three ways.   Deviation
from mean chance expectation (MCE), rather than hit rate, was
used as the measure of the accuracy with which the psi information
was used, to offset the possibility that psi information might lead
to hitting for some percipients and missing for others.   Two variance measures were used to evaluate the run-to-run consistency of
the percipients' performance.   One was the run-score variance,
which indicated whether the average deviation from MCE was consistent from run to run.   A second measure, the subject variance,
was also used.   This measure indicated whether each percipients'
deviation from his or her own average performance was consistent
from run to run.

Sixteen undergraduate volunteers served as the percipients
in the first study.   There were no significant differences between
the overall deviations from MCE in the single target and random
target conditions, suggesting that the increased target redundancy
had not affected the degree to which the psi information had been
used ($F = 0.04$; 1, 8 df; $p > .05$).   The two variance measures,
however, both indicated that the percipients had performed more
consistently in the single target test, since both the run-score
variance (Wilcoxon $T = 25$, $p < .025$, two-tailed) and the subject
variance (Wilcoxon $T = 24$, $p < .01$, two-tailed) were significantly
lower in the single-target condition.   While these results did not
confirm the original hypothesis that target redundancy would increase
the accuracy with which the psi information was used, they did indicate that the target redundancy had influenced the way in which the
psi information affected the guessing behavior.

The same procedures were used for the second study, and
16 new undergraduate volunteers served as the percipients.   Again,
the overall deviations from MCE in the single-target and random-
target tests were not significantly different from each other ($F = 3.22$, 1, 8 df; $p > .05$).   The analysis of the variance measures,
however, only partially confirmed the results of the first study.
The subject variance again showed more consistency in the single-
target condition, although the difference was not statistically significant
(Wilcoxon $T = 41.5$, $p > .05$, one-tailed), but the run score variance
was nearly the same in the single target condition as it was in the random target condition (Wilcoxon $T = 53$, $p > .05$, one-tailed).

It is not clear what the change in the run score variance data from Study 1 to Study 2 means. The other two measures, however, suggest an interesting pattern, indicating that target redundancy may affect the consistency with which percipients use psi information rather than the accuracy with which they use it. There are several things that could produce this effect, involving possible differences in the nature of the information used or the way in which it is used rather than the degree to which it is used, and some of these possibilities would produce identifiable patterns in the percipients' trial-by-trial performances. An analysis of the trial-by-trial data is currently under way.

THE THREE GUNAS AND E S P: AN EXPLORATORY INVESTIGATION

P. V. Krishna Rao and K. Harigopal (Andhra University, India)[†]

According to Samehya yoga of the Indian philosophy system, there are three fundamental aspects (or gunas) to all matter. They are sattva (thought/illumination), rajas (activity) and tamas (inertia). These gunas apply to mind as well, since mind is no more than subtle matter. Some psychologists have regarded the three gunas as three aspects of human temperament. E. G. Parameswaran prepared an inventory to assess the three gunas. The inventory consists of 24 sattva items, 27 rajas items and 29 tamas items in the form of statements in an attitude scale. The subject responds by checking one of the three categories "agree," "disagree," or "doubtful." The gunas are considered to be independent dimensions and the inventory gives separate scores for them.

Yoga texts suggest that preponderance of sattva in one's mind may enable one to obtain siddhis or paranormal abilities, while tamas inhibit them. The present exploratory study was carried out to test whether the asserted relationship between gunas and psi would manifest in a controlled ESP test.

The subjects were 112 (57 male, 55 female) postgraduate students in economics, English literature, and library science at Andhra University. Their ages ranged from 19 to 31.

The personality inventory based on the doctrine of three gunas developed by Parameswaran and Uma, and Lakshmi and Parameswaran was employed to assess the three gunas.

The ESP ability of the subjects was measured using Anderson and White techniques. The ESP targets were prepared by an

---

†Read by K. Ramakrishna Rao.

assistant in accordance with the procedure described by Anderson and White.

The inventory and ESP test were administered to the students in their classrooms by P. V. K. The number of subjects in each class varied from 20 to 30. The order of presentation of the two tests was balanced. For the ESP test the instructions of Anderson and White were modified and given orally to the group. The printed instructions on the inventory were supplemented with oral instruc- tions. The ESP tests and the inventory were scored by the research students of the Department of Psychology and Parapsychology and were double checked.

The data were analyzed using the Pearson product-moment correlation to discern the relationship between the three gunas and ESP. The inter correlation matrix of the three gunas and second- order partial correlations were worked out to control statistically the influence of the other two gunas, while relating each guna to ESP. The subjects were also divided into high and low groups on each guna, taking group mean as the cutting point and the two groups were compared on their ESP scores by a t test.

Only tamas is found to be significantly negatively related to ESP scores ($r = -.2003$, 110 df, $p < .05$). When the influence of sattva and rajas is partialled out, the r between tamas and ESP is barely significant at the .05 level ($r = -.1856$, $t = 1.9629$).

With the exception of the high group on tamas, all other groups scored close to mean chance expectation on the ESP test. The high tamas group obtained a significant negative deviation (dev. = -70, CR = 2.15, $p < .05$, two-tailed). The difference in scoring rate of high and low groups is significant only in the case of tamas ($t = 2.18$, 110 df, $p < .05$, two-tailed). The low tamas group tended to score positively while the high tamas group psi- missed.

GROUP TESTING FOR ESP: A NOVEL APPROACH
TO THE COMBINED USE OF INDIVIDUAL AND SHARED TARGETS

JoMarie Haight, Debra H. Weiner[†] and Melissa D. Morrison
(Institute for Parapsychology, FRNM)

Group testing in parapsychology can be considered comparable to simultaneous individual testing sessions without the personal attention found in the latter. One approach is to treat the group as the unit of analysis by combining the members' responses (e. g. , majority vote) and comparing it to a "group" target. This method orients the group toward a common goal, but necessarily de-empha- sizes the importance of the individual's responses. The present study attempted to design a testing method that would be an effective compromise between these two extremes, that would yield more reliable evidence for psi than is generally obtained in group tests, and would provide a way to explore the effect of group participation on ESP scoring.

The experimenters embedded the task within a "space travel" theme in which subjects were to imagine that they were on a crusade to save the earth from the attack of 24 robot ships. Each subject was given a manila envelope to which was attached two sheets of paper separated by carbon paper. On each sheet was a 48-segment "radar screen" which represented the subject's "view of space" from his individual "spaceship." Inside the envelope between two sheets of construction paper was a computer printout with 24 letters (A-X) dispersed over the page so that a letter was positioned directly behind 24 of the 48 radar screen segments. The location of these 24 "ships" was individually randomized for each printout. Subjects were asked to "blast" the ships with 24 "proton torpedoes" by placing a gummed dot in any segment in which they felt a "ship" lurked ($p = 1/2$). Subjects circled or crossed their dots to leave an impression on the carbon copy. After the copies were collected, subjects opened their envelopes and scored their calls. Responses were independently double-checked and scored by computer (reported analyses conducted on computer-scored calls).

In the explanation of the task, the group had been told that a majority of the members had to hit a ship to destroy it. After individual scoring was completed, a vote was taken separately for each ship; the "destruction" was displayed visually as the removal of a paper ship (identified by its letter) from a star map in the front of the room. Tie votes were placed in a separate category ("damaged but not destroyed"). This method of applying a majority vote (MV) to the number of hits (as opposed to the calls) on individually randomized targets has the advantage of maintaining a distinct individual task, the success on which contributes neatly toward a group goal. Problems of stacking effect or the formation of a conflict between individual and group goals, as might arise in other attempts to create this situation, are avoided.

This test was given to 40 groups as part of a talk on parapsychology. Most groups were high-school classes, though six were junior-high or sixth-grade classes and six were adult groups. In an effort to test possibly more cohesive units, two high-school clubs and one high-school basketball team were tested. The groups ranged in size from eight to 33 with a median of 21.5. Teachers' responses were not included in the MV (majority votes) or other analyses.

Minor changes were introduced in certain sessions with no apparent effect on scoring. The targets for the first three classes were hand-printed and -scored. For one group the fantasy was enhanced by a progressive-relaxation/guided-imagery procedure. A demonstration of the MV technique was added, and for four groups the task was presented without the fantasy element.

The experiment was designed to elicit psi as measured by individual scores and by a significant increase in scoring rate in the MV condition over the enhancement expected statistically. T-tests compared the mean number of hits for each group to MCE (= 12). After corrections for multiple analyses were made, none of the groups showed evidence of psi. The second expectation was evaluated by calculating the cumulative binomial probability for obtaining the observed number of MV hits for the group based on their mean individual scoring rate (i. e., $P_{hit} = \frac{\text{scoring rate } [\%]}{100}$). Tie votes were eliminated. None of the groups individually showed a significant enhancement effect, nor did a t-test comparison of the obtained MV with the expected MV reveal a significant trend toward such enhancement. Analyses for personality-psi relationship and for experimenter effects yielded no consistent results.

A COMPARISON OF SUBLIMINAL AND EXTRASENSORY PERCEPTION USING THE GANZFELD TECHNIQUE

S. M. Roney-Dougal (City University, London)

There are many researchers in parapsychology who have noted a correspondence between the field of subliminal perception and that of psi, e. g., John Beloff, Charles Honorton and James Terry, and Martin Johnson. However it is an area which has not yet been directly researched, even though considerable understanding of sensitivity to psi could be gained by directly correlating an individual's receptivity to these two areas.

In this study, I shall use the Ganzfeld technique since Honorton and Terry, John Parker, and others have shown this to be a reliable method of enchancing whatever psi effects might be present, and the hypnagogic state of consciousness is a more easily attained and controlled altered state of consciousness than, say, hypnosis or meditation. It will be interesting to see whether subliminal perception effects are also enchanced by this technique, thus maybe giving us a greater insight into the whole area of sensitivity to our "subconscious mind."

The methodology to be used is a multivariate one, as this project is purely an exploratory project, giving a look at as many of the factors involved as is reasonably possible. Each subject will undertake a total of six sessions; three Ganzfeld and three non-Ganzfeld. In each group there will be a subliminal, a GESP and a control condition. The stimuli are words that have been chosen so as to evoke certain moods--pleasant, unpleasant or neutral--and have been recorded on tape. For each session that the subject undertakes there will be a completely new word pool so that no subject will at any time know the contents of the pool.

The subject will be, at all times, wearing headphones playing white noise, and it is through these that the subliminal stimuli will be presented. In the psi condition the agent will listen to the tape-recorded stimuli and since he or she will not have the white noise mask, the words will be heard supraliminally. In the control condition, a tape with no words will be played.

During the session the subject will free-associate, and this will be recorded. A record of galvanic skin response (GSR) will be taken on both a pen chart recorder and an FM tape recorder (the latter being subjected to Fourier analysis). After the session the subject will rate the pool of words from which the tape was chosen, according to his or her degree of confidence that the words were or were not presented. Thus three overlapping measures are being taken to ascertain the subject's awareness of the stimuli. The control condition will give a baseline for the subject's GSR activity and for the free-association imagery.

Further, each subject will complete mood, attitude and personality questionnaires and do the Witkin Embedded Figures and the Kinsbourne Eye Movement tests. These will enable me to correlate certain characteristics of the subject, e.g., degree of "globality," with their sensitivity to subliminal and extrasensory stimuli.

Since the design is primarily that of an overview pilot, the data analysis will of necessity be extremely complex. With so little data and so many variables I do not expect significance. I am looking for trends. The word ratings will be analyzed to determine overall significant difference from MCE. They will then be divided into Ganzfeld and non-Ganzfeld groups and will be analyzed to determine whether the two groups differ significantly both from MCE and from one another. They will then be divided into telepathy-subliminal groups and again analyzed. Individual scores will be analyzed on the same bases. A sheep-goat division will be made on the basis of the attitude-personality questionnaires and the resultant groups will be analyzed.

The free-association transcripts for each session will be typed and four copies made. Three of these will be sent to independent judges who will assess which tape was presented. These assessments will then be analyzed for significant differences from MCE and for correlation with the subject's own ratings. Once again the analyses mentioned before will be employed.

The GSR record will be interpreted according to the amount of variation from the resting basal level before, during and after stimulation, and the differences in activity will be analyzed. As far as the Fourier analysis is concerned I have so far not found a single report where GSR has been analyzed by this method. This is, therefore, a complete unknown and I shall merely be attempting to discover what information can be extrapolated.

In conclusion, this project is a general comparative project

synthesizing the relevant variables to enable slightly better understanding of the receptive mode of consciousness utilized in subliminal
and extrasensory perception.

ALTERED STATES AND E S P*

HYPNOSIS AS A PSI-CONDUCIVE STATE:
A CONTROLLED REPLICATION STUDY

Carl L. Sargent (Cambridge University)

There are many studies which claim to show that hypnosis produces significantly higher scoring than the waking-state control condition on ESP tasks.   However, there are many problems involved in interpreting the results of the studies in question.

Most of these studies employed within-subjects experimental designs, in which all subjects are tested in both the hypnotized and control conditions.   Such designs of experiment are inappropriate to the study of the effects of hypnosis on ESP test performance, primarily because subjects are prone to be more interested and better motivated in the hypnosis condition.   In both orthodox psychological, and parapsychological, tasks there is evidence from within-subjects experiments that subjects may (intentionally or not) sabotage their performance in the control condition to enhance the apparent difference between the control and hypnosis conditions.

A second potential artifact, which might affect both within- and between-subjects experiments, is volunteer bias.   There is evidence that volunteers for psychological tasks perceived as threatening or worrying are lower in anxiety than the population from which they are drawn, be this the general or the student population.   Since anxiety is predictive of ESP test performance, and since some subjects do view hypnosis as potentially threatening, it is clear that trait and state variables may be confounded in at least some hypnosis ESP studies.   In within-subjects studies, this might mean that the generalizability of findings from hypnosis studies is low because a highly self-selected, biased population is being tested. The potential artifacts in between-subjects studies are more worrying.   Consideration of them reveals a further weakness in the hypnosis/ESP literature: poor reporting of important details of subject recruitment by researchers.

If a researcher recruits subjects for the control and hypnosis groups in a between-subjects study separately, then clearly the latter group may be less anxious than the former (volunteer bias) and so superior scoring by the hypnosis group (if observed) might

---

*Chairperson: J. G. Pratt, University of Virginia.

be due to state or trait variable differences.   If the researcher recruits subjects and then allocates them to the control or hypnosis
group, two artifacts may be present; first, a general population
bias in anxiety level may limit generalizability of findings, and
second, if the researcher (for example) advertised for subjects "for
an ESP/hypnosis study," and then allocates half of them to a control group, motivational artifacts may be present.   The control subjects may have volunteered because they were interested in hypnosis;
now when they find that they are to be mere controls, they may have
adverse task motivation.   Researchers must give details of just how
they recruit subjects!

     There are many more artifacts in the hypnosis/ESP litera-
ture.   In some studies, subjects have been selected for a hypnosis
group because they were known to be hypnotizable.   Since there are
trait-variable correlates of hypnotizability this procedure leads to
trait-variable differences being confounded with state-variable differences between groups.   Lastly, there is the problem of experimenter motivation, interest and expectancy.   One might expect experimenters to be more interested in and to expect superior performance from subjects in the hypnosis group in a between-subjects
experimental design.   Thus, sensory experimenter effects may be
involved.

     A between-subjects design of experiment was employed in the
present study, which attempted to eliminate as many artifacts as
possible in the study of the effects of hypnosis on ESP test performance.   Forty subjects were tested, 35 males and five females.   The
20 subjects in the hypnosis group and the 20 in the control group
were drawn from minimally overlapping social groups and were all
friends of the experimenter and were contacted personally by him.
All subjects were given the Sixteen Personality Factor Questionnaire
(16PF) before the ESP test.   Control group subjects were told that
the study involved an investigation of personality correlates of ESP
test performance.   All subjects were "sheep" in that they accepted
the possibility of ESP at a general level.   Subjects were all tested
individually.   Prior to the ESP test, hypnosis group subjects were
hypnotized and control group subjects engaged in casual chit-chat
with the experimenter.   All subjects were told to make themselves
as comfortable and relaxed as possible during the ESP test.

     The ESP test comprised two 25-trial runs of clairvoyance
testing with ESP cards using immediate hit-or-miss feedback.   The
experimenter was screened from the subjects and the cards were
concealed in an opaque container.   Subjects paced their own responses and after each response the experimenter noted it down,
carefully withdrew the top card from the pack, and gave the subject feedback.   At the end subjects were given cumulative hit score
and a short (one-minute) break was taken.   The second run was
then completed, subjects told their total score, and dismissed with
thanks.

     Targets were compiled from the Rand Corporation tables and

target packs were prepared by an independent helper who also aided with data checking after the experiment had been completed.

One prediction was made about the outcome(s) of the experiment: in the control group, 16PF Anxiety scores would correlate negatively with total score on the ESP task. This was predicted on the basis of past parapsychological findings and is a subject of particular interest to the experimenter. Therefore there was an interest in the scoring patterns of the control group as well as in those of the hypnosis group. An idiosyncratic interest was exploited in the hope of minimizing the differential experimenter interest artifact noted earlier.

Analysis of 16PF data revealed no differences between groups on Extraversion or Anxiety approaching significance, nor differences between these groups individually or collectively and published norms for the U. K. student population. Analysis of ESP test data did reveal differences. The hypnosis group averaged 11. 90 hits, which is significantly above the mean chance expectation value of 10. 00 (t(19) = 2. 95, p = . 0082, two-tailed) while control subjects averaged only 10. 05 hits. The difference between groups is significant (t(38) = 2. 15, p = . 038, two-tailed).

The correlation between 16PF Anxiety and ESP score in the control group was -0. 41 (p = . 034, one-tailed). The value for this correlation in the hypnosis group was +0. 38 (p = ns). There may be an Anxiety by Condition interaction since the correlation of Anxiety rank with the difference in scoring by matched-rank subject pairs (hypnosis-control) is +0. 59 which is significant (p = . 0067, two-tailed).

Two further aspects of scoring by hypnotized subjects are of interest. First, there is a decline in their scoring rate from run 1 where scoring is strongly above chance (mean score = 6. 50 hits, t(19) = 4. 17, p = . 00052, two-tailed) to run 2 (mean score 5. 40 hits, p = ns). The decline is significant at p = . 0087 (correlated-means t(19) = 2. 95). Second, there is a significant positive correlation between scoring on run 1 and on run 2 (+0. 49, p = . 028, two-tailed). Neither of these features was present in the scoring of control group subjects.

Further analyses indicated no differences between groups in response biases (frequency and first-order alternation response set) nor in mean run time, and that these two variables did not influence results significantly. Extraversion/ESP correlations were insignificant for both groups (-0. 15 for control group, +0. 06 for hypnosis). Mean hypnotic induction time for hypnosis group subjects was 10 minutes 42 seconds and the correlation of ESP score with length of induction period was +0. 29, which is insignificant.

The findings of this study indicate that hypnotic induction methods are effective methods for psi elicitation. Why this is remains to be seen; certainly work remains to be done, for example, in separating the psi-eliciting powers of the induction-as-ritual and the relaxation components of hypnosis. The remarkable achievement of the control group in deviating from mean chance expectation by 0.05 and 0.00 hits in their two runs, in terms of mean scores, is also of some interest. It was exactly what the experimenter wished to observe. Certainly it is of great interest that hypnosis elicits strong positive ESP test performance; it may also be just as interesting that a control group in a between-subjects hypnosis/ESP study has never scored significantly above chance when several of the experimenters involved have had little difficulty in eliciting ESP from waking-state subjects in other experimental contexts.

TWO GANZFELD CONDITIONS: AN EXPLORATORY STUDY

Nancy Sondow (City College, CUNY)

      In a preliminary investigation to explore the effects of two different procedures, which will be called Associations and Feedback, two independent groups ($N_1 = N_2 = 10$) each gave free responses while in 35 minute Ganzfeld isolation with mentation transcribed by the experimenter through a one-way intercom, over a series of five GESP trials with randomly selected target pictures. Possible targets were arranged in packs of four such that the pictures within each pack were as dissimilar as possible in content, dominant colors and form. Subjects later ranked the four pictures of the appropriate pack (double-blind) in order of target likelihood.

      The Association group had four sessions without feedback, associating mentation to each picture before ranking. The Feedback group had four sessions without associating, and feedback after ranking. Both had a fifth session with associations and feedback.

      The two procedures both stemmed from the idea of increasing the recognition of an unconscious psi influence on the seemingly independent direction of one's stream of consciousness.

      It was thought that asking the subject to associate each element of her mentation to each of a group of possible target pictures, looking carefully for all correspondences, might reveal a pattern of thought unconsciously revolving around the target. That is, associations to the correct target may come from all directions. Even if most of them are unimpressive by themselves, taken together they may outweigh a single striking correspondence to the wrong picture.

      Alternately, feedback of a complex target, including a review of all the seemingly related mentation, might reveal individual differences in the pattern of cognitive processing of the psi information buried in the subject's mentation. In this way, feedback might increase a subject's recognition of her own pattern of psi intrusion in her stream of thought, without necessarily increasing either psi frequency, or recognition of psi-mediated internal cues.

Two experienced independent judges each blind-ranked all sessions. To see if judges would be more successful with than without the associations, each of the 60 relevant sessions was judged once with and once without associations.

Forty-one direct hits were found in the 100 sessions (exact binomial p < .0004), where 25 would be expected by chance. The Association group had 28 direct hits out of 50, which is highly significant (exact binomial $p < 3x10^{-6}$) while the Feedback group scored at chance with 13 direct hits.

Comparisons of the two groups using Mann Whitney U tests (two-tailed) ranking hits per subject were significant for the first four sessions (U = 17, p < .02) and for all five sessions (U = 19, p < .02). The difference in scoring between groups in the first session alone is significant (Fisher's Exact p < .02).

Mann Whitney U tests ranking hits per session between groups were also significant both for the first four sessions (U = 8, p < .03) and for all five sessions (U = 0, p < .01).

Blind judges' scores were significant with 23 hits out of 60 (Z = 2.39, p < .02) only when the association material was available. The same protocols judged without associations yielded 15 hits (exactly mean chance expectation).

Replicating Habel, a striking decrease in hit rate was found when sessions run by the experimenter per day increased. The Association group had an 82 per cent hit rate, with 14 hits in 17 trials for sessions run on separate days, a 53 per cent hit rate when two sessions are run on the same day, and a 29 per cent hit rate when three sessions occur on the same day. A two-by-two table of hits versus misses is significant for one versus three sessions per day by Fisher's Exact Method (p < .004). The same trend appears in the Feedback group. Since the Association group had twice as many sessions as the Feedback group in the most unfavorable (three per day) condition, while Feedback sessions predominated in the most favorable (one per day) condition, the superiority in the success rate of the Association group was not partially due to a sessions-per-day effect.

Correlations of ESP success with dream-recall frequency and with subjective estimates of Ganzfeld length failed to replicate.

Results of one judge support the hypothesis that judges would detect more low than high dream recallers' hits. The five high dream recallers had 15 hits out of 25 (Z = 4.04, p < .00007) and Judge 1 had five hits for the same material, with an overlap of four. The five low dream recallers had 11 hits out of 25 (Z = 2.19, p < .03) and Judge 1 had nine hits for the same material, seven of which overlapped subjects' hits, offering some support to the expectation that low dream recallers may have fewer but more straightforward correspondences to targets, and high dream recallers more transformed psi material and better memory for unverbalized details of the Ganzfeld experience unavailable to outside judges.

Post-hoc analyses using Fisher's Exact Method (target versus non-target, chosen versus not chosen) found significant psi-hitting for targets depicting horses (p < . 01), water (p < . 02), fire (p < . 03) and flying (p < . 04).

The major results in this study are the strikingly high scores in the Association group contrasting with the chance results of the Feedback group.   There are several possible explanations.

First, expectation of feedback may have inhibited psi mani-festations for most subjects, either because they may have had a more passive attitude toward the psi task when they expected feed-back, or because anxiety caused by ego involvement in being "tested" may have increased the cognitive noise level and masked the psi input, or because improvement after feedback would seem called for, and most subjects want to please.

Second, associations may have improved the clarity of psi manifestations of most subjects by improving the subject's judging ability.   Third, lack of feedback of psi results may have led to higher scores, either because a more game-like attitude was adopted, or because the active search for clues and reliance on personal insight may have increased some subjects' interest and attention.   Finally, an experimenter effect may have caused the pattern of obtained results.

Since the Association procedure is confounded with lack of feedback in most of the sessions where psi success was evident, interpretation must await future untangling of possible variables. The lower hit rate in the feedback trial of the Association group and the chance results in all five trials of the Feedback group sug-gest the likelihood of psi inhibition caused by expectation of feed-back.   Some support for the anxiety interpretation lies in the fact that subjects in the Association group often spontaneously remarked that they were glad they would not know their results until the series was complete.

In later Feedback sessions, expectation of failure based on previous failure, or anxiety to maintain positive performance, could have adversely affected some subjects' attitudes and contributed to the chance results.   However, the results of the first Feedback session must be examined separately, since other single-session-per-subject Ganzfeld experiments which later revealed the targets to subjects as a courtesy have had significantly high results.   It may be that most subjects in the Feedback group obligingly missed the first target to allow possible room for improvement through feedback.   It should also be noted that feedback was not immediate, and the cognitive analysis approach that was employed may not be suited to many subjects.

Since subjects who reported highest and lowest dream frequency both had more psi success than those in the middle range,
dream recall frequency may not have been a good measure in this
sample to distinguish individual differences in distortion of ESP
material. The question of whether distortion and elaboration of psi
material is more frequent with certain personality correlates might
be explored with other, more sensitive measures.

THE INFLUENCE OF AUDITORY GANZFELD
CHARACTERISTICS UPON FREE-RESPONSE
E S P PERFORMANCE AND MENTATION REPORTS

Rex G. Stanford (Center for Parapsychological Research, Austin,
Texas)

Some investigators have proposed that the favorable ESP
performance often observed under Ganzfeld conditions is due to
reductions in external, somatic and cognitive noise associated with
uniform sensory stimulation in Ganzfeld. Under such circumstances,
it is proposed, the "ESP signal" is easier to detect and recognize.

Theorization by Walker and by Stanford suggests that the
sound (white noise, pink noise, or ocean waves) traditionally used
as the "uniform stimulation" of the auditory Ganzfeld might have
special significance for psi facilitation. Such theorization indicates
that it is not exclusively the uniformity of the Ganzfeld sound--a
factor emphasized in noise-reduction theory--which is of chief importance, but the character of that uniform stimulation. Such
theorization proposes that it is randomness or noise which is
ordered by the psi process to produce ESP "information." Perhaps
listening to the essentially random array of auditory energy found
in the sounds traditionally used for auditory Ganzfeld stimulation
serves to disrupt or destructure patterned, goal-directed, or constrained mental activity. Perhaps it disrupts rational thought and
highly sequential thinking, creating in the cerebral neurons a mode
of functioning more favorable to psi influence, a mode more like
the random mode proposed as of importance in such theories. If
so, the traditional choice of sound for the auditory Ganzfeld might
have been fortuitous. A way to explore this question is to use uniform sound during the Ganzfeld which lacks the random character
of pink or white noise, perhaps a steady musical tone. Noise-
reduction theory, unlike the Walker and Stanford theorization, would,
as it presently stands, suggest no differential influence upon ESP
performance of traditional and musical-tone auditory-Ganzfeld stimuli.

Given these considerations based upon Walker's and Stanford's
theories, we can arrive at deductions about what would happen if a
momentary, unexpected, uninterpretable, auditory interruption were
introduced during auditory Ganzfeld. Any favorable effect upon ESP
performance of introducing this interruption should be greater with

the tone-based Ganzfeld than with the traditional noise-based Ganzfeld, since any favorable effect of the interruption should derive
from its tendency to disrupt ongoing patterned, constrained, cognitive processes and the noise-based Ganzfeld should allow less of
those in the first place.

The basic design of this study was a two-by-two factorial
with independent groups. Eighty unpaid volunteers (42 males, 38
females, mainly of college age or older) were randomly and equally
assigned to the four groups. Independent variables were type of
auditory Ganzfeld (either pink noise or an electronic organ note, E
above middle C, played on the combined flute and trombone voices)
and whether or not the auditory Ganzfeld was interrupted for approximately 2. 5 seconds in mid-session (at minute 7. 5 of a 15-minute
session) by an unexpected, probably uninterpretable, noise (i. e. , a
loud, 60 Hz hum with high-frequency microphonic feedback superimposed on it). Simultaneously with the auditory Ganzfeld all participants experienced visual Ganzfeld produced by half of a ping-pong
ball taped over each eye during relaxation in a recliner chair placed
in the far-back position. At a distance of nine to ten inches,
centered over the face, a 40-watt incandescent appliance lamp inside
a white, rounded reflector illuminated the visual field. Testing of
subjects in the four conditions alternated throughout the study.

It was emphasized to subjects that although this was an ESP
study they should not make a self-conscious effort to perceive the
randomly chosen photograph (on a 35-mm. color slide) which had
been chosen as target. They should simply relax, enjoy the Ganzfeld, and report everything experienced without trying to analyze or
evaluate it, for their intention to do well would automatically mean
that their mentation would tend to incorporate the target. Participants were encouraged concerning the efficacy of the Ganzfeld procedure as an aid to ESP performance. The experimenter who
briefed subjects was blind as to which of the four experimental conditions each would subsequently experience. Subjects were alone
during the Ganzfeld session, and neither the target slide nor the
target designation was present in the room. Utterances made during the 15-minute Ganzfeld session were tape-recorded and were
transcribed by a person who did not know the target for that participant.

The target pool, a total of 36 pictures, consisted of nine
sets of four 35-mm. color slides reproduced from National Geograph-
ic. The four slides within each set had been selected as maximally
different from each other in form and meaning. Two sets of the
36-slide pool were made; one was used in the experiment; the other,
in the judging procedure described below. An assistant who had no
contact with subjects during their testing used the Rand table of
random digits to select, first, the target set for each subject and,
then, the picture within that set. The set and picture designations
for each subject were sealed in an aluminum-foil packet, and that
was not opened until the Ganzfeld session was completed.

After the Ganzfeld had ended, the subject immediately filled out a questionnaire concerning experiences during the session and then rejoined the experimenter. The target-designation packet was opened, and the target slide was projected to provide feedback.

Two typed transcripts were developed for each subject. One, the partial transcript, consisted of the utterances made from minutes 7.5 through 10.5 of the Ganzfeld; for interrupted subjects, this represented the three minutes of utterances immediately following the interruption; for uninterrupted subjects it represented a control period. The other transcript consisted of the entire transcript for the 15-minute Ganzfeld session.

The three judges were all involved with the visual arts as an avocation. Artists were chosen because we felt they might be better able to recognize correspondences of form between subjects' utterances and the pictures. Each judge blindly rated the two transcripts for each subject against each of the four pictures in that subject's set (target and three controls). Rating was done by putting a single slash on a 10-cm. line at the opposite ends of which were the descriptors, "No convincing correspondence" and "Totally convincing correspondence." Pictures were always rated in the A, B, C, D order, and, since the target had been randomly determined, order of rating could not have been a contaminating factor. Judges always read and rated first the partial transcript. This was the important post-interruption or, alternatively, control transcript. It was read and rated first to insure that its rating was not influenced by the material in the other 12 minutes of transcript. Ratings were assessed by measuring to the nearest tenth of a centimeter the distance from the left end of the line to the slash.

Separate ESP scores were developed for each subject for the partial and total transcripts. To derive a subject's ESP score for a given transcript we first computed three separate Z scores, one for each judge's ratings. Such Z scores were computed by subtracting the mean of a judge's ratings for the control pictures from that judge's rating for the target picture and dividing that difference by the standard deviation of that judge's ratings on the control pictures. Finally, we computed the mean across judges of these Z scores. This mean constituted the ESP score for that transcript for that subject; it provided the basis for all the ESP-related statistical analyses.

The analysis of variance for partial transcripts showed no significant main effect, but the interaction of Ganzfeld type with the interruption variable was significant, $F (1, 76) = 3.94$, $p = .05$. The pattern of the interaction means accords with expectations based upon the theories of Walker and Stanford. These partial-transcript ESP means were 3.11 for the uninterrupted pink noise, -1.10 for the interrupted pink noise, 0.23 for the uninterrupted organ note, and 1.78 for the interrupted organ note. The mean for the uninterrupted pink-noise Ganzfeld is significantly above mean chance expectation, t (19) = 2. 15, p < . 04, two-tailed.   The difference of means for the uninterrupted and interrupted pink noise is significant, t (38) = 2. 05, p < . 05, two-tailed.   The difference of means for the un-interrupted pink noise and the uninterrupted organ note is appreciable, but not significant, t (38) = 1. 40, p = . 17, two-tailed.   The difference of means for the interrupted pink noise and the interrupted organ note is of the same magnitude of interest, t (38) = 1. 40.   Other differences of means are negligible.

The analysis of variance for total-transcript ESP also showed the interaction, reflecting strongly the effect of partial-transcript material.   Further discussion of those results will be provided in a fuller publication of this study.

Questionnaire results indicated no effects of experimental conditions which would confound the experiment.   They also provided some evidence, which there is no space to discuss here, that cognitive factors associated with experimental conditions made the study suitable as a test of implications of the theories of Walker and Stanford.   The outcomes of this study suggest, minimally, that the noise-reduction model should be refined to consider the specific cognitive consequences of stimulation; they also suggest that it might well be supplemented by considerations discussed in the theories of Walker and Stanford.

P K STUDIES*

CONFORMANCE BEHAVIOR INVOLVING LIVING SYSTEMS

William Braud (Mind Science Foundation)

Rex Stanford has proposed the concept of "conformance be-havior" as a useful explanatory framework for psychic phenomena. The concept involves an anomalous interaction between physically isolated systems, and encompasses the phenomena of psychokinesis, receptive psi, and perhaps other processes as well (e. g., memory, creativity).   I would like to state the theory in even more general terms than does Stanford, and suggest that under certain conditions, a system possessing a greater degree of disorder (randomness, lability, noise, entropy) changes its organization so as to more closely match that of another system possessing less disorder, less entropy, greater structure.   The greater the number of possible alternative states of the random event generator (REG), and the greater the organization of the structured system, the greater should be the probability of conformance behavior.   Similar theoretical notions are contained in the recent writings of Walker, Mattuck, and Targ and Puthoff.

The present paper marks the beginning of a formal explora-tion of conformance theory within the context of experimental psycho-kinesis.   In the 14 experiments to be described, animate systems serve as the more random systems and the firm intention of an ob-server serves as the more structured system.   Living systems were chosen as the more random systems because of their complexity and plasticity.   The particular living systems used in these investigations were selected not for any intrinsic interest but simply because they were convenient and could be easily quantified.   Several preparations were explored in order to find whether some particular living sys-tems might be more susceptible to conformance effects than others.

Four experiments were conducted with each biological system. One of these experiments consisted of 10 sessions with the investi-gator (W. B.) as observer.   Another experiment involved 10 sessions with Matthew Manning as observer.   For each of the two remaining experiments, 10 unselected volunteers each contributed one session.

Each session involved twenty 30-second epochs.   Ten epochs

---

*Chairperson: Joseph Rush, Boulder, Colo.

were "control" periods during which the observer simply rested and
relaxed without intending for the biological system to behave in a
particular manner.   Ten epochs were "conformance" periods during
which the observer maintained a specified intention for the biological
system to behave in a particular manner.   The epochs were sequenced
in a random order determined by the sequence of a pack of 20 cards,
which was shuffled 20 times at the beginning of each session.   This
epoch-randomizing procedure was used in order to guarantee that
equal numbers of conformance and control epochs were generated.
For each session, the biological activity in the prescribed direction
which was contributed by the 10 conformance epochs was expressed
as a percentage of the total activity in that direction.   For each
session, the percentage expected by chance is 0. 50.   A single mean
t test was used to compare the 10 obtained percentages for each
experiment with the expected population mean (μ) of 0. 50.   This
method of analysis was used so that the results of different experiments might be compared more readily.   Additionally, since all
four experiments of a set were conducted under identical conditions,
it was decided a priori to pool the probabilities of these four experiments, according to the chi-square method recommended by
Guilford.   For each experiment, it was predicted that the biological
activity in the prescribed (intended) direction would be greater during conformance epochs (when the intention was present) than during
control epochs (when the intention was absent).

For all experiments, precautions were taken to eliminate
conventional sensorimotor and conventional energetic and informa-
tional interactions between the biological system and the observer.
This was accomplished by placing the biological system and the
observer in separate rooms, isolated from each other by distance
and by the requirement that no sounds or other signals which might
influence the biological system could be made by the observer while
an experiment was in progress.   The experimenter remained with
the observer throughout the experimental session to assure that the
protocol was followed properly.   He also recorded the target sequence
so that this could not be changed by the observer to fit known experimental outcomes.

Five different kinds of biological systems were used in these
experiments; in all cases, the observer received immediate analog
feedback concerning the momentary state of the biological system.

Experiments 1 through 4.   Concurrent electrodermal activity.
In these experiments, the conformance of another person's spontaneous electrodermal activity to the intention of a motivated distant
observer was studied.   A volunteer sat in a comfortable chair in a
dim room while his skin conductance was recorded via hand electrodes.   This electrical activity was conveyed via shielded cable to
a polygraph in another room 20 meters away.   The observer watched
this polygraph and attempted to activate the record during each of
10 randomly determined 30-second epochs; during 10 control epochs,
the observer rested and did not think of the target system.   There
were 15-second rests between epochs.   Results were quantified by

determining the total amount of spontaneous electrodermal activity (degree of activation) during each epoch, and calculating the percentage contributed by the conformance epochs. Polygraph tracings were scored blind by a scorer who measured and summed amplitudes of all GSR responses during each epoch. For Experiment 1, the mean conformance epoch percentage was 0.59 (t = 3.07, p = .01, two-tailed). For Experiment 2, the mean percentage was 0.58 (t = 2.96, p = .008, one-tailed). For Experiment 3, the mean percentage was 0.59 (t = 2.04, p = .04, one-tailed). For Experiment 4, the mean percentage was 0.47 (t = -0.76, p = .77, one-tailed). The mean percentage for all 40 scores combined was 0.55 (χ^2 = 26.85, df = 2k = 8, p = .002, two-tailed).

Experiments 5 through 8. Spatial orientation of an electric fish. For these experiments, a knife fish (Gymnotus carapo) was placed in a small plastic tank housed inside of a large electrically shielded box in another room. The fish's position was monitored by the strength of the fish's endogenously generated signal (700 Hz, 20 mV) which arrived at two parallel copper plates within the tank. When the fish swam parallel to the plates, a weak signal was generated; a strong signal was associated with perpendicular swimming. This signal was amplified, rectified, and displayed to an observer in another room in the form of an oscilloscope tracing which provided immediate analog feedback concerning the orientation of the fish. The signal was also electronically integrated during each of twenty 30-second epochs. Ten of these epochs were control periods; 10 were conformance epochs during which the observer maintained an intention and visualization of the fish in a perpendicular orientation and of high amplitude tracings on the oscilloscope screen. Control and conformance epochs were randomly sequenced as in Experiments 1 through 4. Results were evaluated by determining the total integrated voltage for all 20 epochs and calculating the percentage of this total contributed by the conformance epochs. For Experiment 5 (with the investigator as observer), the mean conformance epoch percentage was 0.52 (t = 3.26, p = .01, two-tailed). For Experiment 6 (with Matthew Manning as observer), the mean percentage was 0.53 (t = 3.34, p = .004, one-tailed). For Experiment 7 (with 10 unselected volunteers as observers), the mean percentage was 0.54 (t = 2.12, p = .03, one-tailed). For Experiment 8 (with another 10 unselected volunteers as observers), the mean proportion was 0.51 (t = 0.50, p = .31, one-tailed). The mean percentage for all 40 sessions combined was 0.52 (χ^2 = 30.78, df = 2k = 8, p = .0003, two-tailed).

Experiments 9 through 12. Locomotor activity of small rodents. For these experiments, a gerbil (Meriones unguiculatus) which had been deprived of activity for at least 24 hours was allowed access to an activity wheel. Each revolution of the wheel activated a switch which marked a polygraph in a distant room (20 meters away); another pen marked the 30-second epochs and 15-second rest periods. There were 10 control epochs. During each of the 10 conformance periods, the observer sat before the polygraph and maintained an intention and visualization of the gerbil running quickly in the wheel, generating many revolutions and pen deflections.   Control and conformance epochs were randomly sequenced as in Experiments 1 through 8.   Results were analyzed by blind scoring the number of pen deflections during each epoch, totaling these for a session, then calculating the percentage of activity contributed by the conformance epochs.   For Experiment 9 (with the investigator as observer), the mean conformance percentage was 0.55 (t = 1.50, p = .17, two-tailed).   For Experiment 10 (with Matthew Manning as observer) the mean percentage was 0.53 (t = 2.12, p = .03, one-tailed).   For Experiment 11 (with 10 unselected volunteers as observers), the mean percentage was 0.55 (t = 2.33, p = .02, one-tailed).   For Experiment 12 (with 10 additional unselected volunteers as observers), the mean percentage was 0.52 (t = 2.89, p = .009, one-tailed).   The mean percentage for all 40 sessions combined was 0.54 (χ^2 = 28.9, df = 2k = 8, p = .0007, two-tailed).

Experiments 13 and 14.   Prerecorded electrodermal activity; rate of hemolysis.   Only one experiment in each of the next two series was completed before the Convention deadline; those experiments involved Matthew Manning as observer.   Experiment 13 was identical to Experiments 1 through 4 with the important exception that the spontaneous electrodermal target activity had been prerecorded.   Electrodermal activity changes resulted in frequency changes of a voltage-controlled oscillator; these frequency changes were recorded on audio tape and remained unobserved until one to seven days later, when they were decoded and played back to the observer in the form of polygraph tracings.   Thus, the experiment involved "time-displaced" PK and was similar in design to the recent experiments of Schmidt.   The results of this particular experiment, analyzed in the same way as in the foregoing experiments, indicated no evidence of time-displaced conformance behavior.   The mean conformance percentage was 0.47 (t = -0.48, p = .64, two-tailed).

In Experiment 14, the rate of hemolysis of osmotically stressed human erythrocytes was measured while an observer (Matthew Manning) either rested and did not think about the cells (during five control periods) or maintained an intention and visualization that the cells would be protected from hemolysis (during five conformance periods).   Degree of hemolysis was determined by calculating the change in light transmittance at 540 μ (one of the absorbance maxima for hemoglobin) that occurred during each five-minute epoch, using a spectrophotometer.   During each epoch the blood was stressed by a 0.34 per cent hypotonic saline solution at room temperature.   Results indicated that the mean percentage hemolysis score during the conformance periods (0.42) was significantly less than mean chance expectation (t = 8.70, p = 1.0 x 10^{-5}, two-tailed).   Thus, rate of hemolysis was retarded in conformance with the intentions of a motivated observer.

In the exploratory series reported here, four different animate systems were found to be susceptible to a conformance effect.   The "levels of responsivity" of the systems included:

gross behavioral activity of whole organisms (Experiments 5 through 12), peripheral autonomic activity of another person (Experiments 1 through 4), and in vitro cellular activity (specifically, membrane permeability in Experiment 14).   These different systems seemed to be equally susceptible to conformance behavior.   Additionally, the effects appeared to be equally strong for the different observers; it did not appear to matter whether the firm, well-structured intention/visualization was held by the investigator, a selected subject (Matthew Manning), or unselected volunteers.   We plan to explore these and similar living systems in greater detail, not only because they provide useful systems for the study of "psychic healing" analogs in the laboratory, but also because of the light they may shed on conformance theory.

USE OF STROBOSCOPIC LIGHT AS REWARDING FEEDBACK IN A PK TEST WITH PRERECORDED AND MOMENTARILY-GENERATED RANDOM EVENTS

Helmut Schmidt (Mind Science Foundation)

In the experiments to be reported, the subjects tried mentally to affect the duration of time intervals determined by random processes.   In a test run, two types of random time intervals were alternated.   During the "ON intervals," the subject saw a strobe light flashing at a frequency which he had selected as particularly pleasant.   In the "OFF intervals," on the other hand, the subject looked at a practically constant light source.   The subject's PK task was to extend the duration of the ON intervals with the pleasant strobe light, and to shorten the neutral OFF intervals.

Each random time interval was composed of two sections. The duration of these two sections was determined by similar random processes, occurring before or during the test run for the first and second section respectively.

The length of each section was measured by the number n $(n = 1, 2, 3, \ldots)$ of time units, of 5/16 seconds' duration each, in the section.   The random number n for every section was obtained by the repeated activation of an "eight-sided electronic die."   The number n was the number of times this electronic die had to be activated until an "8" appeared.

Thus, the chance probability for a section to last n time units was given by: $P(n) = pq^{n-1}$ (for $n = 1, 2, 3, \ldots$) with $p = 1-q = 1/8$.

The basic source of randomness for the electronic die are radioactive decay processes which stop a high-speed electronic counter at a random time.

Directly before each test run (consisting of eight ON intervals

and eight OFF intervals), 16 such random numbers n were generated
to predetermine the durations of the first sections of the time intervals. This generation took only a few seconds because the "eight-
sided electronic die" was operated at a rate of about 40 trials per
second.

The second sections in the time intervals were determined
during the test run. There, the "electronic die" was activated once
after every time unit and the section was terminated when an "8"
appeared.

In this manner, the prerecorded and momentarily-generated
random events contributed symmetrically to the total time interval
which the subject wanted to lengthen or to shorten, and the subject
could not distinguish, by sensory means, between the two contributions.

The strobe light was provided by two low-intensity incandescent lamps driven by a square wave generator. These lamps
were mounted on a frame for sunglasses so that they did not in-
convenience the subject. The lamps were backed by aluminum foil
and shielded in front by tissue paper so that the subject's field of
vision was illuminated fairly uniformly. The light intensity was
adjusted to the subject's convenience.

The strobe frequency for the ON intervals was selected before the test run to be one that appeared most pleasant to the subject. With a few exceptions, the most pleasant frequency was in
the range between six Hz and 12 Hz. For the OFF intervals, the
strobe was operated at 35 Hz, where the light appeared nearly
constant and psychologically neutral. At this frequency, the light
was only slightly modulated because of the finite response time of
the incandescent lamps.

For this experiment, volunteers were selected for whom
looking at some self-selected strobe frequency was a pleasant experience. The subjects were asked to work most actively on the
ON intervals, trying to extend the duration of these intervals. During OFF intervals, the subjects were to use a more casual, relaxed
approach, trying to shorten these periods.

The subjects first made one or two unrecorded trial runs
and, if they still felt good about the test, they were allowed to contribute recorded test runs. When a subject returned for another
session, he would always begin with one or two unrecorded warm-
up runs after which it was decided whether recorded test runs
should be made on that day.

The main objective of the experiment was to compare the
action of PK on prerecorded and momentarily-generated random
events, rather than a study of personal differences in scoring patterns or a study of the psychological factors related to strobe feedback. Therefore, the quantities of primary interest are the total

(added over all sessions) length of the ON intervals and OFF intervals for the prerecorded and the momentarily-generated sections. These numbers should show whether or not there is an overall pattern favoring the action of PK on either the prerecorded or the momentarily-generated events.

The total experiment consisted of 200 test runs, contributed by 12 subjects. Each of these runs comprised eight ON intervals and eight OFF intervals. The subject's task was to extend the duration of the ON intervals with their pleasant strobe light and to shorten the OFF intervals with the neutral light.

The subjects succeeded in their task with regard to the ON intervals. These intervals were observed to be seven per cent longer than their chance expectancy. This is statistically significant (CR = 4.26) at the .0001 level. The OFF intervals on the other hand, were only 0.5 per cent shorter than their chance expectancy value, which is not statistically significant.

The main objective of this study was a comparison of PK action on prerecorded and momentarily-generated random events. For this comparison, we have to consider the two mentioned sections of each interval separately. Remember that the length of the first section was determined by a random number (1, 2, ...) generated before the test run whereas the corresponding number for the second section was produced while the run was in progress.

Considering the ON intervals, we find that both these sections contribute approximately equally to the total score: The length of the first sections was increased by 6.8 per cent (CR = 2.9) and the length of the second sections was increased by 7.3 per cent (CR = 3.1). For the OFF intervals, neither the first nor the second sections showed significant PK effects.

Thus, the experiment produced significant PK effects acting on momentarily generated random events as well as on prerecorded random events. The results are consistent with the hypothesis that PK acted to the same degree in both cases. This confirms, in particular, the previously reported existence of PK effects on prerecorded targets.

PK WITH IMMEDIATE, DELAYED, AND MULTIPLE FEEDBACK: A TEST OF THE SCHMIDT MODEL'S PREDICTIONS

Melissa D. Morrison[†] and James W. Davis (Institute for Parapsychology, FRNM)

Schmidt's mathematical model of psi predicts that PK scores should be enchanced if each single outcome of a random number generator (RNG) is played back to and observed by a subject several

times. The model also predicts that the time of target generation
should not affect PK scoring; it follows that PK should still be
evidenced if the outcomes of prerecorded RNG events are presented
to the subject.

In an effort to replicate and extend Schmidt's experiments
which support this model, the authors had carried out a pilot and
confirmation study [RIP, 1977]. There was suggestive evidence
that PK occurred on delayed single feedback trials but there was
no sign of enhanced effects in the multiple feedback condition. In
the present experiment, several procedural changes were introduced
to create a testing situation more like that presented by Schmidt.
Given these modifications, the study was intended as a new effort
to test Schmidt's model and only secondarily to confirm the findings
of our own previous work.

As in our earlier study, visual feedback of success at a PK
task was provided by having each subject watch a screen on which
a vertical red line moved toward the right with hits, and toward the
left with misses. An audio tone which rose in pitch with misses
and fell with hits was supplied to the subject through headphones.
Hits and misses were associated with the decisions of an RNG
(p = 1/2) interfaced with the two forms of feedback via the PDP
11/20 computer. The random events constituting the PK trials
were from three categories. In one case, the random decisions
were generated contemporaneously with the feedback presentation;
these constituted the Direct PK trials. In a second category,
labelled the Delay One trials, the behavior of the random generator
was recorded immediately prior to the session and played back to
the subject during the test. The remaining Delay Four trials were
multiple feedback trials in which random generator events recorded
prior to testing were each played back four times to the subject.

The same feedback display was utilized to present a test of
motor skill ability. During this task, which had been included in
our earlier experiments, the subject used a knob to control the
movement of an unstable vertical line and the changing pitch of a
tone. As a subject worked to keep the wavering line in the middle
of the screen, the difficulty of the task gradually increased. This
was accomplished by increasing the intrinsic instability of the line,
eventually reaching a point where control would be lost and the line
would slip completely to an edge of the screen. The trial then
ended and was scored according to the total time elapsed.

Each of 30 volunteer high-school subjects began by carrying
out three trials of the motor skills task. A detailed explanation of
the PK test was reserved until the completion of the motor skills
portion of the session. Instructions to the subject focused on the
desirability of intense, concentrated effort. Each individual was
urged to become as absorbed in the task as he or she could, thinking of nothing else but the goal of keeping the tone low and making
the line move to the right. As aids to concentration, it was suggested that the subject could place a hand on the screen, use vari-

ous types of imagery, chant "right, right, right, " lean to the right,
etc. Most importantly the subject should never "give in" and let
the line slither to the left. This instructional set constituted a procedural change (in line with Schmidt's suggestions) from the more
vague directions offered in our earlier studies.

To begin, each subject pressed a button below the screen.
After a 30-second run, summary feedback was provided. From
the subject's point of view, each run consisted of 300 events, and
his or her goal was to make the line go to the right more than 150
times. Three more identical runs were carried out, followed by a
short break. The experiment was then completed by carrying out
four more runs in an identical manner to the first half of the session. The use of eight short runs with eight scoring subtotals is
another procedural modification based on Schmidt's work. At the
session's end, subjects were provided with a score representing
overall left-right deviations.

The observed deviations of the line reflected the outcomes of
PK trials from the three categories described above, namely,
Direct, Delay One and Delay Four. Targets were generated and
category scores were reported in two sets of four runs apiece,
corresponding to the two halves of the session. Each half was comprised of 400 Direct, 400 Delay One, and 100 Delay Four trials.
Every Delay Four trial was presented once in each of four runs,
alternating throughout with trials from the other two categories.
Hence, the entire session consisted of 1800 PK trials and 2400
feedback presentations.

The experiment was designed as a test of two major and two
secondary hypotheses.

The first main hypothesis stated that there would be overall
evidence of psi in the experiment. This was evaluated by calculating a critical ratio for each of the three categories of PK scoring,
squaring each figure obtained, combining these and evaluating the
total as a chi-square (3 df). In the second main hypothesis, it was
stated that multiple feedback concerning the outcomes of PK trials
would yield scoring enhancement over a single feedback condition.
This was tested by calculating a dependent t (two-tailed) between the
(transformed) scores obtained in the Delay One and Delay Four categories of PK trials. Neither of the two main hypotheses was confirmed, with scores in all three categories nonsignificantly above
chance (Direct = 50. 07 per cent; Delay One = 50. 35; Delay Four =
50. 68 per cent).

The first of two secondary hypotheses (which were based on
suggestions from our earlier work) stated that the subjects' scores
in the two single feedback conditions would show covariance, as
measured by a (two-tailed) Pearson's product moment correlation
between subjects' scores in the Direct and Delay One categories of
PK trials. This yielded an r of +. 35, a suggestive confirmation
(p < . 06, two-tailed) of earlier findings. (An unplanned Spearman's
rho was equal to +. 41, p < . 05, two-tailed.)

The secondary subsidiary hypothesis stated that the subjects' performance on the motor skills task would be systematically related to PK scoring in the two single feedback conditions. This hypothesis was tested by carrying out Pearson's r's between (a) mean motor skills scores and Direct PK scores, and (b) mean motor skills scores and Delay One PK scores. The significance of the relationships was evaluated by combining the exact (two-tailed) probabilities associated with each r through Fisher's Exact Method, and arriving at a single summary probability estimate. The resulting figure was nonsignificant.

Post-hoc analyses were carried out in terms of the main hypotheses concerning overall psi. Single mean t's and CR's based on overall PK scores were nonsignificant. To test the possibility that variation in scoring was greater than that expected by chance, individual CR's (based on each subject's total score) were calculated, squared, and combined to yield a single chi-square. This was marginally significant (χ^2 = 44.84, 30 df; p < .05).

An ad-hoc examination of differences in scoring based on subject familiarity with the laboratory offered the most promising suggestion for future experimental work. Students who had been to the FRNM at least once before scored more positively than first-time visitors. When the planned analysis for overall psi was carried out on second-time visitors only, the combined chi-square was marginally significant (χ^2 = 8.49, 3 df; p < .05), with positive trends in all three categories. The scores for first-time visitors were nonsignificantly negative. A comparison of overall PK scores between the two classes of subjects was marginally significant (t = 2.05, 28 df; p < .05, two-tailed).

Data from the main series of our previously reported study were then similarly analyzed. In brief, the overall PK scores of first-time visitors showed psi-missing (t = 2.91, 12 df; p < .02, two-tailed) while second-time visitors scored at a chance level. The difference was not significant.

Ad-hoc analyses aside, the present study's lack of evidence for overall psi or a multiple feedback enhancement effect implies that we have failed to replicate Schmidt's work. Procedural changes from our previous work were unsuccessful. The Direct-Delay One correlations observed in this and our two earlier experiments are troublesome to interpret in light of Schmidt's model. They suggest the operation of PK on prerecorded targets, but it is difficult to explain the inability to predict the direction of covariance. It is not consistent with the feedback model to admit that identically displayed outcomes from two different periods of RNG activity may well covary inversely rather than positively. Explanations for the correlation which lie outside the Schmidt model need to be considered.

A MEASURE FOR CALL-STRATEGIES

Wilfried Kugel (Technical University, Berlin)

As known from quantitative and qualitative ESP experiments, results seem to depend on individual habits of the subjects. It is possible to investigate these habits by psychological tests but there is the other possiblity of observing the behavior of the subject during the experiment for behavior patterns. In quantitative experiments this is easy to do by investigating the structure of the call series, which has been done by several researchers.

Our research group at the Technical University has systematically investigated call strategies since 1973, especially an effect called feedback susceptibility (FS), the tendency of a percipient to repeat a call if he or she had scored a hit. In 1976 we found a correlation between strong FS and near-chance results. More detailed analyses showed a general correlation between call strategies and ESP hits. We developed a measure especially designed for the FS strategy, but found the concept insufficient for generalization. This paper presents a new concept, which responds to this need. The main problem was to find a formalism for application to different types of call strategies and to obtain independence for any number of trials.

It is easy to detect the existence of a call strategy by comparing the data obtained with theoretical expectancy, but it is not so easy to detect the individual power of a call strategy by using a common statistical method.

It is first necessary to define the call strategy which is of interest. There are many possible call strategies, but only a few are of practical interest. Let us, for instance, investigate the hypothesis that the subject prefers some symbols and avoids others. This hypothesis leads to a statistical one, namely that the frequencies of the symbols in the call series are not the same. In that way every hypothesis about a call strategy might be transformed into a hypothesis about a set of relative frequencies (of n-tuples). Those relative frequencies must expand a complete set of events, that means, their sum equals 1. We will understand this set as an

---

*Chairperson: T. N. E. Greville, Madison, Wis.

estimate for a set of probabilities

$$q = \left\{ q_1, q_2, \ldots q_n \right\} \cdot \sum_{i=1}^{n} q_i = 1.$$

There is another set of probabilities, the reference set, which can be compared with the set q

$$p = \left\{ p_1, p_2, \ldots p_n \right\} \sum_{i=1}^{n} p_i = 1.$$

One might imagine this set as the random probability of occurrence for the symbols. In our example $p_i = 1/5$, using a five-symbol ESP machine. Now we will compare two sets of probabilities. We define a functional $U(p_i, q_i, i = 1 \ldots n)$, which equals 0 if all $p_i = q_i$ and which increases with the difference of the two probability sets. Feinstein gives a formula for such a case:

$$H = -\sum_i q_i \log_2 q_i \leq -\sum_i q_i \log_2 p_i = N.$$

$H = N$ only holds true, when $p_i = q_i$ for all i. Thus we can define a functional $U = N - H$, which is always positive and increases with the difference between the two sets of probabilities. The formula for U follows:

$$U = \sum_i \left[q_i \log_2 (q_i/p_i) \right]$$

A very important quality of the functional U is the additivity: on condition that $p_i(x)p_i(y) = p_i(x, y)$ and $q_i(x)q_i(y) = q_i(x, y)$, $U(x, y) = U(x) + U(y)$, where x is one sample and y another. This gives us an easy way to calculate the U value for a group of independent samples: we simply sum up the individual U's.

The Probability Sets for Three Important Call Strategies

(1) The frequency of symbols in the call series. The following analysis will show the preference of favoring/avoiding symbols or push-buttons. The reference set of probabilities p is given by $p_i = $ const. $= 1/5$, using a machine with five alternatives or five card symbols. The estimates for the probabilities q_i are calculated by $q_i = N_i/N$ where N is the total number of trials and N_i the frequency of symbol i in the call series.

(2) The frequency of pairs of equal symbols and of pairs of unequal symbols in the call series. The next analysis will show whether or not the subject tends to perform more single calls or to call sequences of the same symbol. For a calculation of the reference set of the p probabilities, we have to distinguish two cases: ii pairs (case a) and ij pairs (case b). For estimating p, we use the relative frequencies N_i/N from (1). Under this condition it has been assumed that the second member of a pair is independent of the first. The expected probability for an ii pair is

$$p_{ai} = \frac{N_i N_i}{N \; N}$$

The expected probability for an ij pair is

$$p_{bi} = \frac{N_i(N-N_i)}{N \;\; N}$$

The whole set of p probabilities is therefore

$$p = \left\{ p_{a1}, p_{a2}, \ldots p_{an}, p_{b1}, p_{b2}, \ldots p_{bn} \right\}$$

The corresponding set q describes, in relation to p, the degree of dependence of the second number of the pair in comparison with the first. The measured probability for a pair ii, where G_i^N is the frequency of ii pairs in the call series, is

$$q_{ai} = \frac{N_i G_i^N}{(N-1)N_i} = \frac{G_i^N}{(N-1)}$$

The measured probability for an ij pair is

$$q_{bi} = \frac{N_i(N_i - G_i^N)}{(N-1)N_i} = \frac{(N_i - G_i^N)}{(N-1)}$$

The whole set of q probabilities is therefore

$$q = \left\{ q_{a1}, q_{a2}, \ldots q_{an}, q_{b1}, q_{b2}, \ldots q_{bn} \right\}$$

(3) The frequency of pairs of equal symbols and of pairs of unequal symbols in the call-series when the first member was a hit and feedback was given. Usually the ii pairs of symbols (total) will appear less equal than expected (the U for (2) increases). Looking only at the ii pairs with a hit as first member, a much too large number of ii pairs is noticed. The majority of cases will reveal that persons tend to perform the same call again after a hit, and this was named feedback susceptibility. For the expectance of an ii pair, we may assume that the dependence of the second member on the first is described by the term G_i^N/N_j. Thus the expected probability for an ii pair, where the first member is a hit and where K is the total number of hits and K_i the number of hits of symbol i, is

$$p_{ai} = \frac{K_i G_i^N}{K \; N_i}$$

The expected probability for an ij pair, where the first member is a hit, is

$$p_{bi} = \frac{K_i(N_i - G_i^N)}{K \;\; N_i}$$

The whole set of p probabilities is therefore

$$p = \left\{ p_{a1}, p_{a2}, \ldots p_{an}, p_{b1}, p_{b2}, \ldots p_{bn} \right\}$$

The corresponding set q describes the increased/decreased degree of dependence on the second member by the first member of the pair (under the influence of feedback). The measured probability for a pair ii, where the first member is a hit and where G_i^K is the number of ii pairs with a hit as its first member, is

$$q_{ai} = \frac{K_i G_i^K}{K \, K_i} = \frac{G_i^K}{K}$$

The measured probability for an ij pair, where the first member is a hit, is

$$q_{bi} = \frac{K_i (K_i - G_i^K)}{K \quad K_i} = \frac{(K_i - G_i^K)}{K}$$

The whole set of q probabilities is therefore

$$q = \left\{ q_{a1}, q_{a2}, \ldots q_{an}, q_{b1}, q_{b2}, \ldots q_{bn} \right\}$$

A corresponding U value can be calculated for each of the cases described, whatever further aspects there are that can be defined; by using the formalism described before, it is easy to measure the extent of these aspects. Our investigations showed a strong influence of the strategy on the quantitative ESP results. Therefore it would be important to look at this quantity for a better understanding of the disturbances in statistical ESP experiments. One should always imagine that a subject with completely predetermined behavior, which equals extreme strategy dependence, will hardly have occasion to react to an ESP signal or any signal at all.

As a result of a series of statistical ESP experiments, for every percipient there is one value for the deviation of the hit score from chance $\Delta = [N \cdot p - K]$ and there are three values U_a, U_b, U_c for the three kinds of strategy investigated (all subjects perform the same number of trials).

We do not know anything about the distribution of the U values. As a first attempt we will separate the results into two equal groups: one with smaller Δ-values (the "near-chance results"), the other with higher Δ-values (the "far-chance results"). Now, using the sum of the (independent) U values, we calculate a total U_a, U_b, U_c for each group. We expect the "near-chance group" to show a higher U than the "far-chance group." We now need a significance test for rating the difference.

For samples of any population Pitman has given a test which we will apply one-tailed for two equal groups.

We have n numbers U_i. Numbers equal in value are supposed to be distinguishable one from another. We separate the number into two equal classes of $n/2$. There are $S = C_{n/2}^{n} = \binom{n}{n/2}$ possible separations into two equal groups. For each group a total U will be calculated

$$\sum U_i(\text{group 1}) = U^1 \qquad \sum U_i(\text{group 2}) = U^2$$

The difference between those two values is defined $D = U^1 - U^2$.
There is a particular separation R with the corresponding difference
$D(R) > 0$. Further there is a positive number $M \leq S$. The number
of separations with $D \geq D(R)$ is L. So if $L \leq M$, R will be called
discordant. The probability of a separation's being discordant is
$p = M/S$; p is usually taken as 0.05. Discordant samples are
assumed to derive from different populations. The separation R is
arrived at by chance, using a parameter Δ for separation, which
according to the null hypothesis is independent from U. If we can
separate the numbers discordantly, the null hypothesis, i.e. the
independence of the values Δ and U, can be rejected. The null
hypothesis will be accepted if $L > M$ or $D(R) \leq 0$.

In practice, the number L has to be calculated by computer.
The number of possible separations is increasing rapidly with n.
With today's computer facilities it will be easy to solve the problem
in the area of $S = \binom{20}{10}$. Even when using very fast computers, it
will not be possible to make calculations with n much higher than
30. From $n = 20$ onwards, one should apply approximations. The
significance to be reached depends on S. Therefore the population
as a minimum has to consist of six members to reach the 5 per
cent level, of 10 to reach the 1 per cent level and of 14 to reach
the 0.1 per cent level.

A NEW MEASURE OF BIAS IN FINITE SEQUENCES
WITH APPLICATIONS TO E S P DATA

Lila L. Gatlin (Stanford University)

A new measure of bias in finite sequences is derived from
information theory which characterizes the pattern in any finite
string as the distribution of the components of Shannon's redundancy
vector. This vector is described by the relation

$$R \log a = D_1 + D_2 + D_3 \ldots D_{(m+1)} \tag{1}$$

where R is Shannon's redundancy, $\underline{a}$ is the number of letters in the
alphabet, D_n is the vector component representing divergence from
the most random state at a particular n-tuple level, and $\underline{m}$ is the
memory of the Markov source. Every finite sequence has a characteristic pattern of distribution of its D measures whether or not the
sequence is random under statistical tests. These measures are
not always correlated with classical statistical measures, such as
generalized serial tests using a chi-square metric, and in certain
ranges of lengths can be shown to be theoretically independent of statistical measures. The important concept is that the D measures are
not just highly sensitive statistics. They detect a fundamentally
different kind of ordering in nature.

Although the distributions of the D measures are not precisely normal, they have the same decision properties as normal distributions for two-tailed phenomena and may be standardized by Monte Carlo methods.   A wide variety of algorithmic random number generators all give essentially the same expected values and variances of the D measures as a function of length and alphabet size.

In Tart's book <u>Learning to Use Extrasensory Perception</u> (Chicago, 1976), the Z values of the D_3 measure of the target sequence, or $Z(D_3)^T$ values, are all negative except one, three of them significantly so.   On the basis of chance we would expect less than one of them to be significant and half of them to be negative.   In the guess sequences of the subjects, all the $Z(D_3)^G$ values are significantly negative with magnitudes ranging from -2.36 to -9.05.   This is so highly non-random that statistical tests are superfluous.   The probability of obtaining a result like this by chance is vanishingly small.

Thus it appears that all the subjects without exception have recognized the characteristic negative $Z(D_3)^T$ pattern and exaggerated it in their own guess sequences.   This pattern recognition feat would appear to be "paranormal" if viewed only from the reference frame of classical statistics because the guess sequence of each subject is only 500 symbols long whereas there are 1000 possible triplet sequences from an alphabet of size 10.   The sample is half the size of the sample description space.   Indeed simple statistical calculations at the triplet level are invalid under such circumstances.

However, just as the classical space-time reference frame is often useless in attempting to explain parapsychological phenomena, the reference frame of classical statistics is equally inadequate here.   The broader reference frame of information theory is far more useful.   A significantly negative $Z(D_3)$ value means that the triplet sequences (which are counted in an overlapping manner) are more nearly equiprobable than we would expect on the basis of chance for sequences of this length.   A simple example makes this clear.   Suppose you were trying to guess quartet patterns from a binary source.   There are 2^4 or 16 possible quartets.   Suppose you received the sequence: 00110011... etc.   What would you guess next?   If the source is, in fact, biased at the quartet level to emit preferentially 0011, you could have guessed this quartet bias correctly from the above sequence of length eight which is only half the size of the sample description space.   A more complex but loosely analogous situation exists at the triplet level in the Tart experiment.   If all the target sequences are combined giving a sample of size 5000 which is statistically adequate, $\Delta^2 \psi_3^2$ is highly significant ($p < 10^{-8}$).   This confirms by classical statistics that the target source is highly biased.   Our D measures have detailed this bias at the local level where statistical tests are not even applicable and have shown precisely that the biases in the target and guess sources <u>match</u>.   It is easy to show that matching biases in target and guess sources raise the probability of a hit above the null level.   Hence standard statistical evaluation of such data is not valid.

This does not mean that the data are no longer interesting and valuable. The question remains as to how the subjects have accomplished this remarkable pattern-matching feat. To begin to answer this question we must move into the even broader reference framework of game theory and estimation theory. In any estimation process, there must be some minimal information on which to base a guess and the estimate must be made in time to be effective in scoring. Hence the concept of an optimal estimation length is intuitively obvious and can in fact be demonstrated in the data. If the singlet, doublet and triplet frequencies in the first part of each sequence at various estimation lengths are correlated with those in the whole and these parameters correlated with Z scores, it is found that certain lengths and certain n-tuple levels are optimal for estimation. Within these optimal estimation "windows" in the data the Z scores observed in the experiment are significantly correlated with the degree to which the first part of the sequence is an accurate estimator of the whole.

An estimate of how accurately the subjects are estimating can be obtained by calculating how high a simple Markovian computer strategy would score if it had made 100 per cent accurate estimates of triplet frequencies and simply guessed the symbol most likely to come next, given the preceding two. When the experimental Z score is divided by the theoretical 100 per cent accurate estimator score, it is found that the three significantly scoring subjects with statistically random target sequences would only have to be estimating triplet frequencies with 22 to 24 per cent accuracy to produce the experimentally observed scores. It is not at all inconceivable that such estimates could be made from the sensory feedback; but the feat remains, nevertheless, remarkable since it demonstrates unexpected heuristic skills of the subconscious.

A displacement pattern showing significantly negative Z scores in the ($\pm$ 1) registers which Tart interprets as "transtemporal inhibition" or suppression of information from immediate past and future, can be explained in terms of the triplet bias. Most triplets have all three letters different from each other and most of all possible guess triplets which can be matched against these miss in the ($\pm$ 1) displacement. Hence the observed displacement pattern is one of the most common to be expected in data with a high triplet bias.

In the Martin-Stribic data the pattern in the target source is $Z(D_2) > Z(D_3) > Z(D_1)$ and the subject has matched his guess sequence to this pattern. $Z(D_2)$ is significantly positive in both target and guess and the target $Z(D_2)$ is significantly correlated with scoring rate. In the Tart data, $Z(D_1)^T$ and $Z(D_2)^T$ are both significantly positively correlated with scoring rate and $Z(D_3)^T$ is significantly negatively correlated with Z score.

These findings do not disprove the ESP hypothesis but they offer an alternative explanation of significant scoring in terms of pattern recognition and its exploitation through estimation techniques, game theoretic strategy building and decision by the human mind. It appears that extremely minimal information, not detectable locally by statistical tests, can be utilized by the human mind.   This is a remarkable ability, worthy of scientific study with the potential for opening up new areas of mathematics, particularly those concerned with heuristic processes.

COULD MATHEMATICAL INFERENCE STRATEGIES HAVE INFLATED SCORING IN THE FIRST FEEDBACK TRAINING STUDY?

Charles T. Tart (University of California, Davis)

With increasingly frequent use of immediate feedback of target identity following a call in parapsychology, the question of whether percipients might detect small biases in the target sources and then develop a mathematical inference strategy (MIS) to exploit this bias instead of using ESP becomes important.   Ideally every target digit should be equiprobable and sequentially independent from all previous targets, but in finite sequences there will always be deviations from this.   If targets were the digits zero to nine, as in my original Training Study (C. Tart, Learning to Use Extrasensory Perception, University of Chicago Press, 1976), and, say, eights occurred much more than 10 per cent of the time, a percipient who discovered this could inflate his score by always calling eights.   If eights followed threes at the doublet level too frequently this could also be used to inflate scoring slightly, etc.   Gatlin claims that an MIS strategy was used by the percipients in my original Training Study, so no ESP need be postulated to explain its exceptionally significant result $(p < 10^{-24}$, two-tailed).

Although the overall target distributions of singlets and doublets are random by chi-square tests and Gatlin's D measures, two of the 10 singlet distributions are significant (which is within the range of chance variation) and three of the doublet distributions are significant by chi-square.   Gatlin's triplet measures are probably invalid for the small numbers of individual target sequences.   Although the deviations from randomness are rather small, let us consider whether a MIS could account for all of the results.

Examination of the properties of overall bias measures like chi-square and Gatlin's D measures shows that they are not very useful for indicating how predictable a biased source is.   Since predictability is essential for an effective MIS, rather than lack of randomicity per se, a more direct approach is needed to answer the question.   Several such approaches were examined.

First, if percipients were using a mathematical estimator strategy, we would expect to see the high points of their response distributions match the high points (the most useful predictor points) of their individual target distributions.   At the singlet level, only one of the 10 percipients showed such a match, and no percipient showed a match on high doublets, results strongly at variance with expectations from a MIS hypothesis.

Second, perhaps percipients were only partially successful at utilizing a MIS but still had strong response biases of their own, thus producing the above results.   We would still expect to see most of the significant hitting on the most biased aspects of the target distributions.   But if trials on the most biased aspects of the target distributions are deleted from the results, at both the singlet and doublet levels, an enormously significant amount of hitting is still present, contrary to the expectations of a MIS hypothesis.   Thus actual examination of the data shows that their pattern is quite contrary to Gatlin's MIS hypotheses.

As a more direct approach to the question of how well a MIS could do, Eugene Dronek and I are preparing for publication the results of a powerful, computer-based MIS that we believe is much more powerful than we would expect most human strategies to be. Not only can it do no better than getting less than a third as many hits as the actual percipients got, the internal pattern of the data it generates with respect to temporal displacements is grossly different from the patterns generated by the percipients.   An example of this difference was presented in my Presidential Address last year [RIP 1977].

Examination of actual data, then, not only indicates that the sizes and patterns of biases in the data were too small to be of much use even theoretically for a MIS strategy, it further demonstrates that the percipients did not respond in a way that would be expected by a powerful MIS strategy.   Proponents of MISs as alternatives to ESP should empirically demonstrate that their MISs actually predict questioned target distributions about as well as percipients do, as well as show similar internal patterns, if MISs are to be a serious alternative hypothesis to ESP.

IS ESP ONLY A MISNOMER FOR RESPONSE SEQUENCES CHOSEN TO MATCH INFERRED TARGET SEQUENCES? A REPLY TO LILA L. GATLIN

J. G. Pratt (University of Virginia)

Without going into the intricacies of information theory, I will begin by describing the general features of Gatlin's analysis for patterns in target and guess sequences in plain and simple terms.   The method provides a measure of the degree of patterning--the amount of departure from the expected random sequences when no bias is present.   The target order and the call order are analyzed separately.   Thus far, Gatlin has made this analysis for the distribution of singles, pairs, and triples in the two sequences. Note particularly that the method has dealt only with the degree of patterning.   No efforts have been made thus far to consider whether patterns detected in the target and guess sequences are similar in specific ways regarding the kinds of bias shown.

The fact that the analyses reveal that significant degrees of patterning exist in the sequences is surely not surprising. Indeed, ESP investigators have long known that subjects do not produce random sequences when making their guesses, and it is obvious that the most thorough hand shuffling of the closed ESP pack, for example, can never produce the random order of targets expected from making "open" selections from a given alphabet (in this instance, the five ESP symbols). Even if we grant that both the targets and the guesses show a degree of patterning that deviates in the same direction in the two sequences, we may not assume from this fact that matching the two series will produce high ESP scores regardless of whether the biases are similar in detailed respects. Gatlin omits the essential step of comparing in detail the way in which the targets and guesses are biased. She has reported the results from applying her method to only two sets of data.

In the case of the Tart data the subjects were shown the target after each trial--that is, they were given immediate feedback. This fact obviously makes it important to consider whether the knowledge of preceding targets provided a basis for predicting which one would be presented next. Charles Tart has presented arguments against this possibility as adequately accounting for his subjects' success without invoking the ESP hypothesis.

For the second application of her method to ESP data, Gatlin chose two series done by C. J., the principal high scoring subject in the experiments of Martin and Stribic. In that ESP test the subject called down through or up through the entire pack of 25 cards before he saw the order of the symbols during the checking procedure. After the scoring was done, the experimenter shuffled and cut the pack in preparation for the next run. In this situation patterning of the calls on the basis of the previous order of cards so as to produce a high score on the new order in the next run is not possible. The subject's scoring showed that he knew enough about the particular order of the cards as it existed after the cut to score, on the average, more than the expected number of hits. Even if we wish to think of his performance in terms of responding to patterns in the target sequence, he had to know where the cut was made, and this knowledge could have been acquired only through ESP.

It is easy to demonstrate that the presence of patterning in the targets and calls cannot account for the high scoring. We can give the target order a further cut to provide a control. This does not appreciably change the figures from the Gatlin analysis for the amount of patterning in the targets from those she found for the original cut. When we check the order of calls against the new order of cards, if patterning alone is the key to the subject's success we should again obtain a high score. But this is not the predictable outcome, because all of the possible 24 cuts of the real target pack other than the initial one that was used as the real target pack can be shown, mathematically, to score hits averaging close to chance expectation. Indeed, when the score on the real targets is above

five, the 24 non-target cuts will average very slightly below that
level.   This is true for the reason that the average score from the
25 possible cuts with a closed pack will be exactly five.

There have been many other ESP experiments in which the
subjects scored significantly without receiving any feedback information, either immediate or delayed, on the target sequences.   In
those instances the suggestion that subjects could have applied
sensory-based knowledge of the targets and used normal powers of
the mind to pattern their calls so as to achieve good scores is
obviously ruled out.   Gatlin has generalized too quickly and too
widely from a very narrow data base in her efforts to explain all
experimental parapsychological findings in normal terms.

The three papers of this symposium have been only sum-
marized here.   They are published in full in the January 1979 issue
of the Journal of the American Society for Psychical Research.

PSYCHOPHYSIOLOGY AND PSI*

CONTINGENT NEGATIVE VARIATION AS
AN INDEX OF PRECOGNITIVE INFORMATION

J. W. Hartwell (University of Utrecht)

The contingent negative variation (CNV) is a slow, surface-negative electrical brain wave studied in experiments which emphasize the association (contingency) of two successive stimuli. It was first described by Walter et al. who used the term "expectancy" to describe the primary psychological variable underlying its development. In the present study it is used as a physiological index of information about a future event.

The experiment is organized as a precognition or psychokinesis study. It differs from most other parapsychological tests in several ways. First, no consciously mediated response or guess is required. The analysis is entirely concerned with examining a subject's preparation for the imperative stimulus as reflected in his brain waves. Second, the subject is given a reaction-time task and a psychological set that strongly condition him to focus upon sensory input. This may be considered a disadvantage, as there is a widely-held belief backed by experimental data that paranormal phenomena are more likely to be manifest in situations which minimize the importance of sensory input by focusing a subject's attention internally. Finally, it may be noted that the present study is a highly automated one. All data collection and delivery of stimuli are under the programmed control of a medium-sized laboratory computer. As they are gathered, the data are stored on magnetic discs for subsequent multivariate statistical analysis on the same machine.

The study was designed to contrast two situations which are quite dissimilar in terms of the response expected from a subject. In one instance the subject glimpses a picture of a person of the opposite sex and responds as quickly as possible by pressing a button. In the other instance the picture is of a person of the same sex, and no motor response is made. These two types of pictures (projected transparencies) serve as the imperative stimuli for a CNV study.

---

*Chairperson: Edward F. Kelly, Duke University.

The warning stimuli are also projected transparencies, each of which provides one of three distinct levels of information about the imperative stimulus which follows it.   These slides show a stylized face smiling, frowning, or with no mouth at all.   They are equalized for overall brightness and are projected briefly (about 150 milliseconds).   A smiling face implies that an imperative stimulus depicting a person of the opposite sex will follow, so that the subject should be prepared to make a rapid motor response upon its presentation.   A frowning face means that the imperative stimulus will depict someone of the same sex so that no motor response will be required.   A face without a mouth may be followed by either sex.

One third of the warning slides are of high contrast so that the subject is fully informed about the imperative stimulus which follows.   One third of the warning slides are of very low contrast so that the subject is less well informed about the imperative stimulus.   The brightness of the projected image is adjusted to yield a scoring rate of 75 per cent in a preliminary forced-choice guessing test using only the low-contrast smiles and frowns.   Thus these stimuli are said to be of a low information level.   The final third of the warning slides are also of very low contrast but show no mouths so that they provide no information about the imperative stimulus to follow.   Trials using these warnings constitute the parapsychological portion of the experiment.

Ten subjects (six males, four females) were chosen from those volunteering.   All were previously acquainted with the nature and purpose of the experiment.   The subjects were welcomed as collaborators in the research.   Their questions were answered as fully as possible, and their comments or suggestions were taken seriously.

Experimental sessions were held in the evening when the building was quiet.   Normally three persons were present in addition to the subject.   The author was present on all occasions.   He was usually assisted by two advanced female students who welcomed the subject in English or in Dutch, applied the electrodes, read the standardized instructions and generally tried to provide a hospitable setting.   The entire experimental procedure consumed about two and one half hours per subject.

All analyses were carried out on a seven-variable representation of the CNV waveforms.   The seven variables chosen were the DC component and both phases of the first three Fourier frequency terms.   These variables were chosen following the pilot study in which they appeared to give stronger results than a comparable number of variables formed by averaging over adjacent time points.   Although these variables permit the general shape of the CNV wave forms to be resolved from the background EEG efficiently, they would not allow a detailed analysis of the faster components such as the evoked potential which follows the warning stimulus.   In fact no separate analysis of this portion of the curves was carried out for lack of a well-framed hypothesis.

An extensive analysis procedure, established before any data were collected, was applied separately to each of the 10 subjects and each of the three electrode sites. This procedure aimed at classifying the CNVs from a subject's ESP trials using a reliable discriminant function derived from trials on which the warning stimulus provided some information.   This was not always possible to do, as it sometimes happened that no suitable discriminant function could be fashioned.   For this study a discriminant function was deemed reliable if it was derived from data showing a multivariate difference significant at the .05 level.   Nineteen of the 30 electrodes yielded data with suitable differences.   Every subject contributed at least one such electrode to the analysis, and some contributed all three.   The central electrode position provided the greatest number of reliable discriminant functions, eight, while the parietal site provided six and the frontal, five.

It was thought on a priori grounds that the ESP trials should more resemble the low information ones than those for which full information was provided.   Consequently it was desired to base the discriminant function upon these trials whenever that proved possible. The full-information trials were used only when no significant differences were found in the low-information condition.   Eight of the 19 discriminant functions were based upon the low-information trials alone.   Ten of the discriminant functions were derived from the low- and full-information trials combined, and one was obtained from the full-information trials alone.

The discriminant functions were applied to the CNVs recorded at the corresponding electrodes during the ESP trials.   In this way a single number was assigned to each such trial indicating its position along the dimension which best separates the trials on which the discriminant function was based.   A t test on these numbers reflects the degree of separation found between the two kinds of ESP trials along this same dimension.   In this way the analysis seeks to determine if the ESP trials show differences of the same kind as those evident on trials where information was provided.

The experimental procedure was successful in producing well-developed CNVs.   In the case of the full-information trials the averaged wave forms generally showed clear differences of the expected type when visually displayed.   The low-information trials were less clearly distinguishable for most subjects, and visual differences were rarely apparent for the ESP trials.

Nineteen classification tests were carried out in all.   Only one of these was associated with an a priori probability of less than .05, not an unreasonable result on the chance hypothesis.   The mean classification statistic did not differ significantly from zero for any of the three electrode sites.

This study provides no evidence in favor of the psi-related hypothesis it was designed to test.   Thirteen of the 19 classifications are in the predicted direction, but any real effects fall well

below the sensitivity of the experiment.   The procedures were sufficiently sensitive, however, to reveal the presence of information
in the CNVs to the low-contrast stimuli.   A post-hoc analysis of
the sensitivity revealed that it would have been possible to detect
CNV differences as small as 26 per cent of the size of those observed in the fully-informed condition.

These results do not encourage the widespread adoption of
this experimental technique.   The difficulties and expense associated
with recording and analyzing the data do not recommend the approach
as a screening procedure.   Investigations of this type would appear
to be more appropriate as tools for elucidating the processes of psi
in highly selected subjects.

ESP AND OUT-OF-BODY EXPERIENCES: EEG CORRELATES

John Palmer (John F. Kennedy University)

This is the fourth and last of a series of experiments designed to explore the relationship between free-response ESP and
low level out-of-body experiences (OBEs) experimentally induced in
unselected volunteer subjects.   The results of previous experiments
in the series suggested that there was a positive correlation between
subjective reports of OBEs during the session and ESP scores,
provided that straightforward sensory deprivation procedures were
used to induce the OBEs.   The primary purpose of this experiment
was to confirm this relationship.   Secondary purposes were to explore EEG correlates of ESP scores and the subjective experiential
reports, and to compare systematically the results of sensory
deprivation with a visual Ganzfeld and with the subject merely closing
his eyes.

Twenty subjects, mostly undergraduate students at the University of Virginia, were randomly assigned to the "Ganzfeld" (G)
and "eyes closed" (EC) conditions.   Thus a total of 40 subjects
were tested, 25 females and 15 males.

Each subject met with J. P. in his office prior to the experiment for a briefing, which consisted of a short informal conversa-
tion, a description of the procedure, and the signing of a consent
form required by the University.

Following the briefing, J. P. led the subject to the laboratory,
which consisted of two adjacent rooms.   They first entered the
room where the target picture was located, and the subject was
asked to examine the room and "get a good mental image of it."
EEG electrodes were then affixed bilaterally over the parietal region of the subject's scalp and referenced to the corresponding ear
or mastoid (P1 to A1; P2 to A2).   The remaining electrode was
placed over the external canthus of the right eye to record eye

movements. Electrodes were reapplied if resistance exceeded 20K ohms. The electrodes were inserted into a telemetry device, about the size of a cigarette pack, which was usually clipped to the subject's belt. During the experiment, brain waves were converted by the telemeter to an FM signal which was picked up by an FM receiver in the target room and recorded simultaneously by a cassette tape recorder and a polygraph.

My assistant, Ronald Lieberman (R. L.), then led the subject into the percipient's room and seated him in a comfortable reclining chair. Earphones were placed over the subject's ears and, in the G condition only, halves of ping-pong balls were taped over his eyes such that he could see only a white uniform visual field when a white light was shone into his face. Finally, a button was placed in the subject's left hand. The subject was to press the button immediately after each OBE. The button activated a buzzer in the target room which was recorded on the voice channel of the cassette tape.

When everything was ready, J. P., who was still in the target room, instructed the subject over the intercom to close his eyes for three minutes of baseline EEG recording. J. P. monitored this recording.

J. P. then returned to his office to ascertain the code number of the target picture. As in previous experiments, the target pool consisted of 10 sets (packets) of five pictures taken from photography magazines. The target set and pictures were selected individually for each subject from a random number table. After determining the number, J. P. returned to the target room where the targets were located, removed the selected picture from its packet, and placed it face up on a large, round wooden table near the center of the room. He then seated himself in front of the physiological recording apparatus to begin the induction period.

The induction procedure had been recorded on tape and was played to the subject over headphones. This tape recording was activated by R. L., who remained in the subject's room throughout the induction period and was blind to the identity of the target. The room was darkened except for the second half of the induction period in the G condition.

The first half of the induction procedure consisted of progressive relaxation exercises identical to those used in previous experiments of the series. The subject then listened to instructions which told him what to do during the second half of the induction procedure, which lasted nine and a half minutes. The subject was told either to stare straight ahead with eyes open (G condition) or to close his eyes (EC condition), while a tone consisting of a binaural beat superimposed over pink noise would be played through the headphones. It was suggested that sometime during the session he would experience a floating sensation. At this time he should imagine himself traveling to the target room to identify the target

picture and to press the button upon his return.   As soon as the
second stage was over or the subject was ready to stop, he was to
review in his mind any imagery he received during the session.

While R. L. was removing the headphones, electrodes, etc.,
at the end of the session, J. P. replaced the picture in proper sequential position in its packet, placed the packet on the table along
with the blank rating scales, and left the room before R. L. and the
subject entered.   The ratings were supervised by R. L.   The subject first filled out a questionnaire, similar to that used in previous
experiments, asking him to rate his reactions, experiences and
expectancies at various stages of the experiment.   Included was a
question, to be answered "yes" or "no," as to whether he had the
experience of being outside his body at any time during the session.

Next, R. L. removed the five pictures from the packet and
placed them in a row in front of the subject.   After reading a set
of judging instructions alerting him to likely kinds of correspondences,
the subject was asked to rate each picture independently on a 0 to
30 scale according to its degree of conformance to his imagery
during the induction period.

R. L. then called J. P. back to the lab.   J. P. revealed the
identity of the target and answered the subject's questions.

Subjects in the G and EC conditions did not differ significantly
in how they described their experiences during the session.   However, subjects in the G condition had significantly higher initial expectations of having an OBE ($\bar{x}$ = 2.35 vs. 1.56, t = 2.61, 38 df,
p < .02) and ESP success ($\bar{x}$ = 2.03 vs. 1.48, t = 2.27, p < .05)
than did subjects in the EC condition.   (The scales in question had
a range of zero to four.)   Thirteen of the 20 subjects in each group
answered the dichotomous OBE question affirmatively.

The ESP ratings of each subject were converted to a Z score
by subtracting the mean of all five ratings from the rating given the
target picture and dividing by the standard deviation of all five
ratings.   The relationship between these Z scores and responses to
the OBE question was in the predicted direction but not significant
($\bar{x}$ = +.256 vs. -.077, t = 1.25).   In other words, the mean of
those who answered the item affirmatively was somewhat more
positive than the mean of those who answered it negatively.   The
effect was somewhat (although not significantly) stronger in the G
condition (+.301 vs. -.184) than in the EC condition (+.211 vs.
+.031).   In fact, the mean difference in the G condition (.48) was
almost identical in magnitude to the significant difference (.50)
obtained in the only other experiment in the series where a Ganzfeld procedure was utilized.   Nonetheless, these results provide
only modest support at best for the original hypothesis.   The mean
ESP scores in the two conditions were virtually identical (G = +.132;
E = +.148).

The EEG data on the cassette tapes were digitalized, stored

on disk, and submitted to spectral analysis by Edward Kelly.   Segments of record were eliminated if associated with inordinate eye movement or corresponded to button presses.   The power estimates were reduced in several stages to obtain for each subject non-independent estimates of the proportion of EEG power in the traditional bands of delta (0-3 Hz), theta (4-7 Hz), alpha (8-13 Hz) and beta (14-35 Hz) for each hemisphere of the brain for the baseline period, first half of the test (induction) period, and second half of the test period.   These scores were then averaged in various ways to produce a total of 96 scores per subject.   The data of three subjects had to be eliminated because of digitalization errors.

Ten of the 96 correlations between EEG scores and ESP scores were significant.   The pattern of these correlations indicated ESP scores correlated positively with overall proportion of EEG alpha and negatively with EEG beta.   A composite index consisting of alpha minus beta correlated significantly with ESP scores for the baseline period (Spearman $r = +.34$, $p < .05$).   The correlation for the test period was significant only for the right hemisphere $(r = +.33, p < .05)$, although the correlation for the left hemisphere was quite comparable in magnitude.   While this pattern makes sense in terms of previous research, its post-hoc nature requires caution in interpretation.

None of the 96 EEG scores correlated significantly with responses to the OBE question.   However, three subjects who had more than 30 per cent theta in their baseline EEGs all reported rather strong OBEs as inferred from their open-ended descriptions.

PSI AND COGNITIVE FACTORS*

RESPONSE PATTERNS AND PSI SCORING

P. Sailaja and P. V. Krishna Rao (Andhra University)

H. Kanthamani and Hanumanth Rao carried out three series of experiments on response tendencies and stimulus structure. They found that subjects classified as spontaneous or inhibited on the basis of the number of conspicuous stimuli chosen as their ESP responses showed differences in their ESP scores. The "spontaneous" subjects scored higher than the "inhibited" group to a significant degree. This was consistent in all three series.

The study reported here was an attempt to replicate the Kanthamani-Rao results under dissimilar conditions, so that if the same effect occurred, we could make some progress in interpreting the results. The subjects were students in a Telugu middle school in India and came from families low on the socioeconomic scale, with very little exposure to English. Consequently, the contrast between meaningful and nonsense words was considerably blurred for these subjects, whereas such a contrast was considered to be a salient feature in the Kanthamani-Rao study carried out with American subjects.

The study consisted of two series of experiments. The test format was similar to the one employed by Kanthamani and Rao, but the target words were different. Each response sheet had 21 three-letter meaningful words (MW) and 42 nonmeaningful words (NW). The meaningful words were chosen from a large pool selected from a major dictionary. The nonmeaningful words were chosen from Glaze's list with 40 per cent association value.

The stimuli were arranged in 21 rows. Each row had three words, two NW and one MW. The cell where the MW would be positioned was determined randomly. The target sheets were prepared by P.S., who folded and enclosed each sheet in a piece of heavy paper. This paper was kept in an 8"x12" envelope, which was sealed and numbered. The response sheet was attached to the target envelope and was given the same number as the envelope. The test was one of group clairvoyance.

---

*Chairperson: Irvin Child, Yale University.

P. S. administered the ESP test after giving the group a brief talk on ESP. The subjects were asked to circle one of the three words in each block, using ESP to discover the target word. They were further told that the envelope contained the answers. The instructions were given in Telugu. After the experiment was over, the subjects were asked to (1) rate the score they expected to get by checking one of the three boxes: high, average or poor; (2) their opinion regarding the test they had taken: interesting, in between or uninteresting. The data sheets were independently checked by P. S. and P. V. K.

Fifty female students in the eighth grade in a Telugu middle school (aged 12 to 14) were the subjects in the first experiment. The school caters primarily to girls from middle to low socioeconomic-status families. The subjects had little if any knowledge of English and it is safe to suppose that they could not know any difference between meaningful words and nonsense syllables. The subjects were not told about the nonmeaningful words.

We predicted that the following null hypotheses would be rejected by the results. (1) The number of meaningful words checked by the subjects as ESP responses would have no relationship to their ESP scores. (2) There would be no relationship between the marks the subjects obtained in their English examination and the ESP scores. (3) There would be no significant difference between the ESP scores of subjects who expected to score high and the scores of those who expected to do poorly. (4) There would be no significant difference between the ESP scores of subjects who found the test interesting and those who found it uninteresting.

Two kinds of analyses were made to test the first hypothesis. First, a correlation was worked out between the number of checks on meaningful words the subject made and her ESP score. The second was to compare by means of a t test the ESP scores of the subjects in the first quartile with those in the fourth quartile, arranged in terms of the number of checks made on meaningful words. This analysis was decided because Kanthamani and Rao reported that the subjects who checked five or fewer meaningful words tended to psi-miss while those who checked nine or more tended to psi-hit. Those who checked between six and eight scored at chance.

A product-moment correlation between the number of meaningful words the subjects checked as their ESP responses and their ESP scores gives an r of .40 (t = 3.06; 48 df), significant beyond the 1 per cent level.

There were 12 subjects in the first quartile who checked four to seven meaningful words. They obtained 71 hits in 252 trials, an average of 5.92, where mean chance expectation is 7.00. The 12 subjects in the fourth quartile who checked between 10 and 15 meaningful words obtained 99 hits for the same number of trials, with an average of 8.25 hits. A test of difference between the means gives a t of 2.58, 22 df; p < .05.

The second hypothesis was tested by correlating the most recent English examination marks they took before the ESP test and their ESP scores. The obtained r is -. 06, which is insignificant.

The results were also analyzed to test the relation between subjects' expectations of their ESP scores and their opinion of how interesting the test was. Out of 50 subjects, the 14 who said they would score high obtained 101 hits in 294 trials, a deviation of +3, an average of 7.21 hits. Four subjects who said they would score low obtained 26 hits in 84 trials, a deviation of -2, an average of 6.50 hits. The difference between the two groups is insignificant. As for the second question, only two subjects checked "in between." The rest of the 48 subjects stated that they found the test interesting. Therefore, no useful groupings could be made on the basis of the answers to this question.

The second series consisted of 49 girls from the seventh grade at the same school. These subjects also had very little knowledge of English and were not told that some words were meaningful and other meaningless. The procedure of testing and scoring was the same as in the first series. P. S. administered the test and with the help of B. H. L. scored the record sheets. The results were again analyzed to test the same hypotheses as in the first series.

The 12 subjects of the first quartile checked between five and seven meaningful words and obtained 92 hits in 252 trials. The 12 subjects of the last quartile checked between 11 and 16 meaningful words for 252 trials and obtained 91 hits. Thus, there is hardly any difference in the rate of scoring between the two groups. Pearson's product-moment correlation between the subjects' ESP scores and the number of meaningful words checked gave an r of . 08. Thus, the results of the second series do not support our hypothesis that the number of meaningful words checked is positively related to the subjects' ESP scores. The results bearing on the other hypotheses were also at chance.

The successful replication of Kanthamani and Hanumanth Rao's finding in the first series and the failure to replicate the same in the second may be due to the possibility that the second-series subjects' knowledge of English was somewhat less than that of the first-series subjects. Of course, the knowledge of English of subjects in either group is insufficient for them to recognize any of these words as being nonsensical. The subjects in the first series were more likely to know the meanings of at least some of the words than those of the second series because they were older and had been studying English for a year longer. Therefore, it would seem that some knowledge of English on the part of the subjects may be necessary for this effect to occur. This suggestion is somewhat strengthened by the fact that the subjects' marks in English correlated significantly in both series with the number of meaningful words they checked. In the first series the r is . 29 (p < . 05) and in the second series it is . 48 (p < . 005). The fact

that subjects who had insufficient familiarity with English gave
evidence in at least one series of the effect Kanthamani and Hanumanth Rao found among English-speaking subjects, suggests that
the reason for this effect may not be simply a matter of noticing
meaningful words and nonsense syllables as distinct categories.

The fact that the questionnaire did not separate the hitters
and missers may be attributed to the stereotyped responses the
subjects gave.   Most of them found the test interesting and a great
majority could not decide whether they would obtain good or poor
scores.   In any future attempt to study these questions, perhaps a
five- or seven-point scale may be better than the three-point scale
used here.

FURTHER STUDIES OF MEMORY AND E S P

K. Ramakrishna Rao (Institute for Parapsychology, FRNM)

The apparent similarities between the way memory and ESP
seem to function have led several investigators to explore possible
relations between the two.   While no definite relationships have been
established as yet, several approaches to the study of this problem
have emerged.

Rao and associates reported at the 1977 PA convention three
experiments in which the subjects attempted to recall the meaningful words associated with stimulus trigrams (nonsense syllables).
In half of the trials, the subject had an opportunity to memorize the
associations.   In the other half he had to obtain the associated word
through ESP.

The present study, a continuation of the above, had two ob-
jectives.   The first was to confirm the three suggestions that came
out of previous research: (a) that subjects' memory scores and ESP
scores may be related; (b) that hitters and missers may differ in
their response tendencies in those trials where they fail to hit the
ESP targets; and (c) that if such tendencies exist they may be similar for both memory and ESP misses.   The second objective to
explore was the question whether the meaningfulness of the target
words to the subject would have any effect on his hitting or missing
in an ESP test.   The present paper presents the results bearing on
the first objective alone.

The subjects in this study were volunteers who attended
K. R. R. 's lecture at a science symposium conducted by the Prairie
School in Racine, Wisconsin.   Among the subjects were high-school
and college students, teachers, and local citizens interested in
parapsychology.

The paired-associates learning sheet consisted of 25 trigrams (nonsense syllables) from the same pool as in the previous studies. Each was paired with one of five meaningful words: dark, death, life, light, and self. Four of these were selected for their similar and contrasting aspects. The subjects were also provided with a recall-ESP response sheet which consisted of two columns of trigrams, the 25 previously-seen ones randomly mixed with 25 new ones. To the right of each trigram, a short blank line indicated the space where the subject was to write in his response, i.e., one of the five meaningful words. Thus, the response sheet provided for memory recall, i.e., recall of the appropriate meaningful word associated with the stimulus trigram he had learned before, and for ESP calls, i.e., the subject's responses to the 25 new trigrams which he had not seen before.

The subjects also received an opaque manila envelope (target envelope) which contained all the correct responses to the memory part of the test plus the ESP targets.

The test material also included an association ranking sheet designed to measure the degree to which subjects associated each of the five meaningful words with the other four.

In his opening speech at the symposium, K.R.R. explained the basic concepts and surveyed the evidence for the existence of various types of psi. The audience then broke into three groups. One participated in the ESP experiment conducted by K.R.R.; one went to a biofeedback workshop; and the other viewed a film on parapsychology. The groups were rotated. Thus, the ESP-memory tests were administered to subjects in three batches. Sixty-six subjects were in the first batch, 20 in the second, and nine in the third. At the end of testing the final batch, all the participants gathered again for a final talk by K.R.R.

In all the three sessions the experimenter first briefly explained the nature of the test. Then testing began with the presentation of the paired-associates learning sheet. The subjects were given five minutes to memorize the word pairs. They were then given the recall-ESP sheet and were asked to complete each word pair. After all the subjects had recorded their responses to the stimulus trigrams, they were given the association ranking sheet. After the subjects completed all the sheets, the experimenter briefly explained the scope of the experiment, what he had hoped to find, and answered any questions they had. He also told each group that he would send their memory and ESP scores to the school as soon as the records were scored. These were mailed to the school approximately two months after the test.

The record sheets of the 64 subjects (excluding the two that could not be scored) in the first batch (Group 1) were scored by the computer. The computer input of one of these was messed up and therefore it was hand scored. The record sheets of all the 29 subjects in the second and the third batches (Group 2) were hand scored by K.R.R. and a colleague, H. Kanthamani (H.K.), before being scored by the computer.

The results were evaluated according to two procedures. In the primary analysis, the results of all 93 subjects were combined into one group. A secondary analysis was carried out to analyze the results separately for the 63 eligible subjects of Group 1 and the 29 subjects of Group 2.

The usable memory and ESP scores of 93 subjects were correlated by means of Pearson's product-moment correlation. The obtained r was .18, which has a t value of 1.70 (91 df) and a p < .1, two-tailed.

The association ranks given to a subject's response words relative to target words on all his ESP misses were summed and from this the subject's mean association rank ESP score was computed. Similarly his mean association rank score for memory misses was also obtained. The results were analyzed by two criteria for dividing hitters and missers. According to both of them the obtained t's are in the same direction as those in the previous studies but neither of them is significant.

The subjects' mean association rank scores on their ESP misses were correlated with their mean association rank scores on memory misses. The obtained Pearson's r is .21, which has an associated t of 1.98 (84 df) and a p < .06, two-tailed.

Secondary analyses were carried out to test the same hypotheses separately for the 63 subjects in Group 1 and the 29 subjects in Group 2.

Pearson's product-moment correlation between the memory and ESP scores of the hand-scored data of the 29 subjects gave an r of .53. It has an associated t value of 3.27 (27 df), p < .01, two-tailed. The r for the computer-scored Group 1 subjects was nonsignificant. Thus it would appear that the positive relationship between memory and ESP scores was confined to subjects in Group 2.

The difference between the mean association rank scores of criterion 1 ESP missers and hitters in Group 2 (hand scored) was not significant; but with the computer-scored data of subjects in Group 1, gave a t of -2.24 (50 df), p < .05, two-tailed.

Pearson's product moment correlation between the mean ESP rank association scores and the mean memory rank association scores for Group 2 subjects gives an r of .34. The associated t is 1.70 (22 df); p ≈ .1, two-tailed. The r for Group 1 (computer-scored) is .16; t = 1.26 (59 df).

The most intriguing aspect of the results are the apparent differences between the results of the subjects in the computer-scored Group 1 and the hand-scored Group 2. The mean association rank scores of hitters and missers in the first group are significantly different. But those of the second group are not.

Again, the correlation between the memory and ESP scores of the latter are highly significant while the correlation for the subjects in the first group is completely at chance. These differences could be due to the differences in group composition or subject-experimenter interaction. As it happened, the data of the 29 subjects in batches two and three were hand scored jointly by K. R. R. and H. K. This raises the question whether the differences could be attributed to the so-called checker effect. H. K. had earlier reported a significant positive correlation between the memory and ESP scores of her subjects. At this point, it is clearly impossible to argue convincingly in favor of either of these two interpretations, namely that the differences between these two groups are (1) due to their interactions with the experimenter, or (2) due to the checker effect. Only future research can throw further light on these fascinating possibilities.

EFFECTS OF IMMEDIATE FEEDBACK ON ESP PERFORMANCE: A SECOND STUDY AND NEW ANALYSES

Charles T. Tart, [†] John A. Palmer and Dana J. Redington (University of California, Davis, John F. Kennedy University, and University of California, Davis)

In 1966 one of us (C. T. T.) postulated that the provision of immediate feedback of results to motivated percipients in repeated guessing ESP studies would eliminate the common decline effect and allow some percipients to learn to improve their ESP performance. Percipients with more ESP talent to begin with should profit more from immediate feedback training. The present experiment was designed to replicate and extend the first study of the theory (C. Tart, Learning to Use Extrasensory Perception, University of Chicago Press, 1976) in which very high levels of ESP and no declines were found.

As in the first study, a two-stage serial selection procedure was used, the Selection and Confirmation studies, to locate highly talented percipients for the Training Study. The Selection Study consisted of two quick card-guessing tests in classrooms at the University of California at Davis. The Confirmation Study consisted of two runs of 25 trials each on the Aquarius four-choice trainer, two on a ten-choice trainer, and two more on whichever machine the percipient chose to continue on. The original ten-choice trainer was used through part of the Confirmation Study, but it was replaced midway through by a new ten-choice device, ADEPT (Advanced Decimal Extrasensory Perception Trainer).

The screening was significantly less successful in finding the highly talented percipients for the ten-choice ADEPT than it was in the original study, but we decided to work with them anyway to obtain more data on the lower range of talent. Seven percipients

completed the Training Study (20 runs of 25 trials each per percipient), but as a group their hit scores were close to chance expectation. One individually significant psi-hitter's scores were canceled
by those of an individually significant psi-misser. Five of the
seven percipients showed individually significant trans-temporal
inhibition (contrast between real time and +1 future hitting), suggesting that psi was present in this group but at too low a level to
be affected by brief feedback training.

The screening was more successful for the Aquarius machine, resulting in a talent level similar to that in the original
study, but only three percipients completed the Training Study on
Aquarius. They produced 434 hits when 375 were expected by
chance, $p = 4 \times 10^{-4}$, two-tailed. For both machines, no individual slopes were significantly different from zero, so while no declines occurred, no learning occurred either.

In terms of the learning theory, too few sufficiently talented
percipients were selected by the screening process in this study to
adequately test the theory, so we conclude that the status of the
theory is the same as it was at the end of the original study.

The learning theory application also predicts that learning is
more likely to occur over short, homogeneous time periods with
minimal interference with memory processes, so mean first-half
versus second-half run scores on the ten-choice machines for each
percipient were analyzed. In the original Training Study, percipients
scored significantly higher in the second half of the run; the effect
was concentrated on the last trial of the run. The increments were
positively and significantly correlated with initial talent measured in
the Confirmation Study, as would be predicted. These results were
not significant in the second Training Study, but the correlation of
gain with initial talent was significant for the two studies combined.

INTENTIONAL OBSERVER INFLUENCE UPON
MEASUREMENTS OF A QUANTUM MECHANICAL SYSTEM:
A COMPARISON OF TWO IMAGERY STRATEGIES

Robert Morris, [†] Michael Nanko and David Phillips (University of
California, Santa Barbara, and Science Spectrum)

Our present research is aimed at exploring the effectiveness
of visual-imagery strategies for PK subjects (observers) derived
from a survey of the popular literature on "psychic development"
[RIP 1976, pp. 54-6]. From these we derived two specific observer
imagery strategies, a goal-oriented one and a process-oriented one.

Our pilot study was designed to test the hypothesis that the
behavior of an observable visual display controlled by the processed
noise output of a Zener diode would be significantly biased in the

presence of observers using either of two imagery strategies. Six-teen college-age subjects (observers) were used, 10 males and six females, recruited by posted notices and from personal acquaintances of M. N.

The apparatus consists of a four-module multi-purpose testing system designed for a variety of studies [RIP 1976, pp. 38-40]. It maintains an internally-generated source of random binary decisions by amplifying Zener diode noise with a two-transistor amplifier, then converting the amplified noise to logic levels with an LM 339 comparator. The resulting logic signal is then divided by two to insure that equal time is spent in the high and low states. This random logic signal oscillates at frequencies up to about 200 kHz and it can be sampled and clocked into a shift register whenever a new random decision is desired. A counter-decoder sequencing circuit interfaces this information with a display to the subject and a counter which tallies the number of trials (decisions) and the number of hits (trials in which the decision matched a preselected outcome registered on a special console). In the present studies, the display to the subject consisted of a ring of 16 lights, each light being a red LED that was 0. 4 cm. in diameter. The entire ring was seven cm. in diameter. The binary random decisions were employed to advance the illuminated light one step clockwise or counterclockwise, thus producing a "random walk" back and forth on the circle. The hit counter had been preset to count only clockwise steps as hits.

The procedure for each session was as follows. Each sub-ject was met by M. N. and shown the console containing the Zener diode and processing circuitry. Subjects were told that this was an exploratory test of PK, and that we were testing the effective-ness of two specific imagery strategies for such a task. Each subject was then taken down a hall to a second room, two rooms away from the first (and about 18 feet from the Zener diode and main console), and was seated in an office chair in front of the subject console and the circle of lights. The subject was shown how to initiate a run by pressing a button on the subject console, so that the illuminated LED would shift around the circle 16 con-secutive times at the rate of one shift per 1. 75 seconds. The sub-ject was then told that the task was to bias the lights for each run of 16 trials in either the clockwise or counterclockwise direction, depending on the instructions given the subject in a concealed target envelope. There were eight such envelopes, each of which contained a specific order of directions (clockwise and counterclockwise) for each of 16 runs (the length of the experimental session). This order was counterbalanced for direction within the first eight runs (four clockwise and four counterclockwise) and the last eight runs such that each subject would be asked to influence the behavior of the lights in a clockwise direction for half the runs and counter-clockwise for half the runs. Each of the eight envelopes contained a different specific order of directions. A sample target sheet was used to illustrate these points to the subject.

The subject at this time was also given two specific imagery strategies, a process-oriented strategy ("PK 98") where the subject was asked to visualize "energy" building up inside his or her body, then flowing out to the circle of lights, and assisting their progression in the desired direction; and a goal-oriented strategy ("PK 99") where the subject was asked to point a finger at the light he or she wished to be illuminated next and vividly visualize the light's being lit. The subject was told that both imagery strategies had been suggested by a search of the literature and that we felt that each would be useful for the present task. The subject was asked to relax and take two or three minutes to build up imagery between runs. After eight runs the subject was allowed five minutes to relax and prepare mentally for the next imagery strategy.

The subject was then shown the target envelope, which R. M. had placed on the table earlier in the day, and was told that it contained the experimental target order plus instructions to use either PK 98 for the first eight runs and PK 99 for the second eight runs, or the reverse. Thus each subject used each imagery strategy for half the session, counterbalanced across subjects for order and with the clockwise versus counterclockwise target direction balanced across conditions.

The target order for each session was chosen using a numerical random process by an experimenter not otherwise connected with the study. The other seven target-order envelopes were kept in a drawer in yet another experimental room. Subjects were not told of their location and knew only that their target envelope had been selected randomly from a set and that M. N. did not know the target order.

When M. N. was satisfied that the subject understood the instructions, he told the subject to open the target envelope after M. N. left the room. He then returned to the main console room. M. N. would give the subject five minutes to prepare, then instruct the subject over a one-way intercom to begin run 1. When the trial counter on the main console registered 16 trials, M. N. recorded the number of trials and number of clockwise steps taken (registered on the hit counter). M. N. notified the subject at the end of each run of the run number just completed and the number of the next run. At the end of 16 runs, M. N. would enter the key number of the target sheet, record the target directions for all 16 runs, score the record for total number of decisions in the assigned direction (hits), and give the subject some general feedback. At the end of the session, M. N. would turn over a carbon copy of the unscored record to R. M. for independent tallying. R. M. would also verify that the number of the target sheet matched that assigned randomly to the session and that the target order had been properly recorded.

The random event generator produced decisions in accordance with the subject's instructions (hits) 51.86 per cent of the time ($Z = 2.38$, $p < .02$, two-tailed). Almost all of the positive scoring occurred with the goal-oriented imagery, which produced 52.9 per cent hits and was independently significant (Z = 2.61, p < .01, two-tailed). The difference in scoring between the two groups was not significant (t = 0.872, p = ns). Thus it appeared that an observer effect was present in the data, but was only detected statistically during application of the goal-oriented imagery strategy.

A second study was done both to confirm these results and to explore the functioning of these imagery strategies when concentration enhancement techniques were employed. The subjects were 20 Santa Barbara undergraduates, nine males and 11 females, recruited from parapsychology classes. Ten subjects had indicated on a questionnaire that they had previously been involved in one or more mental development courses such as TM, yoga, or est; ten others had indicated no such involvement. These groups are designated "Experienced" and "Naive" respectively. M. N. was not informed of any subject's background.

The procedure for the first session was the same as for the previous study. Following the first session, M. N. asked the subject to select a preferred imagery strategy and to use it exclusively during the second session two weeks later. The subject was then brought in to R. M. for instructions in two simple concentration exercises to be practiced daily until the second session. One exercise involved concentrating on the sweep second hand of a watch for 10 minutes; the other involved counting one's breaths for five minutes. Two weeks later the subject returned and repeated the experimental procedure, this time using the preferred imagery strategy for all 16 runs. At the end of the session, the subject was invited to describe the experiences in detail and was given specific feedback as to results.

The results of the first session were analyzed by a two-way between-within analysis of variance. Imagery strategy was a significant factor (F = 5.19 with 1 and 18 df, p < .05), with PK 99 scoring above mean chance expectation [MCE] (51.8 per cent) and PK 98 scoring below MCE (48.4 per cent). Experienced versus Naive subjects did not differ overall in their scoring (F = 0.67 with 1 and 18 df, p = ns). However there was a significant interaction between imagery-strategy success and prior experience with mental-development procedures (F = 7.81 with 1 and 18 df, p < .02). Close inspection of the results reveals that this interaction was produced primarily by the Naive subjects, whose hit rate for the process-oriented imagery was considerably below chance (45.7 per cent).

The results for the second session were consistent with those of the first session. Eleven subjects chose to employ process-oriented imagery throughout the session; their hit rate was 49.3 per cent. Eight chose goal-oriented imagery and their hit rate was 52.6 per cent. The difference between these two groups is statistically significant (t = 2.64, with 17 df, p < .02, two-tailed).

In summary, there was consistent evidence throughout both studies that more hits occurred during goal-oriented imagery than would be expected by chance alone (grand total for both studies: 52.4 per cent, $Z = 3.97$, $p < .0001$, two-tailed), whereas process-oriented imagery tended to accompany either chance results or, for some of the Naive subjects, strongly negative results.   At present we can only speculate why results were so poor for Naive subjects; one possibility worthy of follow-up exploration is that the process-oriented imagery was more complex than the goal-oriented imagery and may have impressed many people not already involved with the concepts of various mental-development courses as being rather strange or silly.   The advantage of the goal-oriented imagery appears within as well as between subjects and is maintained even after subjects have been given training in concentration procedures.

Of special interest to those wishing to explore further the effects of an observer upon a physical system is the apparent importance of the structure of the observer's experiences.   Most previous studies have ignored such variables, leaving the subjects to their own devices.   By examining the popular literature directly, we have been led toward at least one imagery strategy that appears conducive to positive results, and possibly to a second.   Further work with the process-oriented imagery should reveal whether it is of no use at all or of use only to those who feel comfortable with it.

MISCELLANEOUS PAPERS*

THE EXPERIMENT OF BRUGMANS, HEYMANS, AND WEINBERG, 1920-1922

E. F. Kelly[†] and S. A. Schouten (Duke University and University of Utrecht)

Previous reports in French and English of this experiment have been terse and fragmentary, based principally on the first seven sessions (187 trials), held between May 1920 and September 1920. Ultimately, however, the experiment consisted of 24 sessions and 589 trials. Having access to original Dutch papers and almost complete copies of the original data, we are preparing the first reasonably complete account of the experiment and its major results. Apart from the extremely high scoring rates, the experiment produced many other results of contemporary interest, including the first physiological data suggestive of a psi-conducive state.

Analyses of target and response data. Although considerable distortions appeared in the overall selection frequencies for targets and responses, the sequential constraints are minimal and unrelated. Hence valid statistical analysis of the data is possible.

Direct hit results. Using Stevens' method to correct for gross inequalities of target and response frequencies, $Z = 29$. For the 233 distant trials alone $Z = 18$. There is no overall difference in scoring between near and distant trials, nor among experimenters. The frequency of exact hits is much greater than expected through chance association of the hits on the attributes separately. Eliminating exact hits, scoring is strongly above chance on letters and slightly below chance on numbers. The scoring is widely distributed over the possible targets, with only a slight suggestion of inverse relationship to target/response frequencies.

Consistent missing analyses. Several analyses were carried out to determine whether erroneous responses were nevertheless systematically related to their targets. When the frequencies of targets and responses are taken into account, a previously reported tendency of responses to enter the physical neighborhood of their targets disappears. An incidental finding is that there is no evidence of $+1$ or -1 displacements.

*Chairperson: Martin Johnson, University of Utrecht.

Analyses of temporal scoring trends. Two principal trends were analyzed, decline effects and tendencies for hits to cluster independently of the scoring rate. There was pronounced decline over the course of the experiment, but no within-session decline. Hits tended strongly to occur in groups, although the groups became smaller and more widely scattered as the experiment went on.

Analyses of response-time data. On all but 17 trials, response time was also recorded. Table and variance analyses of this information reveal a significant tendency for correct responses to be faster, independently of other factors influencing response time such as near versus distant.

Analyses of ambiguous responses. On 131 trials ambiguous responses were recorded. We show that the manner in which these ambiguities are resolved does not affect any of the main statistical results. The sources of the ambiguity remain obscure, although several factors seem to point to van Dam as the most likely candidate. The ambiguous trials are systematically slower, less likely to be hits, and more likely to occur both in the distant condition and with Brugmans as agent. We propose that van Dam made deliberately ambiguous responses when he felt particularly uncertain.

Analyses of physiological results. Two kinds of physiological observations were included in the experiment. First, in some sessions van Dam was given either alcohol or bromide in advance. Second, in some sessions there was continuous recording of pulse, respiration and GSR. Although at present we do not have complete information on these aspects of the experiment, we will at least describe the results which the experimenters themselves reported. Their view was that van Dam's best performances occurred when he succeeded in placing himself in a special psychophysiological state which he called his "passive state," characterized at least in part by deep relaxation.

The statistical objection that the properties of the obtained target orders may be insufficient to support valid analysis of the data, has been eliminated. The methodological objection that the results may be due to auditory leakage from agent to subject is more serious and cannot be decisively overthrown. However, the bulk of the historical and experimental evidence appears to support the experimenters' belief that they had successfully eliminated this source of error. Of particular importance is the fact, ignored by previous critics, that the experimenters were entirely aware of the possibility of sensory hyperacuity and set out deliberately to eliminate it. Even assuming that target-related cues might have been available, moreover, the leakage hypothesis generates several expectations inconsistent with the observed results.

The experiment appears to us to be fundamentally sound. In addition to the dramatic abundance of direct-hit effects, it contains a rich variety of secondary effects some of which have not previously been reported. The aspect of the experiment which seems most significant in relation to contemporary problems, however, is the data suggestive of a psi-conducive state, particularly the stringing results and the physiological observations. The experiment stands as a remarkably substantial and productive early example of the value of intensive within-subject studies of gifted individuals.

AN EXAMINATION OF THE CHECKER EFFECT

Judith Taddonio O'Brien (University of Lowell)

An experiment was conducted to explore the "checker effect" within the context of expectancy. The effect was reported in 1968 by S. Feather and B. Briar in a study which involved asking subjects to complete four runs of precognitive card-calling, and then to guess which two of the runs would be checked by the person who administered the test and which two would be checked by someone else. The targets for the card-calling, and the determination of which runs would be scored by the test administrator and which scored by the other checker were made after the data had been collected. The results of the study showed significant differences between the scores on runs the subjects had accurately predicted would be scored by the test administrator, and scores on those runs which had not been accurately predicted. These differences were not present in the data scored by the "other" checker, however. Three series were reported by Feather and Briar, all yielding the same checker effect.

Kennedy and Taddonio postulated that although the checker effect appeared to be psychological in nature--reflecting a subject's differential prediction of who would score his data--a case could be made for the results being caused by a PK effect on the part of the person actually checking the data. This PK effect could have occurred at the time the targets were being generated. Post-hoc analyses performed on the Feather-Briar data showed significant differences between the data scored by Feather and those checked by Briar, regardless of which person acted as test administrator for a given series. Such a difference may reflect differential motivation or expectancies which operated for them at the time of the data checking. I have suggested that the expectancy held by an experimenter regarding the scoring pattern of subjects on a given psi test can affect the resulting data. The following studies were conducted to assess whether expectancies on the part of the checker can also affect the scoring pattern of subject data.

In the first series, J.O. administered an ESP test to 27 students enrolled in an experimental psychology class at the University of Lowell. The test was given to subjects after an introductory lecture about parapsychology, and participation in the study was voluntary. The ESP test consisted of four runs of precognitive card-calling of standard ESP symbols, and yielded 100 trials per

subject.   After the test session, the record sheets collected from
the subjects were randomly divided into two groups, with the aid of
a series of random 0's and 1's which had been generated by the
PDP/11 computer at the Institute for Parapsychology.   J. O. then
requested that two students working on parapsychological research
projects that semester check the record sheets to give them practice at scoring ESP data.   The checkers were given differing expectancies regarding the scoring direction of the data.   One checker
was "set" for psi-hitting, and the other checker was "set" for psi-
missing.   The two checkers were then given the opportunity to
choose the targets for their respective sets of data.   J. O. had
previously arranged for a large pool of targets, coded according to
the five ESP card symbols, to be generated by the Institute for
Parapsychology.   The targets were arranged in rows of 25 and
columns of 30, and were sufficient for 400 runs of ESP cards.
The two checkers were asked to pick the starting rows for their
data, and then to proceed sequentially from that point as they
scored the data.   The two checkers chose starting points that were
separated sufficiently so that no targets overlapped between them.
After the starting points had been labelled, the checkers were given
their sets of data to check.   All the data were double-checked by
J. O.

The data showed psi-hitting for the set of record sheets
scored by the checker with the psi-hitting expectancy, and chance
results for the set of data scored by the checker with the psi-
missing expectancy.   The scoring rate for data checked by the psi-
hitting checker was 22. 62 per cent, where mean chance expectation
was 20. 00 per cent (CR = +2. 32, p > . 02).   The scoring rate for
the psi-missing checker was 19. 57 per cent (CR = -. 37, p = ns).
The difference between the data scored by the two checkers was
marginally significant (x^2, 1 df, = 3. 77, p. ≈ . 06).   Because this
was a pilot series, all results were evaluated two-tailed.

In the second series, the procedure was essentially identical.
ESP card-calling data were collected from 31 students enrolled in
a psychological research methods course at Lowell, and two additional students were selected to check the data.   The division of the
data into the two expectancy groups differed from the first series,
in that for a given subject, two of the four runs were assigned to
one group and two to the other.   (The subjects had completed one
run per record sheet, making this division possible.)   The change
was instituted to approximate more closely the condition of the
Feather-Briar study, where each checker had scored two runs of
each subject.   The checkers were again allowed to choose the
starting point for their targets from the prearranged pool.   Targets
used for the first series were deleted.

After the data had been scored and double-checked, the results showed a significant difference between the data scored by the
two checkers.   Marginal hitting was present in the data scored by
the checker with the psi-hitting expectancy (scoring rate = 21. 93
per cent, CR = +1. 87, p > . 05, one-tailed), and significant miss-

ing was found in the data scored by the checker with the psi-missing
expectancy (scoring rate = 17.48 per cent, CR = -2.44, p > .01,
one-tailed). A significant difference was found between the two sets
of data (t = 3.84, 30 df, p > .001). The t-test was used in this
series, rather than the chi-square test, to evaluate both the magnitude and consistency of the difference. A correlation conducted between the ESP scores obtained by subjects with the two checkers
was not significant (r = .20), although 24 of the 31 subjects obtained
higher scores with the checker who had been set for psi-hitting.

The results of the two series suggest that checker expectancy
can affect the results of psi experiments in much the same way that
subject and experimenter expectancy can, and hence suggest a possible interpretation of the Feather-Briar results. While the checker
effect may be psychological in nature, the fact that each checker,
both in the present series and in the Feather-Briar study, chose (or
generated) their targets suggests a parapsychological component to
the effect.

It should be noted that a check was made on the effectiveness
of the expectancy manipulation by asking checkers how they felt
their subject would score. In all cases, before actually checking
the data, the checkers' predictions matched the direction of induced
expectancy. None of the checkers, when debriefed about the true
nature of the study, indicated that they had suspected anything, and
all expressed surprise that they had been tricked by J.O.

EXPLORING FOR GROUP EFFECTS AND PREFERENTIAL
EFFECTS IN A REAL-LIFE TESTING SITUATION

Gerald F. Solfvin, [†] Joan Krieger and William G. Roll (Psychical
    Research Foundation)

In previous meditation studies, we have noted preferential
effects in psi scoring. The present study is a continuation of these
explorations in a real-life testing situation that was salient to the
subjects.

The experiment was carried out during a course, "Introduction to Parapsychology," taught by J.K. at the PRF. The class
met one evening per week from 7 to 9 p.m. for eight weeks, of
which six included experimental sessions.

During the first class, the students (two men and seven
women) were each given copies of the Taylor Manifest Anxiety
Scale, Betts QMI Vividness of Imagery Scale (shortened form), the
Personal Orientation Inventory and a Sheep-Goat Questionnaire to
complete and return the following week. The students were also
asked to rank their preference for 13 possible guest lecturers for
the course, and their preferences for six kinds of refreshments

(cookies, ice cream, etc.) that might be served during the classes.

For six of the classes, guest lecturers would be randomly chosen from the pool of 13 in such a way that only the lecturers themselves knew if and when they were scheduled. The refreshments were randomly chosen by an assistant on the day of the class. In addition, individually randomized free-response targets (art print postcards) were prepared for each student each week. These were selected from a pool of four designs, different each week--one with an animal theme, one with a human theme, one with an architectural theme and one with a landscape theme. The students' preferences for these four themes were recorded during the first session of the course.

At the beginning of each class meeting, the students were given a list of remaining lectures and the six possible refreshments and asked to rank their preferences for that evening. They also ranked their preference for the postcard designs. After the preferences were recorded, J.K. placed a target envelope in front of each person and collected the sheets with the students' preferences.

For the psi responses, the target pool for the free-response ESP was displayed at the front of the room for each person to rank according to the correspondence with the postcard sealed in the envelope in front of him or her. Each person made 25 forced-choice (ESP symbols) responses for the target sheets sealed in the envelope beneath the response sheet. Then the students were asked to use their psi to pick out which lecturer would be at the class that night and what type of dessert would be served. After collecting the response sheets, the envelopes were left for the students to open for feedback. The class then moved from the Meditation Center to the PRF library where the students were served their feedback of food and learned who the lecturer for that evening was.

We first asked, "Is there a tendency to bring about the desired lecture or refreshment for the evening?" The original preference rankings--collected prior to the first experimental session--were summed to obtain a majority vote group ranking of the possible lectures and refreshments. Of the 13 lectures, three turned out to be "not possible" by the time of the first experimental session and we eliminated these from the assessment by collapsing the original preference rankings to 10 possibilities. The average preference rank of the lectures that were actually held is 7.5, which is the most extreme result that could have occurred in the psi-missing direction out of 210 possible outcomes! ($p < .01$, two-tailed.)

The six refreshments that were randomly selected with replacement showed an average preference rank (group majority vote) of 3.66, which is well within chance fluctuation of the expected value of 3.5. Interestingly, the degree of group agreement on these preferences, assessed by Friedman's coefficient of coherence, was high for the lectures ($T = 24.65$, $p < .01$), but low for the refreshments ($T = 4.57$, $p = ns$).

Each week each student was asked to give a preference rank-ing of the possible lectures; a preference ranking of the refresh-ments; an ESP ranking of the lecture; and, an ESP ranking of the refreshments. For each of these rankings, we summed the ranks across students to obtain a majority vote. The Friedman Coefficient of Coherence (T), a measure of the degree of agreement among the subjects, was calculated for each group of rankings for which a majority vote was derived.

For all of these categories the average ranks across weeks are not different from chance expectation, nor are the correlations with the coherence measure significant. The preference rankings showed no significant coherence for either the lecture or the re-freshment.

The analysis of the individual art print postcard ranking was carried out in the same manner as in our previous study in which we analyzed for preferential effects.

Separate tables were prepared for the odd-numbered weeks (scoring done after meditation), the even-numbered weeks (scoring done before meditation) and for the combined totals. A similar set of tables was prepared using the weekly preferences of the students. The overall results show insignificant tendencies toward psi-missing in all of the tables.

The forced-choice task with ESP symbols gave overall chance results, as expected, with an average of 5.07 hits per run over 42 runs. The difference between the 20 runs done after meditation (4.80 hits per run) and the 22 runs done before meditation (5.32 hits per run) was not significant ($Z < 1$). However, the first ses-sion showed independently significant psi-missing (22 hits in 7 runs, $CR = -2.45$, $p < .015$, two-tailed).

We hypothesized, and found, a linear trend toward greater coherence in preference and ESP rankings across the six experi-mental weeks for the refreshments, both attaining their highest values in the final session. The same data for the lectures showed no such trend, possibly due to changing perspectives during the course which we shall discuss shortly.

The overall ESP results from this class point towards psi-missing. This would not be expected on the basis of the general response of the students. In fact, the course was extended, at the students' request, for two extra weeks beyond the last scheduled session.

On the other hand, a closer examination of the week-by-week preferences for lecturer shows that the class may not have done so poorly in getting the lectures they wanted. Most people who are taking their first course in parapsychology think they know what they want at the outset, and many come for the same reasons. But after the first couple of weeks, some are disillusioned while some get excited about new things, but most are changed in some way. We may be seeing the results of this process in the weekly preference rankings. The Friedman coherence measure for these preferences, starting with high agreement on the first two weeks but becoming less so (essentially no agreement) during the following weeks, reinforces this interpretation.

Friedman's coefficient of coherence is a promising measure for use in group situations. Particularly, we would look for group psi scoring associated with "significant" group coherence in future studies, and for time trends toward increasing agreement in preferences as the group continues to meet.

The absence of a clear preferential effect is surprising since we found it in our three previous meditation studies.

This study is an exploration of a new approach to experimentation with psi phenomena. It embodies several aspects which are becoming standard features of the studies conducted by the Psychical Research Foundation and which we would encourage other researchers to consider incorporating into their own programs. These features are: (1) experimentation within real-life situations, involving real needs and real outcomes of relevance to the participants in their lives; (2) the shift of focus away from the individual subject, towards the situation as a whole; and, relatedly, (3) carrying out research as a collaborative effort between researchers, students, lecturers, and others in a way that each one may put his or her natural abilities into the project. We can incorporate these and still maintain solid research designs. In a way, this approach bridges the gap between spontaneous phenomena and laboratory research, hopefully capturing the best of both worlds.

Part 5:   Presidential Address

PSI: ITS PLACE IN NATURE*

K. Ramakrishna Rao

The Scottish philosopher David Hume, who stated unambiguously that no evidence is sufficient to establish a miracle, is in a
sense the grandfather of the contemporary critics of parapsychology.
The more sophisticated of these critics, however, find it expedient
on occasion to disclaim their Humean legacy.   For example, Paul
Kurtz, chairman of the Committee for the Scientific Investigation of
Claims of the Paranormal, which spares no effort to debunk the
whole field, has argued that we cannot "legislate antecedent to inquiry, what is true or false.   One must always be open to unsus-
pected possibilities, novel theories, new kinds of discovery.   The
history of science vividly demonstrates the fact that revolutions in
thought can overturn even well-established beliefs, and that ideas
once rejected may eventually be verified" (Kurtz, 1977, p. 42).
Another critic of ESP research pointed out that "modern parapsychological research is important.   If any of its claims are sub-
stantiated, it will radically change the way we look at the world"
(Diaconis, 1978, p. 135).   Obviously, this opinion is not shared
by all the critics.   For example, Ray Hyman says that "if ESP
were proven to be a reality it would not provide a serious threat
to science or other accepted views" (Hyman, 1977, p. 18), and its
import will tend to be "methodological, rather than theoretical or
substantive" (Hyman, 1978).

There is a degree of dissonance in our critics' attitudes--
the belief in the openness of science on the one hand and the belief
that psi is a priori impossible on the other.   Such dissonance leads
one to consider, irrespective of significant data, that the evidence
is inadequate or that the phenomenon is too trivial to merit consideration.   For the same reason, the incongruence between their
general statements of principles and their comments on specific
issues tend to be overlooked by the critics.   One hopes that an
agreement on general principles and approaches would provide the
necessary frame of reference for a meaningful dialogue.   But this
is often frustrated because of the underlying prejudices that can become more important in determining one's beliefs than any stated
principles.

Phillip H. Abelson, editor of Science, is quoted as saying
that "extraordinary claims require extraordinary evidence" (US News

---

*Delivered August 9, 1978.   Debra Weiner and Charles Akers read
the manuscript and made some helpful comments for its improvement.

and World Report, 31 July 1978, p. 41). The logical implication of
this statement is that the strength of evidence required to establish
a new phenomenon is proportional to its incongruence with our prior
notions concerning its existence.   In extreme, then, if one considers
a phenomenon to be impossible, it is within one's right to demand
evidence that is impossible to obtain.   This is what some critics of
parapsychology have attempted to do.   When the requirements set
by a critic for acceptable evidence are met by further research,
another critic will come up with new ad-hoc explanations for positive results.   This can go on endlessly because their unstated assumption is the one made by David Hume concerning miracles.   The
history of science is replete with examples that render Hume's assumption untenable.   However, some of our critics who readily see
the weakness of any a priori denial of psi do no better than mask
their implicit Humean prejudice by assertions of the openness of
science to anomalous phenomena while making demands that are
impossible to satisfy.

I can speak from my own personal experience how well-
intentioned, intelligent and informed men and women can have mental
blocks when their long-standing belief systems are questioned.

I have two long-time Indian friends who in their gentle way
tried to persuade me to change my research interest in parapsychology to something more conventional and consequential.   They
made no secret of their disdain and displeasure at what they perceived to be an able man going astray.   They sincerely wanted to
help.   We had long, sometimes difficult, discussions on this subject.
The central thesis of one of them was that psychic phenomena are
too anomalous and incongruous with the current corpus of science to
be true, no matter what the evidence is.   His method of disposing
of the evidence for psi was somewhat similar to that of B. F.
Skinner, who lamented, "The genetic endowment responsible for our
behavioral processes cannot fully protect us from the whims of
chance, and the statistical and scientific measures we devise to
bring our behavior under the more effective control of nature are
not adequate for the extraordinary complex sample space in which
we live.   Science has not ignored some underlying order; it has
not yet devised ways of protecting us against spurious evidences of
order" (1977, p. 11).

The other friend, who would patiently listen to my side of
the story, finally conceded on statistical grounds that psi probably
exists but then he exclaimed, "What good is this stuff--it is too
trivial to be of any value or interest!"   One would think that the
manifest contradiction between the respective positions of these men
would be sufficient to expose the weaknesses in their arguments and
that a confrontation between them would have settled the questions
of the existence and importance of psi phenomena.   Unfortunately,
the outcome would not be as simple as that.   Our intellectual
biases, like our emotional prejudice, tend to make us overlook those
arguments which conflict with our prior beliefs and make us reinforce those which are congruous with our biases.   Consequently, to

one of my friends, psi appeared to be profound but unreal, to the other it seemed real but trivial. In either case it was not worth the effort, they thought.

I wish to share with you this evening my reasons for dis-agreeing with my well-meaning friends. I will argue that psi is neither nonexistent nor trivial. It is both real and profound. It is real because the evidence is inescapable and the criticisms of it are unfair, false and unable to explain away much of the experi-mental evidence. It is profound and exciting because it has sub-stantive implications for our understanding of the nature of man and his place in nature.

I

To this audience it is hardly necessary to review in any detail the reasons for my belief in the reality of psi. Psi exper-iences have been reported throughout the recorded history of human-kind. Evidence for the existence of psi has been obtained under controlled conditions by dozens of scientists widely scattered across the globe. Psi effects such as declines and missing (Rao, 1977a) that are not anticipated by the original investigator have later been discovered in the data. People who were too afraid or too reticent to publish their data because of their controversial nature are known to have obtained significant psi results. I do not really see how someone like Dr. Kurtz could have any alternative to accepting the reality of psi. C. E. M. Hansel, who is often referred to for a final word on parapsychology by those who do not believe in it, concluded his magnum opus ESP: A Scientific Evaluation thus: "a great deal of time, effort and money has been expended but an acceptable demonstration of the existence of extrasensory perception has not been given. Critics have themselves been criticized for making the conditions of a satisfactory demonstration impossible to obtain. An acceptable model for future research with which the argument could rapidly be settled one way or the other has now been made available by the investigators at the United States Air Force Research Laboratories. If 12 months' research on VERITAC can establish the existence of ESP, the past research will not have been in vain. If ESP is not established, much further effort could be spared and the energies of many young scientists could be directed to more worthwhile research" (1966, p. 241).

If these are the final words of the critic, no one who is familiar with the recent parapsychological research could reasonably doubt the existence of psi. Helmut Schmidt and the work that followed his first experiment involving the random event generators and the automatic recording devices, which are no way inferior to the VERITAC, meet all the demands made by Hansel for an accept-able psi experiment. The overwhelming evidence that Dr. Schmidt and others have accumulated should suffice to convince an open-minded skeptic.

Informed skepticism has a place in science. If the best of
parapsychological research is among the best in behavioral research
from the standpoint of design and data collection, part of the credit
should go to the critics who did their best to find possible loopholes
and artifacts. Occasionally, however, one wonders whether they
did not go beyond the limits of rational discourse, as when G. R.
Price (1955) attributed significant psi results, which were not otherwise explainable, to "a few people with the desire and the ability
artfully to produce false evidence for the supernatural," a statement
which he has since retracted (Price, 1972).

The same journal which published the article by Price, has
in a recent issue (July 14, 1978) another critical article by Persi
Diaconis who describes himself as both a statistician and a magician.
It would appear that it is just as easy to publish in Science if you
are a critic of parapsychology as it is difficult if you wish to
present some evidence in favor of psi. One of the common strategies of the critics, the one that Diaconis unhesitatingly embraces, is
to set up straw men and shoot them down, to raise pseudo-problems
or problems the parapsychologists have long ago recognized and
solved.

I will refer to the article by Diaconis (1978) in some detail
because it exemplifies both the dissonance of many of our critics
toward psi as well as the inherent weakness of their arguments
once they abandon the Humean position.

Diaconis states unambiguously that "modern parapsychological
research is important." He acknowledges that Feller's criticism of
the statistics used by J. B. Rhine and his coworkers was wrong,
and concedes that many parapsychologists are statistically sophisticated. He even credits the parapsychological community with solving "numerous statistical riddles in its own literature." Yet, in
the same breath, he accuses parapsychologists of violating elementary
statistical assumptions. He writes as though parapsychologists are
unaware of the statistical problems related to feedback and multiple
analyses. The fact of the matter is that these problems have been
discussed in the parapsychological literature, and procedures for
correcting for any artifacts arising from them are well known to
most parapsychologists.

"A common problem in the evaluation of ESP experiments,"
Diaconis states, "is the uncertainty about what outcomes are to be
judged as indicative of ESP" (p. 131). On the face of it, this
statement is tantamount to saying that parapsychologists do not con-
duct experiments, but only make ad-hoc observations. Obviously,
this is not what he means. He seems to say that parapsychological
experiments are so loose-ended that it is difficult to make any
sense of the evidence. This is simply not the case and displays
on the part of Diaconis a serious lack of understanding of the way
parapsychological experiments are carried out.

The first book any student of parapsychology needs to read

is Parapsychology: Frontier Science of the Mind by Rhine and
Pratt (1957). This book makes a clear distinction between exploratory research methods and methods of verification. A critic who
does not grasp this distinction between exploratory and confirmatory
studies has simply not done his homework and cannot talk meaningfully about parapsychological experiments. It is suggested in the
book that a pilot experiment be carried out before undertaking any
elaborately designed project because "the many uncontrolled variables
... are especially likely to cause trouble in investigations with so
elusive a capacity as psi" (Rhine & Pratt, 1957, p. 26). The
triviality of Diaconis' criticism becomes obvious if one looks at the
two statistical requirements of the Journal of Parapsychology, a
leading journal in the field:

> (1) The precise statistical formulation of the hypoth-
> esis (or hypotheses) being tested in a research report
> should be concisely stated and listed in advance of the
> presentation of the results. It is recommended that the
> type of statistical test(s) that are planned be given along
> with the hypothesis.

> (2) Any statistical analysis not previously stated as
> preplanned should be accompanied by a brief statement
> of the motivation or circumstances leading to that analy-
> sis, and the probability value should be in close enough
> proximity to this statement that its association is obvious
> [Cover, page 3, March 1978].

It is amazing that Diaconis should commit the same errors
which he wrongly accuses parapsychologists of making. His
criticisms of psi experiments are not applicable to much of the
serious research in the field and where they are applicable they
have already been discussed in the parapsychological literature itself. "The confusing and erratic experimental condition" he has
witnessed at the Harvard demonstration would seem to anyone well
acquainted with psi research to be more an indication of the limitations of his exposure to parapsychological experiments than a true
and typical picture of the field. To be brief, I shall confine my
comments to his remarks regarding the experiments with the special
subject, B.D., carried out at the Institute for Parapsychology.

His criticism of the Kelly and Kanthamani experiments
(1972; Kanthamani & Kelly, 1974a, 1974b) is two-fold. It concerns
informal design and cheating by the subject. The evidence for these
criticisms is not obtained either by an examination of the actual
experiments or of their reports in professional journals, but from
his own observations of B.D.'s informal performance in another
place and setting.

It would seem that the accusation of "informal design and
evaluation" is more apt to the observations of Diaconis relating to
the Harvard demonstrations than to the experiments of Kelly and
Kanthamani, since the critic's arguments are almost wholly based

on observations obtained under conditions more informal than any
he chooses to criticize.   What he refers to as uncontrolled experiments were, in fact, informal presentations to a group at Harvard.
They can in no sense be construed as experiments.   It is difficult
to see how observations made during such informal presentations
could be cited to invalidate the results obtained under a different
set of experimental conditions which he does not even attempt to
criticize.

Apart from this fatal methodological flaw, one wonders how
relevant are his observations to the findings claimed by Kelly and
Kanthamani.   "A major key to B. D. 's success," states Diaconis,
"was that he did not specify in advance the result to be considered
surprising.   The odds against a coincidence of some sort are
dramatically less than those against any prespecified particular one
of them.   For the experiment just described, including as successful outcomes all possibilities mentioned, the probability of success
is greater than one chance in eight.   This is an example of exploiting multiple end points" (p. 132).   The implication of this
statement is that in the experiments reported by Kelly and Kanthamani, B. D. 's results are at least in part due to "exploiting multiple
end points."   This is patently false.

Not surprisingly, Diaconis refers only to a part of the first
report of Kelly and Kanthamani which deals with their exploratory
work with cards, leaving out other parts where B. D. could not have
used any tricks.   The fact of the matter is that this report also
presents significant results obtained with Schmidt's four-button
machine and with a dice machine which leave no scope for sleight-
of-hand tricks.   Kelly and Kanthamani (1972, p. 188) specifically
state that B. D. 's card trials in their exploratory research cannot
be considered as scientific evidence for ESP.   Subsequent research
as reported in the second paper (Kanthamani & Kelly, 1974) was
aimed at confirming under controlled conditions the suggestions that
came out of the exploratory work.   In the second report to which
Diaconis refers, the subject B. D. obtained three times more the
number of exact hits than expected by chance.   Such a result gives
a Z score of 12 and one does not have to be a professor of statistics to appreciate the fact that an inconceivably large number of
multiple end points would have to have been available to the subject
or experimenter to dig up such an improbable result on the hypothesis of coincidence.   However, the fact is that neither the subject
nor the experimenter was allowed such multiple ends as Diaconis
wants us to believe.

The second criticism is based on cheating by the subject.
Diaconis accuses B. D. of employing sleight-of-hand tricks in the
Harvard presentations that he had witnessed.   Among the observations he made are "I saw him glance at the bottom card of the deck
he was shuffling" and "BD secretly [emphasis added] counted the
number of cards between the card he had seen and the selected
card" (p. 132).   To accuse someone publicly of cheating, I would
think that we should have something more evidential than "I saw

him glance at the bottom card. " The critic cannot use one set of standards for evaluating evidence for psi and another set for convincing himself there was fraud in the experiment. Would Diaconis be convinced that B. D. has ESP if someone with training and a background similar to that of Diaconis has testified that he did not see B. D. use sleight-of-hand when he obtained significant psi scoring?

If one of my colleagues who is also a professional magician had told me that his broken watch was paranormally mended by Geller and that he saw Girard paranormally bend an aluminum rod, it would not convince me that Geller and Girard are psychics; we need to have something more than informal observation. We need data and we need to know the conditions under which the data were obtained so that we can reach sound conclusions. The hypothesis of Diaconis is more ad hoc and multiple ended than anything he criticizes. In support of his accusation, he should provide more objective evidence than he has. It would have been a simple matter if the subject's movements were monitored through video recording, if they had any reason to believe that B. D. would use such sleight-of-hand tricks. Again, one would ask what evidence Diaconis had for concluding that B. D. had "secretly counted. " One would hope that he appreciates the difference between the statement, "BD could have secretly counted," and the one he actually makes, "BD secretly counted.... " If one could confuse inference for observation, is it not possible that one could also mistake imagination for actual perception?

Apart from the ad-hoc hypotheses and post-hoc surmises he makes, the shallowness of Diaconis' criticism becomes obvious when one looks into the actual experimental set-up and realizes that none of these hypothetical tricks are appropriate for explaining the results obtained in the Kelly-Kanthamani experiments with B. D. To dismiss the results of controlled studies on the basis of speculative inferences drawn from ad-hoc observations made at informal "performances" is just another indication of the Humean prejudice against those phenomena that do not seem to fit into the current corpus of science. And that Science chose to publish a paper with such glaring gaps between evidence and conclusion, gaps which can be filled only by one's prejudice against parapsychology, makes one wonder whether Science itself is free from the Humean inheritance.

The criticisms of Diaconis have not shaken in the least my belief in the existence of psi. In fact, if the arguments of Diaconis are the best any critic can muster, I believe the case for psi is strong and irrefutable. This does not mean that everyone will find the evidence convincing. Given a fertile imagination, even intelligent and stable individuals who are neither paranoid nor disoriented tend to engage in all kinds of ad-hoc reasoning. Adolph Baker illustrates this beautifully with reference to his friend who refused to believe, at one time, that the Russians orbited an astronaut because "they are perfectly capable of fabricating such a story out of whole cloth" (1970, p. 103).

II

My second friend, who has the necessary scientific training, sees the pitfalls of ad-hoc reasoning and is therefore willing to concede that psi may exist.   But his initial prejudice leads him to raise questions of a different sort.   What difference does it make, really, he asks, even if one accepts that psi exists, as long as it is so elusive, unpredictable and inconsequential?   In a typical card-calling experiment, he argues, it is not even possible to pinpoint a trial and say that "here is ESP."   In several experiments that gave significant results, parapsychologists themselves were unable to agree who was, in fact, the source of the effect--the subject or the experimenter.   There is little hope of learning to use psi for prac-tical benefits; repeatable experiments are still not in sight.   The information that is supposed to be gained through ESP is too trivial, insignificant and uncertain to hold any hope that it would displace or supplement sensory communication.   What is it, then, queries my friend, that you hope to accomplish in your research, besides per-haps convincing a few more people?

My friend, of course, knows that I do not generally contribute to and am not fascinated by the science-fiction projections of what psi might accomplish in the future.   I have little fear that psi, in the near future, will be used to control the minds of men.   I do not believe that psi will ever be a substitute for our sensory-motor functions.   I doubt whether psychic healing is anywhere near com-peting with conventional therapies.   I do believe, however, that psi interacts with our normal functions and to some degree, determines how we function.   And this is important because a greater under-standing of psi may contribute to our better functioning.   Also, psi seems to point to levels of reality and of our being that we have so far ignored.   And this will have revolutionary consequences for our understanding of man and his place in nature.

Before I take the quantum leap and discuss the implications of psi, I will briefly go over some of the basic things that we seem to know about psi.   These may provide the empirical grounding or at least the starting point to some of the speculations I will subse-quently discuss.

At various times during the past quarter of a century of my involvement in parapsychology I have asked myself the questions, What do we know about psi other than that it exists? and What have been the lines of progress so far and what areas hold promise for the future?   One of my first exercises to answer these questions was to analyze and compare the bibliographic entries in my card file for the first two decades of my active involvement in the field, 1955-1974.   In 1975 I attempted to make a comparative review of published parapsychological reports during the years 1955 to 1964 and 1965 to 1974.   At the outset, I found a 50 per cent increase in published research papers from the first to the second decade. Interestingly, even though most parapsychologists consider that psi had been conclusively shown to exist well before 1955, a number of

papers whose main objective was to provide further evidence for
the existence of psi continued to be published in our professional
journals.   During the years 1955 to 1964 more than 40 such experimental reports appeared.   There does not seem to be any slackening
of such effort during the subsequent 10 years.   There were as many
as 53 papers whose main contribution was limited to providing further evidence for psi.   Thus, while our professed objective is one
of attempting to understand psi, we have not given up the endeavor
to obtain more and better evidence.   Reporting such evidence did
not preclude criticisms of research.   There were nearly 25 published reports critical of parapsychological research in the period
1955 to 1964.   In the following decade there were as many as 35
reports of criticism and countercriticism.   A recent and welcome
trend is for parapsychologists themselves to criticize each other's
research on methodological grounds.

There have been perceptible increases in reports on the
following areas from the first to the second decades: altered states
of consciousness; historical and review papers; methodology; personality, psi and cognitive processes; and the relation of parapsychology to other disciplines.   Papers on spontaneous cases, survival
and theory remain at about the same level.   The only area where
there is a marked decline in the number of published reports is the
one involving target variations, experimenter differences and differences in test conditions.

There has been a significant increase in the use of free-
response target material in ESP research.   In PK research, significant departures from the traditional dice experiments were made
with the introduction of random event generators.   Also of interest
are investigations on the effect of PK on living systems and greater
openness to the study of static PK.

Despite technological advances allowing new types of psi experiments and increased methodological sophistication in experimental
research, the riddles of psi are still with us.   The effect of subject
variables such as personality is far from being conclusive.   We
still do not seem to know whether it is a better strategy to work
with selected or unselected subjects.   As for target content and
conditions, not much of any consequence has been added to our
knowledge of such variables since 1955.   The initial assumptions
that the physical aspects of targets and their location in time and
space may not have any intrinsic effect on psi functioning continue
to be entertained by most researchers in the field.   The role of the
experimenter has come to be increasingly complicated with the
realization that his psi may be the source of the observed effect.
The evidence for unintentional psi has further blurred the neat distinction between the subject and the experimenter.

What has impressed me most, however, was the fact that
what seemed to be a salient finding at one time appeared to be
quite trivial at another time.   Take for instance, the question of
telepathy versus clairvoyance.   The conceptual distinction between

these two terms was made quite early in the history of systematic parapsychology. For many years there was a controversy over the state of evidence for one against the other. One could even identify national stereotypes on this question, the British by and large favoring the telepathy hypothesis and the Americans, clairvoyance. My very first experiment in parapsychology was prompted by my youthful enthusiasm to solve the question of telepathy and clairvoyance once and for all. This attempt proved abortive as the "beautifully" designed experiment gave no evidence of psi.

After years of intense attempts to demonstrate "pure" telepathy and "pure" clairvoyance and the heated exchanges to explain telepathy by clairvoyance and precognition and clairvoyance in terms of telepathy, we are now led to a position where the traditional distinction between the two as two distinct modes of psi seems to be rather pointless and where telepathy and clairvoyance simply appear as a single ability operating on diverse target materials. The range of targets seems to be immense indeed, as subjects are known to succeed in guessing images in someone's mind as well as electromagnetic activity inside a computer. Again, recent evidence seems to suggest that the distinction between ESP and PK may be misleading in some crucial ways. Already theoretical attempts to reduce one to the other have been made with some degree of plausibility (Schmidt, 1975; Stanford, 1977, 1978; Walker, 1975).

I recognize that we may not all agree on what is the most significant aspect of psi we have been able to discover so far. It seems to me that the most salient findings have in some sense a negative tone. We seem to know more about the conditions that do not constrain psi functioning than those that would enhance it. This is somewhat paradoxical because the occurrence of psi itself is sporadic and elusive. I have come to think that these findings are quite important in that they may lead us to an appreciation of the true place of psi in nature. The physical aspects of psi, such as size, shape, color and form of the targets, do not seem to have any intrinsic effect on psi. Neither do space and time and the causative complexity of the psi task. Any hypothetical relationship of distance to ESP must assume that there is some energy transmission between the subject and targets which is inhibited by the distance factor. But if precognition is a fact, as we have strong evidence to believe that it is, what is the nature of this transmission that occurs between the subject and the not-yet-existing target? Thus, the evidence for precognition and the success of ESP experiments over long distances lead me to believe that space and time are not constraining variables as far as psi is concerned. Another significant negative is the relative ineffectiveness of task complexity in constraining psi. Stanford (1977) has reviewed the relevant literature and concluded that "the efficiency of PK function is not reduced by increases in the complexity of the target system" (p. 375).

If psi is unconstrained by space and time and the complexity of the task and if the psi situation is such that distinctions between

thought and matter, cognition and action, subject and object become
less than meaningful, it would seem that psi may function beyond the
familiar categories of understanding, and point to a state of being
which cannot be properly classed as mind or matter.   Psi phenomena raise the question whether there exists a realm of reality beyond the phenomenal world of appearance that is primarily a product
of our information-processing capabilities and mechanisms.   One
may rightly wonder whether we are not dealing here with the Kantian
"thing in itself. "   Also, it would seem that it is just for this reason
J. B. Rhine (1953) and others have emphasized the notion of the
nonphysicality of psi.

Another characteristic of psi phenomena is the apparent lack
of any discernible connection between a psi event and its assumed
cause.   This led C. G. Jung to postulate that psi belongs to a
class of synchronistic acausal events (Jung & Pauli, 1955).   In
order to make any sense of synchronicity as an explanatory hypothesis, we have to assume a kind of omniscience on our part and
regard archetypes as nonlocal in the sense that they can function
independently of space-time constraints (Rao, 1977).   Yet the problem of communication between the individual and the archetypes remains unresolved.   We need to explain the dirigibility aspect of
psi--i. e. , the synchronization of archetypal activity with the wishes
of the subject or the experimenter in a successful psi test.

Unlike spontaneous psi, laboratory effects involve a connection between someone's intention and the subsequent observation of
an effect.   Without such an intention or expectation, observed effects
would be no more than improbable coincidences.   It is this intentionality, often stated in terms of expectations and experimental
hypotheses, that gives meaning to coincidences.   But the intention
itself, it seems to me, is not the cause of the observed effect in
the sense of a formal or efficient cause.   Only in a teleological
sense can the intention be considered a cause of a psi effect.   This
point is becoming increasingly apparent in the attempts to regard
psi as goal oriented.

What about, then, nonintentional psi effects?   In the sense
of an effect obtained in a planned laboratory experiment, nonintentional psi is a misnomer.   The usefulness of this concept is at
best limited to focussing attention on the possibility that the source
of a psi effect may not be the subject as is traditionally assumed.
Insofar as the experimenter intends or wishes a particular outcome
in an experiment, whatever psi that may be evidenced by that experiment is largely intentional.

III

If you now allow me to leave the stable empirical base of
research and take a flight to not-so-secure heights of intellectual
fantasy, I will share with you my distant gaze of psi from the skies
of speculative thought.   The gaze at this point is somewhat hazy as

our conceptual framework is still misty.   My vision is to a degree
obscured by the clouds of acquired biases in favor of an orderly
universe compatible with commonsense world views.   So I cannot
promise to present to you a clear, much less an accurate picture
of psi.   Perhaps we can gain a perspective that would stimulate
further search for psi laws when we return to our base and resume
our research.   If some of you fear at this point that I am about to
palm off on you some Oriental nonsense, I am afraid your fears
may not be unfounded.   I assure you, however, that I will attempt
to match such nonsense with an equal amount of its Occidental
counterpart.

    Our attempt to understand psi in some ways parallels the
attempts of some of the Indian thinkers to understand the nature of
the Brahman, the supreme self.   It is suggested, for example, that
the best way to grasp the Brahman is to strip it of all the contents
of experience through a process of elimination.   This process of
successive denial of attributes in describing Brahman is expressed
in the famous formula "neti, neti (not this, not this)."   The denied
attributes include all the things and relations we find in the world,
including spatial, temporal and sensory attributes.   Brahman is
something which is neither limited in space and time nor is distinguished from other objects.   It is both the subject and the object.
In a sense, it is undifferentiated subjectivity or non-objective consciousness.

    Brahman is the same as Atman for the Advaita Vendantins.
Atman is undifferentiated pure consciousness, timeless and spaceless.   It underlies each and every individual person.   Atman as
supreme consciousness is devoid of such distinctions as subject and
object that are so characteristic of our normal consciousness.
Ordinary consciousness or thought is a process whereas Atman is a
state of being.   The statement in Chandogya Upanishad, "tat tvam
asi (thou art that)" referred to as the mahavakya, or the "great
saying," expresses the relationship between the individual consciousness and the supreme consciousness.   The relationship is one of
identity but represents a progression from phenomenal consciousness
to pure consciousness.   In a sense the supreme consciousness constitutes the ground for our individual consciousness.   Thus, tat tvam
asi is the assertion of a common ground that links the individual to
the Brahman.

    The individual is a curious combination of both reality and
appearance.   Insofar as Atman constitutes the ground of the individual, it is real, but in its phenomenal aspect with its stream of experience, the individual is mere appearance.   The phenomenal consciousness according to Sankara continually strives towards one end
or another.   It acts like an agent controlled by the upadhis (mental
processes) that limit our understanding.   Thus, the individual consciousness that manifests a systematic unity of experience constitutes
the empirical being or self that is defined in terms of bodily conditions.   But this empirical being is not all that we have because within each of us we have also a supreme consciousness that acts as the

ground and witness or sakshin. The Atman is called sakshin when
the mind of the individual acts as a limiting adjunct to the supreme
consciousness. The sakshin is thus conceived as the constant witness of the individual's experiences, a screen on which the experiential phenomena are played. It is important to note that according
to Sankara, the individual person is neither a part of, nor different
from, nor a modification of the supreme consciousness. It is
Atman itself steeped in avidya or nescience. It is the upadhis
within us that limit the understanding of the Atman. According to
this theory of limitation, known as the avacchedavada, the individual
person is the Atman limited by his mind. There is also another
theory, called pratibimbavada, to account for the relationship between the individual and the supreme consciousness. According to
this theory, the individual consciousness is a reflection of the
supreme consciousness in the mirror of avidya or nescience. The
reflection is as real as the image but its clarity is a function of
the state of the individual. Just as the reflection of a person in a
pool of water differs depending on the state of the water, whether it
is clear or dirty, calm or turbulent, the reflection of the supreme
consciousness in an individual self depends on the state of the avidya
of the individual in whom it is reflected.

        To sum up, then: the ultimate reality is the pure being and
it is the supreme consciousness. The empirical being or the individual consciousness is a phenomenal manifestation of the supreme,
limited by the mind, the intellect, the senses and the body. The
supreme consciousness not only provides the necessary support to
the individual but also acts as the witnessing consciousness throughout the life history of the individual. It is possible to transcend
the limitations of our bodily conditions and achieve understanding of
the supreme.

        Advaita distinguishes between four states of consciousness.
They are the waking state, the dream state, the state of deep sleep,
and the transcendental state. In the waking state the content of our
consciousness is largely determined by external objects. It is the
state where consciousness is processed by the whole set of our
psychophysical system. Dream consciousness is made up of the
same stuff as the waking consciousness but unlike waking consciousness its content is not empirically real. The deep-sleep state is
characterized by the abeyance of all distinctions including the distinction of subject from object. The Mandukya Upanishad describes
the fourth state of consciousness thus:

        They consider the fourth to be that which is not conscious
        of the internal world, nor conscious of the external
        world, nor conscious of both the worlds, nor a mass of
        consciousness, nor simple consciousness, nor uncon-
        sciousness, which is unseen, beyond empirical deter-
        mination, beyond the grasp (of the mind) undemonstra-
        ble, unthinkable, undescribable, of the nature of con-
        sciousness alone wherein all phenomena cease, un-
        changing, peaceful and nondual [Mandukya Upanishad, 6].

Recently Karl Pribram (1971), the distinguished neuropsychologist, proposed a holographic model of brain and consciousness. There are striking similarities between some of Pribram's ideas on the relationship between the brain and the world and the advaita speculations on the Brahman and the individual self.

According to Pribram, the brain function is holonomic in that it partakes of both computer and optical information processes. "The brain is like a computer in that information is processed in steps by an organized and organizing set of rules. It differs from current computers in that each step is more extended in space--brain has considerably more parallel processing capability than today's computers" (Pribram, 1978). Again, unlike today's computers, memory storage in the brain is holographic. Pribram believes that his holonomic theory, besides providing models that would help us precisely explore in the laboratory such cognitive processes as memory, attention and problem solving, has possibilities for the study of consciousness. Ordinary consciousness, he says, is "achieved by a mechanism (somewhat like a hologram) that disposes the organism to locate fresh experiences and performances at some distance from the receptive and expressive interfaces that join organism and environment." One of the reasons for this conclusion is the similarity between sensory processing and physical holography as, for example, in Bekesy's findings (1967) in which the subject projected the somato-sensory source into space when a set of phase-related vibratory stimuli were applied to two of his limbs.

Pribram goes on to suggest that the world itself may be a hologram. Following David Bohm's (1973) distinction between explicate and implicate organizations relative to structural and holographic processes, Pribram makes a similar distinction for perceptual processes. Our current scientific analysis gives us knowledge about extrinsic properties of the physical world. Pribram argues that even the intrinsic properties (such as the stoneness of stones) are knowable. In fact, he says

they are the 'ground' in which the extrinsic properties are embedded in order to become realized.... [T]he intrinsic properties of the physical universe, their implicate organization, the field, ground or medium in which explicit organization, extrinsic properties, become realized, are multiform. In the extreme, the intrinsic properties, the implicate organization is holographic. As extrinsic properties become realized, they make implicate organization become more explicit. This implies that the uncertainty of occurrences of events is only superficial and is the result of holographic 'blurring.' Thus, a random distribution in as much as it is based on holographic principles is not haphazard but determined.

All this makes Pribram conclude that there is "no more mystery to

the mystic than to the induction process that allows selective de-
pression of DNA to form now this organ, now that one."

Obviously, much of the above is as speculative as advaita
metaphysics, even though the language of Pribram is closer to a
scientific formulation.   I do recognize that even if it is the case
that the brain processes involved in such activities as memory retrieval are in some sense holographic, it does not follow from this
that the universe itself is a hologram.   One would hope that Pribram
would work out the implications of the enlarged holographic model
encompassing the entire universe to man's nature in general and
paranormal phenomena in particular.

The similarity between Pribram's ideas and the advaita
speculations concerning the nature of the universe is quite apparent.
The holographic universe is very much like Sankara's Brahman, the
ultimate or first-order reality.   The holonomic brain resembles in
essentials the individual self, the jiva.   The advaita belief that the
world of our experience is a mere appearance or a second-order
reality is also implied in Pribram's theory.   Both seem to hold
that the primary reality provides the ground, the field or the
medium for the secondary reality as it manifests in our experience,
and that the form of the processed reality is very much a function
of our physical system.   Again, they seem to hold that while the
primary reality in itself is in principle unknowable at the level of
our sensory awareness, it may be knowable in another dimension.
There is thus the possibility of transcending the ordinary state of
awareness and achieving consciousness without content.   When such
a state is achieved, the brain may function as a hologram of the
universe so that it attains a state of omniscience.   In the language
of advaita, when the veil of avidya is removed, we have the knowledge of the absolute.   It is interesting to note that according to
advaita vedanta, perception involves the mind's taking on the form
of the object perceived.   Antahkarana (the mind) is of the nature of
light and is capable of assuming various forms so as to give us
corresponding perceptions of objects.   The mind in advaita occupies
an intermediary position between conscious subject and unconscious
matter and thus makes the interaction between the two possible at
the empirical level.

It is the potential for omniscience on the part of an individual
organism that makes the advaita and holographic theories attractive
to a psi theorist.   However, the concept of omniscience implies a
kind of determinism which is in a sense negated by some parapsychological phenomena.   While ESP can be contained within a deter-
ministic framework, PK, it would seem, requires more than a
closed block universe; PK requires an open system that enables
mental effort to bring about physical changes that cannot be accounted
for in cause-effect sequences.

I shall not attempt to pick loopholes (of which there are
doubtless many) in the advaita theory or the holographic model or
to draw out more explicitly their implications for parapsychology.

These are better left to their opponents and proponents.   Instead I
will attempt to reconstruct a necessarily simplistic and mostly
speculative picture of the universe in which psi may make some
sense--a picture, it may readily be seen, inspired by Sankara
vedanta and to a lesser degree by Pribram and Bohm.   At this
stage the picture may not be as elegant as the advaita theory or as
provocative as the holographic model.   But, hopefully, it may lead
us to a line of research that will enable us to understand psi a
little better.

IV

        Reality, it seems to me, has many layers.   In the core,
it is undifferentiated and stable.   On the surface it has distinct forms
that are ever changing.   The core reality is progressively differentiated so as to give us the appearance we have of it in surface
reality.   In the outer layers things are relatively insulated from
each other.   The interaction between them can be understood in
causal terms.   But within the inner layers distinctiveness and in-
dividuality are obscured and even obliterated as things merge into
each other.   Subject-object dichotomies become meaningless.   Consequently, causality as it is commonly understood and the space-
time characterization of reality lose their significance and relevance.
The reality as actualized in the outer layers is implied in the
inner layers in the same way the oak tree is implied by the acorn.
The relations between things across a layer are causal and the relations between layers themselves is teleological.

        In other words, the outer layers of reality are explicate
forms of what is implicate in the inner layers.   The process of the
universe is one of making explicate what is implicate in the core
reality.   To put it differently, reality at its core contains the grand
plan or design to which the unfolding universe conforms.   The
process by which the grand plan gets implemented, I venture to
hazard, is psi.   So conceived, psi is a fundamental process in
nature, a process through which nature communicates with its
constituents.   Nature is so organized that its constituents inevitably
conform to the grand design.

        A crucial stage in the differentiation of core reality, i. e.,
the evolution of the universe, is the emergence of the self that can
perceive itself as distinct from the rest.   From such self-perception
arises subjective awareness.   The self, it would seem, is a nucleus
which interacts with the contiguous constituents which provide the
material for weaving around itself a world of its own.   This weaving is accomplished by the structures that process reality, which at
once mask the essential reflexivity of the self to relate as a nucleus
to core reality and create the notion of the individual agent.   The
flowing stream of experience represents the encounters of the self
with what is perceived to be reality.   Insofar as we share similar
structures, our experience of reality tends to be similar and we
are able to meaningfully communicate with each other.

An essential feature of the self is its intentionality which enables the differentiated being (individual organism), now only remotely related to the core, to carry on the process of becoming. There is then, in the self, an instance of an interface between the implicate and explicate organizations. The implicate organizations are mediated through psi and are essentially teleological. The explicate organizations are bound by chains of causation. The intentionality of the self reflects both the teleology of implicate structures and the causality of surface reality in which it partakes. The interface between the implicate and explicate structures established in a selfhood makes a reciprocal relation possible. Not only do the intentions of the self reflect the grand design, but they also influence on appropriate occasions the peripheral phases of the design itself. Thus, we find that the constituents of nature conform to its design and that the intentions of the constituents, when suitably directed, have tangible effects on the design itself.

Intentions then have two sorts of effects. They affect surface reality directly through sensory-motor operations. They can also affect surface reality by affecting the reality plan to which all constituents of nature must conform. The former is achieved through what may be called "temporal" processing, while the latter seems to involve "depth processing," namely, a psi-mediated "reverse" contact that is established by the self as it is sinking back into its primordial condition of unity with the rest of reality. The "live" intentions of the submerged self get assimilated into the periphery of the grand design. As the constituents of nature conform to the design, the intentions bring about "paranormal" changes in surface reality. Depth processing may be holographic in the sense Pribram has implied, or it may involve the process of abaissement, as Jung put it, which makes the psyche open to the direct impact of archetypal factors.

The processes that generate immediate experience of surface reality are fundamentally temporal in nature. Our most immediate experience seems to be a product of integrating temporally separate events with an interval of approximately 100 milliseconds into a unitary impression. Compatible events are fused in experience and the incompatible and structurally different ones are omitted. This is accomplished at rapid speeds by our central nervous system. There is evidence that alterations of the interval of integration could result in changes of experience. These unitary impressions are further integrated with past and future events to give us experiential continuity and even to establish or select goals. Attention deployment or volition, central to cognitive control, has two dimensions, attentional focusing and attentional scanning. I suspect that these same dimensions of our cognitive control when applied to a mental event in a nontemporal way may enable us to have access to psi. A nontemporal application of our cognitive structures may enable us to experience the effects of our implicate organization.

It would seem that yoga may be a means of achieving control of nontemporal cognitive functioning. According to yoga, the chitta,

or the psyche, is in a state of continuous change or fluctuation.
These fluctuations are called chitta vrittis. The purpose of yoga is
to attain a state in which these fluctuations are completely restrained
and controlled. We are told that such a state can be achieved by
practicing certain psychophysical exercises that include meditation
and concentration. The object of most of these exercises is to enable one to concentrate and attain attentional control. Dharana, or
concentration, results in narrowing the focus of attention, perhaps
to a single event. Controlled expansion of this focus is achieved
by meditation or dhyana. And a prolongation of dhyana results in a
standstill state called samadhi where one has consciousness without
content, or attains a state where one perhaps can more directly
partake in the implicate structures of core reality. Yoga and
similar techniques may enable us to do such depth processing as is
necessary to have access to nature's grand plan. It is claimed by
certain practitioners of yoga that during the higher stages of yoga
one loses personal identity, transcends subject-object dichotomies
and gains an intuitive grasp of reality as well as paranormal experiences.

          I am not sure that at this stage any of us are willing to bet
that such control over psi is ever possible. But results of experimental research (Schmeidler, 1970; Osis & Bokert, 1971; Dukhan &
Rao, 1973; Matas & Pantas, 1971; and Rao, Dukhan & Rao, 1978)
involving meditation and similar techniques to alter the normal mode
of our cognitive function have met with a fair amount of success
warranting some optimism, if not conviction. Honorton's (1977)
review of experimental studies bearing on psi and internal attention
states in general and meditation in particular makes a strong case
for a possible relation between psi and the control of attentional
processes through such means as meditation.

                                   V

          Two kinds of psi are implied in what has been said so far.
I propose to call them constitutive and epistemic psi. Constitutive
psi is involved in natural processes. Epistemic psi is mediated
through the intentionality of nature's constituents. What we now
study in the laboratory is of the latter kind. Since psi is essentially a process that belongs to implicate organizations, it is logical
to raise the question whether we can ever study and understand psi
by means of methods that manipulate only physical or psychological
variables. J. B. Rhine (1975), who more than anyone else is
responsible for the development of research methods in parapsychology, himself has wondered whether such methods would ever
lead to an understanding of psi, and has stressed the need for
developing parapsychological methods that would make use of what
he called psi "fingerprints. " I do not believe that the true import
of Rhine's revolutionary stance on parapsychological methodology has
received its due among parapsychologists. It seems to me that
Rhine's call for psi methods is his recognition of what appears to
be psi's essential feature of manifesting in certain identifiable ways.

Inasmuch as our behavior is determined by the ongoing explicate as well as implicate organizations, it follows that psi is involved to a degree in our daily activities. In a few rare instances psi is the sole determinant of an outcome in our behavior. Sometimes the explicate and the implicate organizations act independently and may conflict with each other, resulting in the suppression or distortion of the input of one or the other. More often the inputs from both the sources mix and fuse and result in behavior that is indistinguishable from the normal but at the same time unexplainable in terms of meaningful explicate organizations.

I postulate that there is nothing that is purely random either in the universe or in our behavior. All behavior is determined either by the explicate organizations or the implicate organizations or by a combination of both. It is likely that apparent random behavior is an area where we may more likely encounter psi. The fact that the logically derived theories of probability are neatly supported by empirical data suggests a balancing function in nature. It would appear that such a balancing is essential for keeping intact the integrity of our cognitive function. The differential effect and similar psi effects seem to be a consequence of such a balancing.

That psi may be involved in more ways than in recognizable psi experiences has implications for understanding not only certain facets of our behavior but also some of the basic processes in nature. This fact renders parapsychology one of the most interdisciplinary of all subjects. There is perhaps no subject of inquiry that has no connection with psi. Take for example evolution. There are no agreed probability formulae among mathematicians and biologists to satisfactorily explain how our biosphere has evolved the way it did by mere random mutation and selection. The inherent difficulties involved in the classical Darwinian position has led at least one eminent biologist, Sir Alister Hardy (1965), to speculate that psi may interact with the physical system in the evolutionary process and thus, would account for some of the gaps left by the classical selection theory. Others, like John Randall (1975), see the possibility that psi may have even a more direct role in the origin of life and its subsequent mutations. Jule Eisenbud argues that "any psi-mediated factor that could work in confluence with and complement normal determinants influencing behavior might just tip the balance in one direction or the other" (1976, p. 45). He suggests that psi may effect the balance of adjustment "by facilitating the coming into each other's range of those predatory pairs whose ultimate encounter would tend to fulfill particular ecological requirements" (1976, p. 45).

In physics, Walker (1975) and others have suggested that "will," identified with hidden variables, may determine the collapse of the state vector for a physical system at the quantum level with infinitely small diverse potential states.

A basis for psi in our normal volitional processes is sug-

gested by John Eccles (1977).   Again, Jan Ehrenwald argues elo-
quently in a recent book that "psi phenomena do not stand apart
from the rest of human experience.   They are part and parcel of
the same overreaching psychosomatic continuum ranging from the
mindless strivings of the instinct to Samadhi or satori, from
metabolism to gut feelings, from transcendental meditation to artis-
tic creation" (1978, p. x).   He suspects the presence of psi in
psychotherapy not only in striking experiences where psi may be
involved, but also in what he calls doctrinal compliance, in which
a patient seems to provide evidence for the therapist's theories; in
mutual reinforcement of emotionally-charged attitudes resulting in
the patient's positive therapeutic responses, and in the blocking of
beneficial therapeutic effects in a manner analogous to psi-missing.

The intertwining of psi with some of the normal psychological
processes may be illustrated in connection with Robert Rosenthal's
(1975) interpersonal expectancy effects.   Of course, Rosenthal himself did not claim any such connection.   For those who are familiar
with psi effects and experimenter expectancy effects, the connection
is not, however, too strenuous to make.

The influence of the experimenter on the performance of the
subjects was recognized almost from the beginning of systematic psi
research.   J. B. Rhine et al. (1940) wrote:

> The kind of experimenter actually in contact with the
> subjects may be of the first importance.   His person-
> ality may be a determinative factor in the experimental
> environment.   The investigator, then, may find it most
> advantageous to conduct his first exploration in the
> selection of assistants whose personalities and attitudes
> are suitable.

> The methodology at this important point may consist
> in great part of the art of handling people successfully.
> All the skills and methods that can be devised by the
> experimenter for conveying encouragement, inspiring
> confidence, implanting a realization of the importance
> of the tests, and arousing and maintaining an ambition
> to perform well in the tests will be decidedly to the
> point [p. 341].

Recent reviews of experimenter effects in psi research
(Kennedy & Taddonio, 1976; White, 1976) have referred to some 75
studies in which the experimenter seemed to be a significant variable.   In some of these studies, however, variables other than
experimenter's expectancy (such as attitudes and personality) have
confounded the results.

There appears to be three kinds of experimenter effects in
psi research.   First, the experimenter-subject interaction at the
psychological level seems to be a significant variable.   These
effects are like the ones Rosenthal and his associates attempted to

study. In a study by Honorton et al. (1975) for instance, the subjects with whom the experimenter interacted in a "friendly," "casual" and "supportive" manner obtained significantly higher ESP scores than those whom the experimenter treated in an "abrupt," "formal" and "unfriendly" way. As expected, the subjects with positive interactions guessed significantly better than chance expectation and the subjects with negative interactions scored significantly below chance expectation.

Second, some subjects are able to receive psi signals and are able to act in response to them unintentionally. A good example is an experiment by D. J. West and G. W. Fisk (1953). The subjects in this study, who did not know that two experimenters were involved in the preparation of targets, obtained, as predicted, highly significant results when they were guessing the targets prepared by Fisk, while their scores on the targets prepared by West were at chance.

Third, there is evidence that the experimenter or his agent could intentionally influence the subjects' physiology through the mediation of psi. Recently William Braud (1978) was able to obtain significant evidence suggesting that the electrodermal activity of his subjects could be influenced from a distance and with precautions taken to eliminate conventional sensorimotor and energetic interactions.

Therefore, it is not unreasonable to expect that at least some of the experimenter expectancy effects described by Rosenthal could be mediated by psi. That the experimenter expectancy effects may have a psi source is also suggested by the apparent similarities between familiar psi effects and the experimenter expectancy effects:

Apart from their somewhat elusive and evanescent nature, these effects seem to occur more frequently with certain experimenters than with others.

With some experimenters the effect may be the opposite of what was expected.

The experimenters who produce negative effects seem to share some psychological characteristics as distinct from those who produce positive effects (Rao, 1966; Rosenthal, 1976).

If it is the case, then, that expectancies create situations where they become realized, and if some of these realizations cannot be accounted for in terms of sensory-motor interactions, one may, with some imagination, see the substantive implications of psi for the study of interpersonal relationships. As a mediator of expectancy effects, psi may have important implications for those processes that are intended to influence behavior, such as propaganda, psychotherapy, persuasion and education. Again, psi may be just as significant as such nonverbal interactions as gaze and mutual gaze, in mediating feedback during interpersonal encounters. This vast area of interpersonal behavior is still untouched by para-

psychologists.   The role of psi in bringing people together or in
breaking their ties is something that we should look into.

   The ideas I have attempted to outline have two other implications for research.   First, the locus of psi control may lie in our
attention-deployment mechanisms.   Therefore, experimental manipulation of variables that influence attentional processes may provide us
with insights bearing on the connection between psi and cognitive
functioning.   Second, insofar as psi functioning is basically teleological and acausal, the question of the complexity of the psi task cannot be stated in causal terms.   Therefore, it is not surprising that
causal complexity appears to be irrelevant as a psi-limiting condition.   According to our theory, volitional and teleological complexities and not causal complexities would affect psi.   The greater the
volitional strength and congruence and the lesser the dissonance between the experimental "goal" and nature's grand design, the greater
is the probability of the occurrence of a laboratory psi effect.
Thus, I see a necessary complementarity between epistemic and
constitutive psi.   The congruence between nature's design and the
purposes of its constituents, I venture to speculate, would speed up
the evolutionary process.   Also, microscopic psi effects could have
significant consequences in the surface reality because the complexities that seriously limit interactions at the surface level cannot act
as psi deterrents.

   I do not know if my stated purpose of arguing for the importance of psi and finding for it a significant place in the universe is
somewhat obscured by my excursions into Oriental philosophy and
speculative theorizing.   If there is any sanctimonious breast-beating,
not uncommon among Indians writing on Indian thought, it is wholly
unintended.   Psi is important not because the Orientals have thought
so for centuries.   It is important not because it is anomalous and
questions some of the so-called basic laws.   Rather, its importance
lies in its potential for making the interface between the volitional
self and the brain more meaningful and purposive and in providing
empirical grounds for believing that the picture of the universe as
painted on the space-time canvas with the colors of our senses is
not the only possible one.   The restoration of the self as an active
interface between explicate and implicate structures in the universe
is bound to have a profound impact on the future of psychology, and
perhaps of science in general.

<h2 style="text-align:center">REFERENCES</h2>

Baker, A.   Modern physics and antiphysics.   Reading, Mass. :
   Addison Wesley, 1970.

Bekesy, G. von.   Sensory inhibition.   Princeton, N. J. :   Princeton
   University Press, 1967.

Bohm, D.   Quantum theory as an indication of a new order in
   physics.   Part B.   Implicate and explicate order in physical
   law.   Foundations of Physics, 1973, 3(2), 139-168.

Braud, W. G.   Conformance Behavior Involving Living Systems.
    In W. G. Roll (ed.), Research in Parapsychology 1978.
    Metuchen, N. J.: Scarecrow Press, 1979, 111-114.

Diaconis, P.   Statistical problems in ESP research.   Science,
    July 1978, 201, 131-136.

Dukhan, H., and Rao, K. R.   Meditation and ESP scoring.   In W.
    G. Roll, R. L. Morris and J. D. Morris (eds.), Research in
    Parapsychology 1972.   Metuchen, N. J.: Scarecrow Press,
    1973, 148-151.

Eccles, J.   The human person in its two-way relationship to the
    brain.   In J. D. Morris, R. L. Morris and W. G. Roll (eds.),
    Research in Parapsychology 1976.   Metuchen, N. J.: Scarecrow
    Press, 1977, 251-262.

Ehrenwald, J.   The ESP experience: A psychiatric validation.   New
    York: Basic Books, 1978.

Eisenbud, J.   Evolution and psi.   Journal of the American Society
    for Psychical Research, 1976, 70, 35-53.

Hansel, C. E. M.   ESP: A scientific evaluation.   New York:
    Scribner's, 1966.

Hardy, A. C.   The living stream.   London: Collins, 1965.

Honorton, C.   Psi and internal attention states.   In B. Wolman
    (ed.), Handbook of Parapsychology.   New York: Van Nostrand
    Reinhold, 1977, 435-472.

Honorton, C.; Ramsey, M., and Cabibo, C.   Experimenter effects
    in extrasensory perception.   Journal of the American Society
    for Psychical Research, 1975, 69, 135-150.

Hyman, R.   Psychics and scientists: "Mind reach" and remote view-
    ing.   The Humanist, May/June, 1977, 37, 16-20.

Hyman, R.   Psi: A challenge to critics and believers.   Contem-
    porary psychology, 1978, 23, 644-646.

Jung, C. G., and Pauli, W.   The interpretation of nature and the
    psyche: Synchroncity; and the influence of archetypal ideas on
    the scientific theories of Kepler.   New York: Pantheon Books,
    1955.

Kanthamani, H., and Kelly, E. F.   Card experiments with a special
    subject.   I Single-card clairvoyance.   Journal of Parapsychology,
    1974, 38, 16-26.   (a)

Kanthamani, H., and Kelly, E. F.   Awareness of success in an ex-
    ceptional subject.   Journal of Parapsychology, 1974, 38, 355-
    382.   (b)

Kelly, E. F., and Kanthamani, B. K.   A subject's efforts towards
  voluntary control.   Journal of Parapsychology, 1972, 36, 185-
  197.

Kennedy, J. E., and Taddonio, J. L.   Experimenter effects in
  parapsychological research.   Journal of Parapsychology, 1976,
  40, 1-33.

Kurtz, P.   The psychology of belief.   The Humanist, May/June,
  1977, 37, 42-43.

Matas, F., and Pantas, L.   A PK experiment comparing meditating
  versus nonmeditating subjects.   Proceedings of the Parapsychological Association, 1971, 8, 12-13.

Osis, K., and Bokert, E.   ESP and changed states of consciousness
  induced by meditation.   Journal of the American Society for
  Psychical Research, 1971, 65, 17-65.

Pribram, K. H.   Languages of the brain: Experimental paradoxes
  and principles in neuropsychology.   Englewood Cliffs, N. J. :
  Prentice-Hall, 1971.

Pribram, K. H.   Consciousness: A scientific study.   Journal of
  Indian Psychology, 1978, 1, 95-118.

Price, G. R.   Science and the supernatural.   Science, 1955, 122,
  359-367.

Price, G. R.   Apology to Rhine and Soal.   Science, 1972, 175, 359.

Randall, J. L.   Parapsychology and the nature of life.   New York:
  Harper & Row, 1975.

Rao, K. Ramakrishna.   Experimental parapsychology: A review and
  interpretation.   Springfield, Ill. :   Charles C. Thomas, 1966.

Rao, K. Ramakrishna.   Some frustrations and challenges in parapsychology.   Journal of Parapsychology, 1977, 41, 119-135.
  (a)

Rao, K. Ramakrishna.   On the nature of psi.   Journal of Parapsychology, 1977, 41, 294-351.   (b)

Rao, K. Ramakrishna, Durkhan, H. and Rao, P. V. K.   Yogic
  meditation and psi scoring in forced-choice and free-response
  tests.   Journal of Indian Psychology, 1978, 1, 160-175.

Rhine, J. B.   New World of the mind.   New York: William Sloane
  Associates, 1953.

Rhine, J. B.   Comments: Psi methods reexamined.   Journal of
  Parapsychology, 1975, 39, 38-58.

Rhine, J. B., and Pratt, J. G. Parapsychology: Frontier science of the mind. Springfield, Ill.: Charles C. Thomas, 1957.

Rhine, J. B., Pratt, J. G., Stuart, C. E., Smith, B. M., and Greenwood, J. A. Extra-sensory perception after sixty years. New York: Henry Holt, 1940.

Rosenthal, R. Experimenter effects in behavioral research. New York: Irvington, 1976.

Schmeidler, G. R. High ESP scores after a swami's brief introduction in meditation and breathing. Journal of the American Society for Psychical Research, 1970, 64, 100-103.

Schmidt, H. Toward a mathematical theory of psi. Journal of the American Society for Psychical Research, 1975, 69, 301-319.

Skinner, B. F. The force of coincidence. The Humanist, May/June, 1977, 37, 10-11.

Stanford, R. G. Are parapsychologists paradigmless in psi-land? In B. Shapin and L. Coly (eds.), The Philosophy of Parapsychology. New York: Parapsychology Foundation, 1977, 1-18.

Stanford, R. G. Toward reinterpreting psi events. Journal of the American Society for Psychical Research, 1978, 72, 197-214.

Walker, E. H. Foundations of paraphysical and parapsychological phenomena. In L. Oteri (ed.), Quantum physics and parapsychology. New York: Parapsychology Foundation, 1975, 1-44.

West, D. J., and Fisk, G. W. A dual ESP experiment with clock cards. Journal of the Society for Psychical Research, 1953, 37, 185-197.

White, R. A. The limits of experimenter influence on psi test results: Can any be set? Journal of the American Society for Psychical Research, 1976, 70, 333-369.

BRIEF GLOSSARY

AGENT In telepathy, the person whose mental states are to be apprehended by the percipient. In GESP tests, the person who looks at the target.

CALL An individual guess to a specific target.

CLAIRVOYANCE ESP of a physical event.

DECLINE EFFECT A decline in scoring during a series of trials.

DIFFERENTIAL EFFECT A differential scoring rate between two procedural conditions within the same experiment.

DISPLACEMENT An ESP response to a target other than the intended one.

DT [Down Through] PROCEDURE The clairvoyance method in which the cards are called down through the pack before they are checked.

ESP [Extrasensory Perception] Information obtained by a person about an event without the use of known means of information.

ESP CARDS Cards bearing one of five standard symbols: circle, cross, square, star, and wavy lines.

FREE VERBAL RESPONSE METHOD (FVR) Any procedure in which the range of targets is not known to the subject, such that he or she is free to make any response desired.

GANZFELD A method to induce an altered state of awareness by placing halved Ping Pong balls over the eyes, hereby creating a uniform visual field.

GESP [General Extrasensory Perception] Any method designed to test the occurrence of ESP which permits either telepathy or clairvoyance or both to operate.

MATCHING PROCEDURE Any procedure in which the subject matches one set of cards (or objects) against another.

OUT-OF-BODY EXPERIENCE (OBE) A state in which one's "self" is experienced to be located at a specific place outside the physical body.

PERCIPIENT   The person who is receiving information through
    ESP, especially information coming from an agent or sender.

PK   see   PSYCHOKINESIS

POLTERGEIST   see   RSPK

PRECOGNITION   ESP of a future event.

PSI   Psychic ability in general, including ESP and PK.

PSI-HITTING   Exercise of psi ability in a way that hits the target
    at which the subject is aiming.

PSI-MISSING   Exercise of psi ability in a way that avoids the tar-
    get the subject is attempting to hit.

PSYCHIC   Pertaining to psi; also, someone who is a sensitive.

PSYCHOKINESIS (PK)   A physical effect produced by a person
    without known intermediaries.

PSYCHOMETRY   The ESP method in which an object (known as a
    token object) is used to obtain information about events associated
    with it.

RETROCOGNITION   ESP of a past event.

RSPK   Recurrent spontaneous psychokinesis.

RUN   A group of consecutive trials.

SENSITIVE   An individual who purportedly has strong psi ability.

SPONTANEOUS CASE   An unplanned natural occurrence apparently
    involving psi.

SUBJECT   The person whose psi ability is being tested.

TARGET   The aspect of the subject's environment toward which he
    or she is asked to direct his or her psi ability, such as an
    ESP card or a rolling die.

TELEPATHY   ESP of a mental event.

THETA   Pertaining to aspects of the self which appear to survive
    death.

TOKEN OBJECT   see   PSYCHOMETRY

TRIAL   A single attempt by the subject to use his or her psi ability.

ERRATUM

Research in Parapsychology 1977

I should like to call attention to an error that has crept into the Presidential Address I gave to the Parapsychological Association in 1977, with respect to the signs of some correlation coefficients. In the section titled "Persistence of Inhibition," the three correlation coefficients dealing with the relationship between a lack of hit doublets and real time hitting should be +.70, +.40, and +.60 (p. 239), for what the data showed is that the more real time hitting by a percipient, the greater the deficiency of hit doublets.

Charles T. Tart

NAME INDEX

Abelson, P. H.   159
*Adamenko, V. G.   75-7
Akers, C.   159
Anderson, M.   95-6

Bailey, A.   18
*Bailey, K.   63-5
Baker, A.   165
*Barber, T. X.   vii
*Barker, D. R.   52-4
Barrett, W.   49
Barron, F.   40
Bauer, E.   4
Becker   22
Bekesy, G. von   172
*Beloff, J.   1-2, 11-2, 15,
   16, 40, 63, 98
*Bender, H.   2-5
*Bibeau, J.   86-7
*Bierman, D. J.   10, 56-8
*Bisaha, J. P.   68-70
Blissenbach, D.   60-1
Bohm, D.   172, 174
Bokert, E.   176
*Braud, W.   35, 40, 70-2,
   78, 111-5, 179
Breederveld, H.   10
Briar, B.   153, 154, 155
Brugmans, H. I. F. W.   9,
   151, 152

Capra, F.   15
*Child, I. L.   67-8, 139
Comte, A.   19
Constantinov, B.   5

*Dal Corso, D.   59-60
Dale, L. A.   40
*Davis, G.   70-2
*Davis, J. W.   56-7
Dean, D.   40, 44
de Argumosa, Prof.   5
de Beaupré, Anne   20
Dennis, M.   8
Diaconis, P.   159, 162-5
*Drewes, A. A.   27-8
Dronek, E.   129
*Drucker, S. A.   28-9
Dukhan, H.   176
*Dunne, B. J.   68-70
*Duplessis, Y.   5-6

Eccles, J. C.   36-8, 178
Ehrenwald, J.   178
Einstein, A.   17
Eisenbud, J.   177
*Eisler, W.   80-2, 84-6
*Ejvegaard, R.   6-7
Eliade, M.   18

Feather, S.   153-5
Feller   162
Féré, C.   5
Fisk, G. W.   179
Fox, C.   82-3

Galin, D.   41
Garfield   30
Garrett, E. J.   25, 28-9
*Gatlin, L. L.   125-8, 129-
   131
Geller, U.   78, 165

---

*Convention participants are identified by asterisks.

189

SUBJECT INDEX

Acupuncture   20, 75
ADEPT   145
Age
    differences   32, 47, 51, 87,
    in RSPK cases   60, 61, 62
Agents
    Eleanor Sidgwick as   26
    relationship between subject and   27, 53, 112
    RSPK   60, 61, 62
Alchemy   18
Allgemeine Zeitschrift für Parapsychologie   3
Alpha   36-8, 41-3
Altered states   18, 20, 50, 53, 66, 76, 98, 167; see also Ganz-
       feld; Hypnosis; Cognitive variables; Relaxation
American Society for Psychical Research [ASPR]   30, 50
Amsterdam   9, 10
Analyzer effect   see Observer effects; Experimenter effects; Check-
       er effect
Andhra University   95, 139
Anesthesia   21-3
Anpsi [animal psi]   10, 77-8, 80-2
    and observer effect   56-7
Anxiety   32, 101, 103, 106
Apparatus (ESP)   35, 63, 136, 145-6
Apparatus (GESP)   38-9, 40, 41, 88-9, 99
Apparatus (PK)   36-9, 56, 57, 77, 79-80, 112-6, 118, 146-7, 164
Apparitions   8, 51; see also Visions
Archetypes   169, 175
Arousal   see Cognitive variables
Association
    free   99
    of mentation to target   104-7
    of stimuli   132-5, 142-5
Astral projection   see Out-of-body experiences
Astrology   3, 7, 18
Atman   16, 170, 171
Attitudes   28, 33, 48, 50, 106, 178
    of parapsychologists   54-5
    toward death   32
    toward healing   19, 23
    toward parapsychology   2, 3, 6-7, 8, 102, 159, 160, 161, 165
Auras   51